Aiding Eyak

Alaska's Orphan

Jay Miller, PhD, ed

© 2019

Contents

1   Eyak History by Anna Nelson Harry in Eyak & English

7   A Preliminary Sketch of the Eyak Indians Copper River Delta, Alaska
by Frederica de Laguna 1937

15   Eyak by Frederica De Laguna 1990

26   A History of Eyak Language Documentation and Study:
Fredericæ de Laguna in Memoriam by Michael E. Krauss 2006

    26 The Pre-Russian Period, 1778-1791
    31 The Russian Period, 1792–1867
    49 Summation of Russian Period
    50 The American Period, 1867 to Present
    54 Frederica de Laguna
    57 Published and Archival Results
    58 Linguistic Results
    61 Note on the Name Eyak
    62 Eyak Language Work after de Laguna
    67 Summary of Work before Krauss
    69 Eyak Speakers 1961 to Present
    73 Chronology and Results of Krauss's Eyak Work

84   Anna Nelson Harry (6 January 1906 – 1982) Lament for Eyak
by Michael E. Krauss

86   Language of the Land by Marilee Enge 1994

89   Last Words, A language dies by Elizabeth Kolbert 2005

95   Eyak Stories in English bt John FC Johnson 1988

    95 Old Man Dude >> Raven and Echo Raven and the Grass Blanket Raven
Steals the Fisherman's Bait Raven and the King Salmon Raven Robs
His Partners Raven and the Owners of the Tides Raven and Magpie /
The Woman Who Married a Bear The Man and the Land Otters The
Porcupine Dance The Giant Mole The Giant Devilfish

contents

97   Johnny Stevens >> Raven and Echo Raven Steals the Sun Raven and the Owners of the Tides Raven Teaches the People Raven and the King Salmon How Raven Became Black Raven Marries Raven and the People with the Magic Canoe Raven and the Killerwhales Raven Turns War Parties into Rocks Where Old Raven Made the Earth

101   Galushia Nelson >> Raven Makes the Rivers and Other Geographical Features Ugly Baby Crow Old Raven Was Walking in Back of the Waves Old Raven and Magpie Where Raven Went into a Whale Where Old Raven Pitched the Seals Eyes Together I Am Light Raven Pretends to Use His Body as Bait Raven and Porcupine Raven Raises an Army in the Sky Raven Journeys to the End of the Earth Porcupine and Beaver in Partnership Porcupine and Beaver Wolverine and Fox Were Cousins Wolverine Man Taken by the Fish People Turned into a Groundhog Living with the Black Bear Brown Bear People Porpoise People Blackfish People He Came Back To Shore Together With The Seal People Boy Turning into a Loon Where a Man Killed Lots of Land Otters The Big Mouse Giant Animals Alder People and Sun People Calm Weather's Daughter (diiyeextsii)   Around-The-Lake-People (maaqudati 'a 'ah daxunhyuu) Wolf People Tree People One-Eyed Frog The Man and the Salmon Tail The Man Who Fed A Starving Animal The Girl and the Dog A Tlingit War Story The Man Who Killed His Children The Man Who Left His Wife The Illegitimate Child Good For Nothing The Little Girl Who Played With Dolls Taking Away by Owl Taking Away by Checkers People Salmon Boy

134   Lena Nacktan >> Mosquitos and Water Bug Man Fixes Crane's Beak Bear-Man Killed Bride Eats Only Liver Witch Jealous Wife Walks On Water Shaman Aleuts Punished for Beating Eyak Woman Preacher Tempted by Land-Otter Girls Aleuts Betrayed Eyaks

135   George Johnson >> Raven At Controller Bay Shaman Causes Ice Breakup Qadyyina and the War with Aleuts

141   Anna Nelson Harry >> Raven Cycle (III) Ravens and Mother of Pearl Canoe War with Aleuts Giant Strawberry Old Husband and Young Wife Wolverine People Lake-Dwarves Two Sisters Woman and Octopus Wolf-Woman Blind Man and Loon Eyak History and Language

155 Sue Abraham >> The Legend of a Tlingit Warrior: Kaa-Tee-Na-Ah The Tlingits and Aleuts Battle in Controller Bay

156 Herman Kitka Sr >> The Aleuts Trapped At The Guyot Glacier in Icy Bay Ravens Party House (*Ka-Ta-Ton-Hit*) in Controller Bay Tlingit Migration in and out of Alaska The Birth of the Tlingit Bear Clan

158 Eyak Wiki

165 index 167

Preface

Eyak has a special place in the world, as well as Alaska, where its language was the first to go dormant. As a unique language split off 3,000 years ago from Proto-Athapaskan and the larger stock of Na-Dene, its special role remained elusive during Russian, Spanish, and American explorations and occupations. Finally, Michael Krauss, a linguist at the University of Alaska, devoted himself to learning to speak with and record the last fluent Eyaks, mostly women.

This book begins with the bilingual text titled Eyak History, as told by the gifted Anna Nelson Harry. In the 1930, Frederica de Laguna, a precocious student of the famous Franz Boas, began archaeological, ethnographic, and folkloric studies of Alaska and encountered Anna and her husband Galushia, who proved that Eyak was both exceptional and under threat. With Danish scholar, Kaj Birket-Smith, she drafted the preliminary sketch that leads off this compendium, followed by her mature statement for the Smithsonain. As he retired, Krauss published the tour de force overview of the growing scholarly awareness of Eyak, especially during the Russian and American occupations of Alaska, along with tributes to the final speakers who conversed with, shared, and helped him. Two of the last speakers are then highlighted. Finally are assembled many English versions of Eyak stories. Since Krauss was initially hired to teach college French in Alaska, it is more than ironic that the newest speaker Guillaume Leduey is himself French. The Wiki entry summaries key features of Eyak grammar and more recent history, including the 2019 passing of Krauss.

EYAK HISTORY*

1 Dik'da<u>x</u>unhyu•q* q'aw I•ya•qda•t, dik'dak Ana<u>x</u>anaqda•t da<u>x</u>unhyu•k'a'łe•q.
   No people* were at Eyak, nor were there people at Alaganik.
2 <u>X</u>i•t <u>x</u>adaqdach'aht q'unhuw da<u>x</u>unhyu•, aw t'a<u>x</u>ksga'* a<u>x</u>ya'li' saqehł
   From way upriver it was the people, they boated down in those cottonwood*-like canoes.
3 A•ngy•'nuwya'<u>x</u>* q'uhnu•li' saqehł.
   Down the Copper River* it was they boated.
4 Da'aw a•n ida• ya<u>x</u>gu•ndi'ahwa•łx q'uhnu• ya<u>x</u> daqe•<u>x</u>.
   Following along the way that river flows around they were boating around.
5 Aw'a'n' saqchłinu', k'uda'uhtk.
   They came upon them, eggs.
6 Ne•tl'da'<u>x</u> k'uda'uhtklax isał'anhł.
   First they saw eggs.
7 Aw dasałqa't'kłinu•.
   They boiled them.
8 Aw u'saq'e•'ł da'<u>x</u> k'udadzu•, k'udat'u' wa<u>x</u> dasałił.
   They tried them and (they were) good, they got lots of them.
9 *Da•'wax gaqe•łdawa• q'uhnu• Ana<u>x</u>anaqda' saqehł.
   *As they were still boating they arrived at Alaganik.
10 Ana<u>x</u>anaq da•<u>x</u> daq saqehłinu'.
   They boated upstream by Alaganik.
11 U•t q'uhnu• ya•n' salahł.
   There they settled down.
12 Lisya'a•ł, ne•ti'da•<u>x</u> yahtga'aw <u>x</u>a•n' sałiłinu•*.
   Spruce-boughs, first they made something like houses*.
13 Awt'a•xt* quhnu• wa<u>x</u>i•t'eh.
   In those* they lived.
14 Saht<u>x</u> q*aw wa<u>x</u> i•t'eh da•<u>x</u> q'uhnu•, ta'xts'*, ya•n dla•sakukł lis, ta'xts',
yaht, ta'xts'ayaht, aw <u>x</u>a'n' dasałiłinu•, aw ta'xts'ayaht.
   They lived thus a long time and then, *ta*'xts', wind•fallen trees, *ta'xts'*, houses,
   ta'xts'-houses, they made them, those *ta'xts'-houses.*
15 *Wax q'uhnu•, da-'wa<u>x</u>yu• lehdawa• q'uhnu•, idehdah daxu'ya'<u>x</u> –
al tl'e•yu', tl'e•yu'yaht, tle•yu' wa<u>x</u> sałiłinu•, yaht u<u>x</u>a'.
   *Thus it was, upon doing so over and over it was, really veritable –
   this hemlock, hemlock-houses, they got hemlock, their houses.
16 Yaht <u>x</u>a•n'dasłił, k'uda'luw.
   They built houses, big ones.
17 K'ugu•nt'u' g̱ałe'łinu.
   They were becoming populous.
18 *Ahnu• ne'tl'da•'<u>x</u> yi•nhmu• li' sa<u>x</u>ahł, dik' dage'<u>x</u> q'e' asda<u>x</u>ahłq.
   *Those first ones who boated down, they never boated back upriver.
19 Dik'u•da' q'e' asda<u>x</u>ahłq q'aw.
   They didn't boat back there.
20 Ahnu• ahnu•'iht yi•nhinu' q'e' li' sdixahł.
   Those (who had been left) behind them boated down in another fleet.

21 Q'e' li' sdiqehł*.
     Another group* boated down.
22 *Wax q'uw daxunhyu• I•ya•qda•t.
     *Thus there were people at Eyak.
23 U'ch'aht q'uhnu• I•ya•q.
     Thence Eyak.
24 Sałxwa'ł.
     It became summer.
25 Gałxwa'ł.
     It was becoming summer.
26 Xwah.
     Summer.
27 Yax ixada•xa•'k'.
     A group of canoes would travel around.
28 Yax ixada•xa•k'.
     A group of canoes would travel around.
29 Ne•tl'da•x xa•n' sałił, axakih.
     First they made them, dugout canoes.
30 K'uda'luw t'axksk*, aw ya•n' dla•sagahqł.
     Big cottonwood*, they chopped them down.
31 Aw q'uhnu' axakihda•x xa•n' sałił.
     Those they fashioned into dugout canoe form.
32 Awya' q'uhnu•, yax daqe•x, I•ya•qya'ch'.
     In those it was, they boated around, into Eyak Lake.
33 *Aw t'axksk, a•, aw lis, aw q'e' u'saq'e•'ł.
     *Those cottonwood, er, the spruce, they tried that next. [150]
34 Aw k'udzu• q'e' sdiłe'ł.
     That turned out to be another good thing.
35 K'u'luw ax, aw lisch'aht q'e' xa'n' sałiłinu•.
     Big canoes, they made them anew from spruce.
36 *Wax q'uhnu• I•ya•qda•t, I•ya•qya'x q'e•daq sdixahł.
     *Thus they were at Eyak, they boated back upstream to Eyak Lake.
37 Q'e•daq sdiqehłinu'.
     They boated back upstream.
38 Aw I•ya•qda't, udagalehyaq' aw sałiłinu•.
     That Eyak area, it pleased them.
39 U•t ya•n' salahłinu•.
     They settled down there.
40 U•t ax q'e' xa•n'sałił.
     There they made some more canoes.
41 U•dax aw *Eyak Lake*ch' saqehł da'x, k'ut'u' te'ya', gi•nga•ndaq*, awlax isał'anhł.
     Then they boated to Eyak Lake and, many fish, ripe reddened salmon*, they saw them.
42 *Wax q'uhnu• dik* q'e'yax adaxa•k'q.
     *Thus they didn't boat around any more.
43 Da'u•t wax sat'u'ł.
     They settled right there.

44 Da-'wax u•t wax i•t'eh da'x q'uw, uyahsh, wax q'uw k'ugu•nt'u* k'usałe'ł.
    They remained living there and then, their children, thus there came to be many of them. [151]

45 I•ya•qdalahgayu'* saqe•gayu• da'lałxa'ginu•, I•ya•qda•t.
    The Eyaks* kept having children, at Eyak.

46 Wax q'aw k'ugu•nt'u' I•ya•qda•t da•sałe'ł.
    Thus we became many at Eyak.

47 Wax q'uw I•ya•qdalahgayu• da•yiłeh, I•ya•qch'*.
    Thus we are Eyak people, at Eyak*.

48 Ayaq wax i•lih'a't'eh da•x q'uhnu• al a•nguda'ch', a•nguda't gadi•q'ach', ge•łta•kyu•lu'qa•.
    They when they felt like it then to the mouth of the river, to the breakers
    at the river-mouth, to get seals.

49 Xi•t qi'ch'aht li' saxahłda•t dik' ke•łta•kyu• k'a'łe•q.
    Yonder at where they had boated down from there were no seals.

50 Dik'dak k'ut'u' a't ałe'q, aw te'ya' u•da' daq galah.
    Neither were they very many, the salmon that might swim up thither.

51 Aw li' saxahł da•x awlah u'satahłinu•, łi'q' ya•yu•.
    They boated down and they found out about that, everything.

52   Ke•łta•kyu•, gi•nga•ndaqyu•, al sahxwayu•, al k'uda'uhtkyu•, awlax isał'anhł, al yax
xada'ya•xyu", na'xak, ch'aq'i•nq'yu•.
    Seals, ripe reddened salmon, these cockles, these eggs, they saw them, these birds,
    geese, mallards.

53 Wax q'al al I•ye'q* anh sałe'ł.
    Thus this Eyak became a home.

54 *Itl'a•ndaya'tdik awa•, k'ugu•nt'u' gałe'ł da•x Itl'a•ndaya'ch' awa', lah q'e' sdiłe'ł.
    *Mountain Slough too though, [152] they were becoming populous
    and at Mountain Slough for its part, it became another village.

55 *Cordova, dik'* Cordova *lah ał'e'q.*
    Cordova, Cordova was not a village.

56 Aw I•ya'qya'tq'a'aw, lah yiłeh.
    It was at Eyak Lake, that was a village.

57 Dati•q'a•l Xalahsdia•gayu• u•da' isał'anhł da•'x q'aw *Cordova, Cordova* lah sałe'ł.
    Already now White People arrived there and then Cordova, Cordova became a town.

58 I•ya•qdalahgayu• u•da' – I•ya•qdalahgayu•, dik' a't k'ugu•nt'u' q'e a'dałeq.
    Eyaks thither – Eyaks, they aren't very many any more.

59 *Cordova*hda•t salahłinu•, I•ya•qch'aht q'a'aw, u'da' lah salahł.
    They lived at Cordova, from Eyak it was, they moved thither.

60 *Cordova*hda' lah salahłt da•x, da'awtl I•ya•qya't, uqa'x yi•nhinu' I•ya•qya'ch' q'e' adaxa•k'.
    They moved to Cordova and, nevertheless at Eyak Lake, some of them would
    boat back to Eyak.

61 I•ya•qya't q'e' wax dat'uhinu'.
    They would live some more back at Eyak.

62 Dik' łinhqda•tq.
    Not in one place.

63 Al Xalahsdla•gayu• k'usałe'ł da•x q'al, *Cordovo*hda•t da• wax sat'u'ł, lahq', lahq', da• wax i•t'eh.
    There came to be these White People and, we settled at Cordova, in town, in town, we lived.

64 Daxunhyu• wax sat'u'ł.
    People thus settled.

Notes

0. Recorded on tape, Yakutat, May 28,1965, and first transcribed with the help of Lena Nacktan, Cordova, June 5, 1965.
1. Daxunhyu' means both 'people, humans' and specifically 'Eyaks', so that the sentence does not necessarily imply that these places were previously uninhabited. Anna does not mention any previous inhabitants, however, though it is known that the Eyak-Alaganik area was previously Chugach territory. See Introduction.
2. Cottonwood is rare in and perhaps not native to the Cordova Eyak area; the word *t'a'ks(k)* is probably a very old borrowing from Athabaskan (e.g. modern Ahtna *t'aghes*). The reference here may in fact be to birchbark, not part of the modern Eyak culture (cf notes to 30 and 33).
[148 EYAK HISTORY]
12-13. yahtga' 'house•like' and missing the normal *da-* prefixes used in reference to houses, so not rated grammatically as real houses; otherwise forms should be dasałiłinu: (12), awdat'a'xt (13).
14. Neither Lena nor Anna could identify the exact meaning of ta'xts', only that it was some kind of tree or bark, out of which canoes and houses were said to have once been made, but no longer. Ta'xts'ayaht was also the name of a village and a Raven House in Gravina Bay. Anna herself seems to mean here that it is a fallen tree of some kind. It is also uncertain whether in this whole section (12-16) on house-building they are building a single (community) house or many houses.
15.   Loose sentence structure. Da-'waxyu• 'all sorts of ways' or 'that way over and over', presumably tryiqj to build a better house, finally succeeding in building a "real" house of hemlock, such as described by Gatushia in Birket-Smith and de Laguna 1938: p. 32. According to Anna here, the Eyaks had first to build shelters of spruce-boughs, then of ta'xts', before learning to build houses of hemlock.
18, 21. Here, as elsewhere in this text, Anna shifts back and forth between -qe 'travel by (one or more) boat(s)' and -xa 'travel in fleer of boats' for describing the movements of these groups, awkward in either case to translate directly into English.
22.   Anna apparently implies here that this second group settled Eyak, the first group having settled Alaganik.
30, 33. Cf note to 2. The classic Eyak dugout is of course made of spruce, not cottonwood (or birchbark).
36. It has not been clear whether it was the first (Alaganik) group or the second (Eyak) group, or both, involved in the fleet traveling around in 27-28, or in the canoe-making of 29-35. Here the q'e•- could mean, as before, either movement of a subject back co starting point, or renewed movement of the subject farther on. or movement of a new subject in turn over the same area as a previous one, such that these sentences could refer either to the second (Eyak) group reaching Eyak for the first time, then boating westward to the mouth of the Eyak River (about eight miles farther west than the mouth of Alaganik Slough, cf note to #9), turned back upnver and upland ascending the Eyak River to Eyak; or to a return of the first and/or second j group to Eyak, after having boated around; or to (he voyage upriver to Eyak of a new group (the Alaganik group). In any case in modern times there was no clear distinction between the Alaganik and Eyak groi the population being fluid between them, with of course constant communication.
41. Chugach word, with *–ng–* as in English 'singer'.

43. Or 'They didn't (traveling by boat) turn/go back'; this could mean either that the second group (Eyak) in last ceased their wanderings, as translated, or that the first (Alaganik) group came tojoin the second at EyikJ for good, preferring Eyak to Alaganik; Alaganik, however, remained an important village until 1892 or 1893, as mentioned in the Introduction.

45. I•ya•qdalahgayu• 'inhabitants of Eyak, Eyaks', here and hereafter in this text refers to the Cordova Eyaks in general, but probably not to other Eyak-speaking people (from Controller Bay cast).

47. I•ya•qch' 'towards Eyak', or, as here, 'continuous or repeated motion toward or development at', thus 'we became more and more people at Eyak', or 'we became more and more associated with Eyak (Village)'.

53. Partly English pronunciation.

54. The location of this village (more likely villages or camps) is uncertain. Lena states that it was at a "big beach, way below Mountain Slough," which would be at Tsa'laxa̱łluw ('big gravel'), on the coast between the mouth of Mountain Slough and Point Whitshed, or that it was above Lisyaq' daq gali•'ah ('where water runs up into trees'), which was somewhere along Mountain Slough.

EYAK HISTORY [152-3]

1 There were no Eyaks at Eyak, nor were there any Eyaks at Alaganik. The Eyaks came from far uprivcr, in boats made of something like cottonwood. They came down the Copper River. They were following along the river in their boats. They found eggs. They first saw eggs. They boiled them, tasted them, and they were good, so they gathered a lot of them. Continuing along they came to Alaganik. They went up past Alaganik. There they settled down.

12 Of spruce boughs they first built shelters, and lived in those. After living a long time like chat they then built houses of *ta'xts'*, wind-fallen trees; *ta'xts'-houses* they built. So after many attempts, they made true houses, of hemlock. They made their houses of hemlock. They built large houses.

17 They were becoming many, those first people who came down the river in their boats, and they never went back upriver. More people after them came down, in turn. That's how Eyak was established. It was Eyak after chat.

24 Summer came and they would go around by boat. They made their first dugout canoes. They chopped down large cottonwood, and fashioned that into a canoe. They went in that into Eyak Lake. Then they tried spruce instead of cottonwood. That too was good. They carved large boats out of spruce.

36 They went back up by Eyak into Eyak Lake. They liked it at Eyak, and settled down there. They made more boats there. They went by these to Eyak Lake and saw many fish, ripe salmon. So they no longer wandered, but lived right there.

44 As they remained living right there, their children became many. The Eyak villagers kept having children, at Eyak. That's how Eyak became populous. Thus we are Eyaks, at Eyak Village. When they felt like it they would go to the mouth of the river, to the breakers, to get seals. Over where they had come down the river there are no seals. Nor are there many salmon, that swim up that far. When they came down the river they found out about all these things. They saw seals, ripe salmon, cockles, eggs, birds, geese, mallards.

53 So Eyak became a village. They were becoming numerous at Mountain Slough, and Mountain Slough became a village too.

55 Cordova was not a village. The village was at Eyak. Whites arrived there and Cordova became a town. The Eyak people were no longer very many. They moved here from Eyak. After they moved to Cordova still some of them would go back to Eyak, and live there again, not being in just one place. As there came to be these whites, we moved to Cordova; the Eyaks lived in town.

A Preliminary Sketch of the
Eyak Indians Copper River Delta, Alaska
By Frederica de Laguna

THE Eyak Indians, whose original territory included the mouth of the Copper River and the eastern edge of Prince William Sound, Alaska, were first mentioned in 1788 as the *Ugalachmuten* in the reports made by the Russian explorers Ismailof and Botscharof to Shelikof (see the German translation of Shelikofs report in Pallas, VI, 7, 1793, p. 218 ff). From that day until the present this little tribe have been discussed by a succession of writers under a variety of names, most of which, like Ugalachmuten, are corruptions of Uṅalaɣmiut, the name by which their Eskimo neighbors designate them. Partly because the form of the name is Eskimo, partly because the Eyak were supposed to live on Kayak Island, an island actually occupied by the Eskimo, and because the Eyak have borrowed some elements of Eskimo culture, a number of writers have assumed these people to be Eskimo. A number of others have confused them with the Atna, the Athabaskan-speaking group who live above them on the Copper River. Because the Eyak were in close contact with the Tlingit, who were expanding from the southeast, and because Eyak culture contains traits obviously borrowed from the Tlingit, other writers have considered them as a branch of these people. The Handbook of American Indians (II, 1910, p. 862) has only succeeded in increasing the confusion by describing the 'Ugalakmiut* as "a tribe of Alaskan Eskimo ... so far metamorphosed by contact with the Tlingit as to be more properly Tlingit than Eskimo.'

I first visited the survivors of this tribe in 1930 and at that [64 PHILADELPHIA ANTHROPOLOGICAL SOCIETY] time learned enough to suggest the hypothesis that the Eyak 'are an Athabaskan-speaking people who have pushed down the Copper River to its mouth, separating the Eskimo of Kayak Island from their neighbors in Prince William Sound' (The Archaeology of Cook Inlet, Alaska, 1934, p. 156). The ethnological researches conducted by Dr. Kaj Birket-Smith and myself in the summer of 1933, and the information supplied me by Colonel W.R. Abercrombie who visited the Eyak in 1884, have supported this hypothesis and form the basis of this preliminary sketch. The final report is being prepared jointly by Dr. Birket-Smith and myself.

The name 'Eyak,' by which these Indians call themselves in speaking English, is a corruption of Iɣíáq'Dɛláqɛíyú, 'people of Eyak,' from Iɣíáq', one of their two principal villages. They claim as their territory the mainland from the eastern edge of Prince William Sound (Cordova Bay) to Cape Martin, excluding Kayak and Wingham Islands which were originally held by the Eskimo, later by the TIingit. The vocabulary which Norman Reynolds and I collected has been examined by Dr. Boas and Dr. Sapir. The latter reports that the phonetic system is suggestive of Tlingit, and the language itself may be a new dialect of the Na-Dene group, coordinate with Athabaskan on the one hand and Tlingit on the other. Certainly it is not Eskimo, nor any known dialect of Tlingit or Athabaskan. Some rather striking differences in the words given by two informants suggest that even within the Eyak itself there may have been dialectic differences, though this would be surprising to find in a tribe that numbered some 150 to 200 individuals, when intercourse between the two main villages seems to have been intimate.

The material and spiritual culture of the Eyak represents a rich blending of Interior Athabaskan, southwestern Alaskan Eskimo, and Tlingit elements. In sketching the culture I shall do little more than point out the more striking borrowings, since this phase of the problem is being exhaustively studied by Dr. Birket-Smith for the final report.

The Eyak house was a rectangular structure, built entirely above ground, with walls of vertical planks mortised into a [65] frame of horizontal logs at top and bottom. The gable roof of planks and bark was supported on a ridgepole that ran through the center of the smoke hole. The doorway was square, with a plank door suspended on rawhide hinges. The fireplace was in the middle of the dirt floor; the smoke hole protected by a movable wooden wind-break. Across the back and sides were small sleeping rooms for the several families, roofed and floored with planks, illuminated by lamps of clam shell or roughly hollowed stone cobbles, and entered by means of sliding doors. They were furnished with grass mats on the floor and walls; the bedding was of skins and a goat's hair blanket; the common pillow was a long sloping board. Besides these communal houses, there were also smaller houses accommodating a single family. The village contained smoke houses where fish and meat were cured, and meat caches, like those of the Interior Athabaskans, small box-like houses set on high posts.

In each village was a fort or stockaded enclosure built of upright logs. Near it were the two potlatch houses of the two moieties, in front of which was a post carved to represent the moiety bird, raven or eagle. In 1884 Abercrombie found people living in these potlatch houses, sleeping on top of a high broad platform that ran around the two sides and across the back, and storing their belongings in lockers under it. Each locker door was carved with totemic crests (?) in typical Northwest Coast art style. These potlatch houses were used as guest houses for visitors, as public halls, and for the feasts and ceremonies conducted by the moieties.

Near the village was the graveyard, where the dead were buried or where their ashes were stored. The graveyard was surrounded by a picket fence, and each individual grave was similarly enclosed. A tall post, the top of which was carved to represent a raven, with other unrecognizable animals below it, was seen by Abercrombie in one of the village graveyards. Many of the individual graves had smaller carved graveposts at the head of the small house-like box that held the ashes of the dead.

The Eyak built wooden dugout canoes, and it is apparently from them that the Prince William Sound Eskimo learned the [66] art. The small Eyak hunting canoe had a cleft prow, like the small canoe of the Yakutat Tlingit. The cleft was formed by the projection of the keel below the ordinary prow, and this facilitated handling in waves or swift currents. The larger traveling canoe, holding from ten to sixteen occupants, was sometimes equipped with mast and sail. The paddles had a pointed blade and crutch handle; a long paddle was used for steering the big canoe. There were also special canoes built for racing, and large canoes for war, the latter carved with a raven's or an eagle's head on the prow. To some extent the Eyak made use of the Eskimo kayak for sea-otter hunting, and there were also war canoes, made of goat or seal skin, like the Eskimo umiak.

The Eyak made crude snowshoes, with three cross-bars, webbed only between the first two bars. For bringing home game they made an emergency sledge of branches. While they bred large dogs for hunting, dogs were never used for hauling the sled or packing loads. Just as children inherit the name of a dead relative, so dogs were named after dead dogs. There was no taboo against feeding animal bones to dogs, as among some Athabaskan groups, but it was considered unlucky to kill a dog at any time.

Men wore their hair tied behind in a bunch, women and girls had a long single braid. Shamans let their hair hang somewhat longer and looser than other men. The faces of both sexes were painted (only for dances?). Women (and men?) were tattooed around the wrist with awl and thread, and women burned their wrists to harden themselves to pain. Both men and women wore earrings, women wore nose rings. Men wore finger rings of native copper, traded from the upper Copper River. Milk teeth, nail pairings, and hair were disposed of in special ways to keep them from witches.

The dress of men and women was like that of the Eskimo, and consisted of shirt, trousers, boots, mittens, and gloves. The inner or summer shirt was worn with the fur next the body, and lacked a hood. The outer shirt, worn over it in winter, had a hood attached. With the summer shirt a separate skin cap or hood might be worn, but the Eyak lacked [67] both the Eskimo hunting helmet and the Tlingit basket hat. In rainy weather the men wore a gut-skin shirt like the Eskimo *kamleika*. Trousers were worn in winter. The women's summer boots left bare the leg between the boot top and the hem of the shirt. The men went barefooted in summer but in winter wore a short boot leaving their knees bare below the trousers. On war expeditions they wore an apron and when fishing a breech-clout. Men and women also had robes, something like those of the Tlingit, made of small animal skins sewn together. Shamans wore special costumes, masks, and belts when practising. Taboos relating to clothing forbade women to dress in fresh sealskins, and also prohibited the mixing of land and sea animal skins in the same garment. This taboo is certainly inspired by the Eskimo restrictions separating land and sea animals, though the Prince William Sound Eskimo applied it to food, not clothing, and the Eyak lacked the taboo in respect to food.

Among the other items of material culture we may mention the heavy Northwest Coast and southern Alaskan Eskimo adze, stone axes and wooden wedges for splitting logs, hand and cord drills for making fire and drilling holes, ulos [ulu], crooked knives with blade of beaver tooth, double-bladed copper knives like those of the upper Copper River Indians and the Tlingit. Food was roasted on spits over the fire or was boiled with hot rocks in spruce root baskets. Wooden storage boxes were not made after the Tlingit pattern (also copied by the Prince William Sound Eskimo) of one long plank steamed and bent around to form the side, but were of five pieces, the sides mortised into the bottom, though they were carved in Northwest Coast art style. There were also pails and storage vessels of bark, wooden bowls and plates for serving food, spoons of wood, baleen, and goat horn. Twined spruce root baskets were decorated with false embroidery of colored grass in typical Tlingit patterns. Pack straps were used to carry loads and babies. Sewing thread was made of twisted sinew, but no needle was used. Ropes were of rawhide or bast. Abercrombie describes pipes made of pottery, imperfectly [68] fired, with stems of hollow arrowwood. This is the only reference we have to pottery among the Eyak.

Mountain goats were hunted by driving them towards hunters in ambush, the dogs assisting. Bears were hunted with spears at the winter dens, or were killed in deadfalls or with the automatic bow. Fox and lynx were caught in snares; beaver, mink, and martin in deadfalls; weasels in box traps. Land otters and wolves were not hunted because they were supposed to be transformed human beings. (Compare with Tlingit and Prince William Sound Eskimo belief.) The Eyak did not hunt walrus for the same reason, and were afraid to attack fur seals, porpoises, or whales, though there was no taboo against using the meat of those they found dead. The bows had sinew backing; the arrows were equipped with three half-feathers and a barbed bone head, and were kept in wooden quivers or under the hollow stool in the hunting canoe. Harbor seals were clubbed or harpooned on sand-bars, less often harpooned from the canoe. The harpoon used for seals and salmon had a detachable barbed head with tang; and the seal harpoon was sometimes equipped with a float of an inflated seal stomach. The sea otter harpoon-arrow was identical with that used by the southern, Alaskan Eskimo. Birds were shot with bow and sharp (not blunt) arrow, or, when moulting, were driven together and clubbed. The loon was not killed, because a boy had once turned into one.

Salmon was the most important item in the Eyak food supply. They were caught in fish traps like those of the upper Copper River Indians, with two-pronged fish spears, with big dip nets, or with harpoons. In fishing with dip net or harpoon, two men generally worked together, one man catching the fish, the other dispatching it with a club. Halibut, cod, sand-sharks, trout, and whitefish were caught with compound hooks, a piece of quartz fastened to the shank acting as lure and sinker. The bait was a clam, a lump of seal fat, or some salmon eggs, depending on the type of fish sought. Herring and oelachen were caught with a two-pronged spear like a rake or a dip net from the canoe, with fire used to attract them. [69]

Like the Tlingit, the Eyak were divided into two exogamous matrilineal moieties, Eagle and Raven. Within these were partially differentiated groups, supposed to be descendants of some Tlingit who had been adopted into the tribe. The sub-groups were the 'Wolves' (within the Raven moiety) and the 'Bark House People' (within the Eagle moiety). At the head of each moiety was a chief, one of them the tribal chief, who led war parties. Below each moiety chief was a sub-chief, and there seems to have been a chief or leader of each moiety in each village. The office passed on death to the brother (failing a brother, to the maternal nephew?). The communal hunts were under the leadership of a chief. It was principally the chiefs who owned slaves (captives or the children of captives), and one of these might be killed at the funeral of a chief's son or daughter. Though the chiefs and their families were generally distinguished by garments of rare furs decorated with dentalium shells, there does not seem to have been any fixed hierarchy of rank. In addition to the chiefs, there was some man (in each village ?) who acted as peacemaker to prevent quarrels, and who carried a painted paddle, like the ceremonial paddles of the Northwest Coast, as a badge of office.

Though a large number of Eyak myths and tales mention chiefs and slaves, there is not one that mentions the moiety or potlatch, the moiety ceremony, and this leads us to suspect that the dual division of the tribe was an institution borrowed in comparatively recent times from the Tlingit. The potlatch houses, for example, have typically Tlingit names. The use of one of the kinship terms, sɪtɬta also suggests a time before the moiety was instituted. This term is used by a man towards his father's sister's son (his future brother-in-law under the system of cross-cousin marriage), and by the woman towards her female cross-cousins, whom her brother calls 'sweetheart.' However, she also uses it for her co-wife, her husband's brother's wife, and the man uses it for his wife's sister's husband, individuals belonging to the same moiety as the speaker and who now could not possibly marry into the speaker's family. This makes us suspect that the term was originally [70] applied to cousins of the same sex as the speaker, at a time before moieties were established.

Within the family the oldest brother had authority over his younger brothers and sisters. The prospective groom 'slaved' for his future parents-in-law, and there is some evidence that he lived in their house for a short time after marriage, though he afterwards took his wife back to his own house. The son-in-law avoided his mother-in-law, and one tale suggests that the father-in-law and daughter-in-law were forbidden to speak to each other. Joking and 'rough-housing' were permitted between brother- and sister-in-law, but grown-up brothers and sisters were not allowed to speak to each other or be alone together. There was polygyny but not polyandry, the sororate, the junior levirate, even involving the taking of the elder brother's wife during his lifetime. Men sometimes exchanged wives or offered them to guests. Between men of the same moiety a partnership might be arranged, but there were no secret societies. There was no village endo- or exogamy, no moiety or family regulation of house sites, fishing or hunting territories.

Murder, or even the accidental injury of a member of the opposite moiety, or of a member of the offender's own moiety living in another house, called for payment of damages to the victim's family. Grievances were aired in public by the singing of insulting songs, as among the Eskimo.

The religious beliefs of the Eyak are very similar to those of the Eskimo. They conceive of all things, animate and inanimate, as having souls, or spirit owners, shaped like human beings. Those of the animals are located in the heads. For this reason, when a hunter has made a kill he cuts the eyeballs of his game, so that the animal cannot see him, and caches the head in a secluded place, so that the animal's soul may be reincarnated. The tail, blood, and entrails of a fish are thrown back into the water. No particular respect was shown the bear, though the hide was lowered three times over the carcass before being removed. A hunter never spoke about what game he hoped to kill, or made a sled in advance to bring home the meat, for this form of boasting would spoil his luck. The [71] Eyak also had a simplified form of first salmon ceremony. The man who caught the fish washed and dressed in clean clothing. He cooked the fish because no woman was supposed to touch it, and it was eaten by every one in the village except menstruating or pregnant women. It is the souls of people and things which are seen in dreams, and it is the soul which leaves the body in dreams, shamanistic trances, and in insanity. At death the soul leaves the body, but is revived by the sun to become reincarnated in a child. A child was named after a dead relative of the same sex in the mother's family, and was supposed to be the deceased, actually returned to life, with all his or her peculiarities. There was no taboo against mentioning personal names, except that of a dead person, but it was impolite to address a person by his name.

At puberty the girl was secluded in a special hut or in a sleeping room in the house for several months, during which time she ate from special dishes, sucked water through a bone, and used a bone scratcher to scratch her head. Menstruating women ate from their own dishes, and at the end of their five-day period purified themselves with a cold bath. Menstruating and pregnant women were not supposed to see, touch, or eat fresh meat or fresh fish, for fear of offending the animals. Other food taboos applied to expectant mothers were designed to protect the health of the child. The mother was not secluded at childbirth, though all the men had to leave the house. The husband was not allowed to hunt during his wife's ten-day confinement, and at the end of that period both purified themselves in a bath of devil-club infusion.

The death and potlatch customs suggest those of the Tlingit. When a person died, the body was kept in the house for four days, during which time members of the opposite moiety prepared it for burial or burning, watched beside it, and entertained the relatives with songs and stories. The dead person's property was either buried with him, or was saved to be burned or given away at the death potlatch. There was thus no inheritance of wealth except for the dogs and house, and unfortunately we were unable to get specific information about these. The bodies of slaves and witches were always [72] cremated (Contrast with the Tlingit belief that the body of a shaman could not be burned). The dead were removed through an opening made in the wall of the house. Several months or even years after the death, the relatives would invite the members of the opposite moiety to a potlatch. The chief of the deceased's moiety acted as host. Food was put into the fire for the dead, as were those of his belongings saved for this occasion. If a member of the opposite moiety wanted one of these things, he might offer something in exchange, to be kept by the relatives. Food was served and gifts given to the guests in order of rank, and each recipient was addressed by his potlatch name, that is, by the name of a dead and not yet reincarnated member of the hosts' moiety. In accepting, he would answer that he took the gift or food, not for himself, but for some dead relative of his own. In this way all the dead were supposed to share in what the living enjoyed. The chief of the guest clan and those who had attended the corpse received the greatest number of gifts. Persons who had sung songs requested by the hosts, or who had given the best animal impersonations at the festivities following the potlatch proper, received special prizes. Somewhat similar feasts and giving of gifts celebrated the building of a new potlatch house. It should be noted that while there was a certain rivalry between moieties there was none between chiefs. The potlatch was not an occasion for overwhelming the guests with gifts to be returned at ruinous interest, nor did it lead to the bankruptcy of the hosts. Potlatches might be held in honor of any dead person, man or woman, of whom the relatives had been fond.

Feasts and dances were also held in the potlatch house to entertain guests. The two performances held in honor of Abercrombie and his party were actually plays. The shaman, dressed as Raven, told the story, incident by incident; his assistant acted as stage manager; dancers in masks and appropriate costumes acted out the play with dialogue. They were accompanied by drummers and by a chorus of women; the two old women who led the chorus enlivened the performance with repartee. Musical instruments used at potlatches were the hollow log drum, tambourine, whistle, and rattles worn or [73] carried by the dancers. While the Eyak know a great number of Raven tales, including the story of the theft of the Sun by the Raven-baby, one of the plays witnessed by Abercrombie enacted the theft of the Sun by the sea mammals. The other recounted the massacre of the Russian exploring expedition up the Copper River in 1847.

Various taboos and magical observances show a blending of Eskimo, Athabaskan, and Tlingit elements. A man might not hunt during his wife's confinement, nor until the body of a dead housemate had been taken from the house. Women were not supposed to touch a man's weapons, nor step over them or a man's legs (Athabaskan). While her husband was hunting or chopping wood a woman was not supposed to leave the village, make a noise, wash clothes, or sew on new garments (Eskimo). When a boy made his first kill, the meat and gifts were distributed. Bad luck in hunting, sickness, or spells could be counteracted by the use of the devil-club in certain ways. The devil-club as a purifying agent is also found in Tlingit practice. Sexual abstinence was observed by shamans during the period of their novitiate and before attempting a cure. It was enforced between the widower and a surviving wife for a few months, and a widow had to wait some time before remarrying. Fasting was practised by relatives on the first day following a death, by warriors before a fight, and by all when a warrior had been killed. The shaman fasted often during the period of his novitiate. The general fast and sexual abstinence may be considered as a means of provoking the pity of the supernatural forces and keeping the body pure and receptive to their blessings. It may also be the traditional expression of grief. Bathing in cold water, as among the Athabaskans and Tlingit, was not only a part of the physical training of boys and men, but was also a means of purification.

Men who lived like women were termed 'good-for-nothing' and had no supernatural powers. The Eyak distinguished between witches and shamans. The former were men or women who had obtained their evil power from handling skeletons. They could fly through the air and change into animal or bird form at will. They could kill a person by [74] making a piece of his clothing or nail-parings rot, or by touching him with the dog skin which they wore when acquiring their power. Sickness was generally attributed to witchcraft. A witch might be detected by the shaman and killed, or else forced to pay a fine.

A man or woman might become a shaman. The power was apt to be inherited, even though it would not manifest itself until the person had passed puberty. The first manifestation of the spirit helper was in a dream. After a period of fasting, bathing in cold water, purging with devil-club infusion, the novice went alone into the woods to fast and receive his power. The spirit might appear in animal or human form, and the shaman would make a doll in that same form to embody his power. The spirit also taught him his song. A shaman might have any number of helpers. Shamans could cure the sick by singing, laying on of hands, sucking out the disease, etc. They could also kill or bewitch by spells. They could fortell the future, find lost or stolen property, bring good luck in hunting or in war, walk on hot stones and handle fire, walk on the surface of the water, free themselves from bonds, give ventriloquist performances, etc.

The sun seems to have been worshipped at one time, and prayers were said to it. Northern lights shine when some one is dying. Thunder is caused by a huge bird like a raven. When trees are split by lightning this is supposed to be the work of a creature that wanders through the woods with its crying baby on its back. It brings good luck if a man can take off his clothes, run and touch this animal (Compare with Tlingit belief). Bad weather is caused by abortion, concealment of an illegitimate child, playing with boats, sleds, or a buzz in winter, by touching a fresh-water clam, or when an adolescent girl looks at the sky. Good weather can be brought back by a number of spells, most of them involving the use of fire. Generosity towards the poor or towards starving animals is rewarded by good luck. The Eyak believed also in monster animals, dwarfs who live beside a lake, giants (Tree People), and man-eating Wolf People.

Among children's toys and games the Eyak knew the [75] popgun, blow gun, whip sling for dart, throwing stick for pebbles, top, buzz, string figures, and hide-and-seek. Girls were not allowed to play with dolls in human form. Adults games were the stick game, tossing wooden disks at a mark, shinny, shooting matches, foot and canoe races, wrestling, and gambling with dice.

In this brief sketch I have attempted to outline the culture of the Eyak and show the various elements which have mingled here at the mouth of the Copper River.

PUBLICATIONS OF THE PHILADELPHIA ANTHROPOLOGICAL SOCIETY

Volume I

Twenty-fifth Anniversary Studies

Edited by
D. S. DAVIDSON

Philadelphia

UNIVERSITY OF PENNSYLVANIA PRESS
London: Humphrey Milford: Oxford University Press
1937

sketch

CONTENTS

	PAGE
THE STICKFAST MOTIF IN THE TAR-BABY STORY — BY W. N. BROWN	1
GODS AND HEROES ON MAYA MONUMENTS — BY MARY BUTLER	13
THE SIGNIFICANCE OF FOLSOM AND YUMA ARTIFACT OCCURRENCES IN THE LIGHT OF TYPOLOGY AND DISTRIBUTION — BY J. L. COTTER	27
FOOT FORMS OF POTTERY VESSELS AT PLEDRAS NEGRAS — BY FRANK M. CRESSON, JR	37
THE RELATION OF TASMANIAN AND AUSTRALIAN CULTURES — BY D.S. DAVIDSON	47
A PRELIMINARY SKETCH OF THE EYAK INDIANS, COPPER RIVER DELTA, ALASKA — BY FREDERICA DE LAGUNA	63
INDEX MOLLUSCA AND THEIR BEARING ON CERTAIN PROBLEMS OF PREHISTORY: A CRITIQUE — BY LOREN C. EISELEY	77
CROSS-COUSIN MARRIAGE IN THE LAKE WINNIPEG AREA — BY A. IRVING HALLOWELL	95
THE EMERGENCE OF A GENERAL FOLSOM PATTERN — BY EDGAR B. HOWARD	111
AUSTRALIAN CULT TOTEMISM — BY NATHANIEL KNOWLES, JR	117
LATE ARCHAEOLOGICAL SITES IN DURANGO, MEXICO — BY J. ALDEN MASON	127
FRIENDSHIP AS A FUNCTIONAL MOTIVE IN CERAMIC TYPES OF EASTERN NORTH AMERICA — BY SAMUEL W. PENNYPACKER, 2ND	147
COMPOSITION OF 'TORTS' IN GUAJIRO SOCIETY — BY VINCENZO PETRULLO	153
IDENTIFICATION OF MAYA TEMPLE BUILDINGS AT PLEDRAS NEGRAS — BY LINTON SATTERTHWAITE, JR	161
CATAWBA MEDICINES AND CURATIVE PRACTICES — BY FRANK G. SPECK	179
FIJIAN DREAMS AND VISIONS — BY DOROTHY SPENCER	199
THE SCOPE OF THE RITE OF ADOPTION IN ABORIGINAL NORTH AMERICA — BY H. NEWELL WARDLE	211
MARRIAGE AMONG THE BABUDJA IN SOUTHERN RHODESIA — BY HEINZ A. WIESCHHOFF	221

Eyak

Frederica De Laguna

The Eyak ('e₁ak) speak a language that is related to the Athapaskan family as a coordinate branch of a larger grouping called Eyak-Athapaskan.[1]* This grouping may be remotely related to Tlingit.

Territory

In the eighteenth century the Eyak were living on the 300-mile long shore of the Gulf of Alaska between the Tlingit-Athapaskan people of Dry Bay and the Chugach Eskimo of Prince William Sound. Their original homeland extended from Italic River, east of Yakutat, westward to Cape Suckling and probably included the mainland shores of Controller Bay, although the Chugach held the islands (fig. 1). Kayak Island in 1741 was the hunting territory of a Chugach Eskimo band, the *čiłqaɣmiut* (*Tyitlqarmiut* in Birket-Smith 1953: 20), named after "Chilkat" village on Bering River at the head of the bay, but they may never have occupied it. An Eyak clan obtained their beaver crest in the vicinity, suggesting early Eyak occupation of the mainland despite Chugach claims, and the name Chilkat itself is of Tlingit origin.

By the late eighteenth century the Yakutat area Eyak were dominated by the expanding Tlingit. In the early nineteenth century Tlingitized Eyak from east of Cape Suckling drove the Chugach from Controller Bay, while more purely Eyak people pushed on to the Copper River delta (fig. 2) and to Cordova, just inside Prince William Sound. By the late nineteenth century the only relatively pure Eyak were those living in this last area, where they [190] had a village named Eyak. Evidence for these movements is provided by historical records, traditions of the Tlingit proper, the Yakutat Tlingit, and surviving Eyak of Cordova (Swanton 1909: 64-69, 154-165, 326-368; Birket-Smith and De Laguna 1938; De Laguna 1972, 1: 210), and by place-names. Many place-names from Cordova to Cape Suckling are Chugach in origin; those from Cape Suckling to Yakutat and farther east are often Eyak (or Tlingit translations).

The Eyak have evidently lived on the Malaspina-Yakutat Forelands for a long time and, prior to Tlingit expansion, may have lived even farther south. Their culture, minus Eskimo borrowings and recent acquisitions, suggests what once may have been characteristic of present

---

[1] *The phonemes of Eyak are: (plain voiceless stops and affricates) *d*, λ, ʒ, ǯ, g, g^w, g, ʔ; (aspirated stops and affricates) t, ƛ, *c*, *č*, *k*, *q;* (globalized) t', ƛ̓, c', č̓, k', *q'* (fricatives) ł, *s*, *š*, *x*, *x*^w, *x̲*, *h;* (nasals) m, *n;* (resonants) *w*, *l*, *y;* (short plain vowels) i, *e*, *a*, u; (long plain vowels); i•, *e•*, *a•*, *u•*, (short nasalized vowels) į, ą, ų (long nasalized vowels į•, ą•, ų• . All short vowels occur before *h* and before a ʔ that is in the same syllable (not intervocalic); in other positions only i, *a*, and u are found and *a* is [ə]. Information on Eyak phonology is from Krauss (1963-1970a: 8, 1982: 23-24); the transcription of Eyak words into this orthography has been provided or checked by Michael E. Krauss (personal communications and communications to editors 1974, 1984, 1986). The short vowels are written as in Krauss (1982), which writes *a* for [ə] whether this is the reduced form of *a* (in prefixes) or the reduced form of e, *u*, and *i* (in stems); another solution to this problem of phonemic overlap would recognize a phoneme /ə/ and write the reduced vowels as /ə/ in stems and as /ə/ and /i/ in prefixes.   [1990]

Northern Tlingit territory (Birket-Smith and De Laguna 1938; De Laguna et al. 1964).

The Eyak formed four regional groups, none a "tribe" in any political sense. These groups were, first, the Eyak (proper), since 1800-1825 in the Cordova-Copper River area (former Chugach Fig. 1. territory). Second were the Eyak on the mainland of Controller Bay, who were becoming Tlingitized by 1850; they were sometimes called Chilkats from their village at the head of the bay. Third were the Eyak of the Gulf of Alaska coast between Capes Suckling and Yakataga, who were also being Tlingitized by 1850 and were sometimes called Yakatags from a village near Cape Yakataga. Emmons (1903) designated them as Guth-le-uk-qwan or Qwolth-yet-kwan from their main village on Kaliakh River and included with them the Tlingitized Eyak of Controller Bay. The fourth group lived around Yakutat Bay and are now completely Tlingitized.

Within this whole area 47 sites have been identified as having been at one time occupied by the Eyak (De Laguna 1972: 58-106). Archeological investigations have been made in Controller Bay by Ketz and Johnson (1985) and in Yakutat Bay by De Laguna et al. (1964).

Environment

Eyak groups living on the morainic shore, 15 miles wide at its maximum, between the open Gulf of Alaska and the mountains of the Saint Elias, Robinson, and Chugach ranges (10,000 to 18,000 feet high) tended to be isolated 56790] both from each other and from their nearest neighbors. Canoe travel was dangerous except in the shelter of offshore bars; safe landing places could be found only inside the mouths of rivers or behind the islands of Yakutat and Controller bays. Sudden squalls, strong winds, fog, and rain, with heavy winter snows demanded human adaptation to damp and cold, but not to severe freezing.

Yet the surf brought to the outer beaches the precious flotsam of the Pacific: bamboo, spars with drift iron, and stranded whales and sea lions (which the Eyak used but dared not hunt). Advances and retreats of the great piedmont

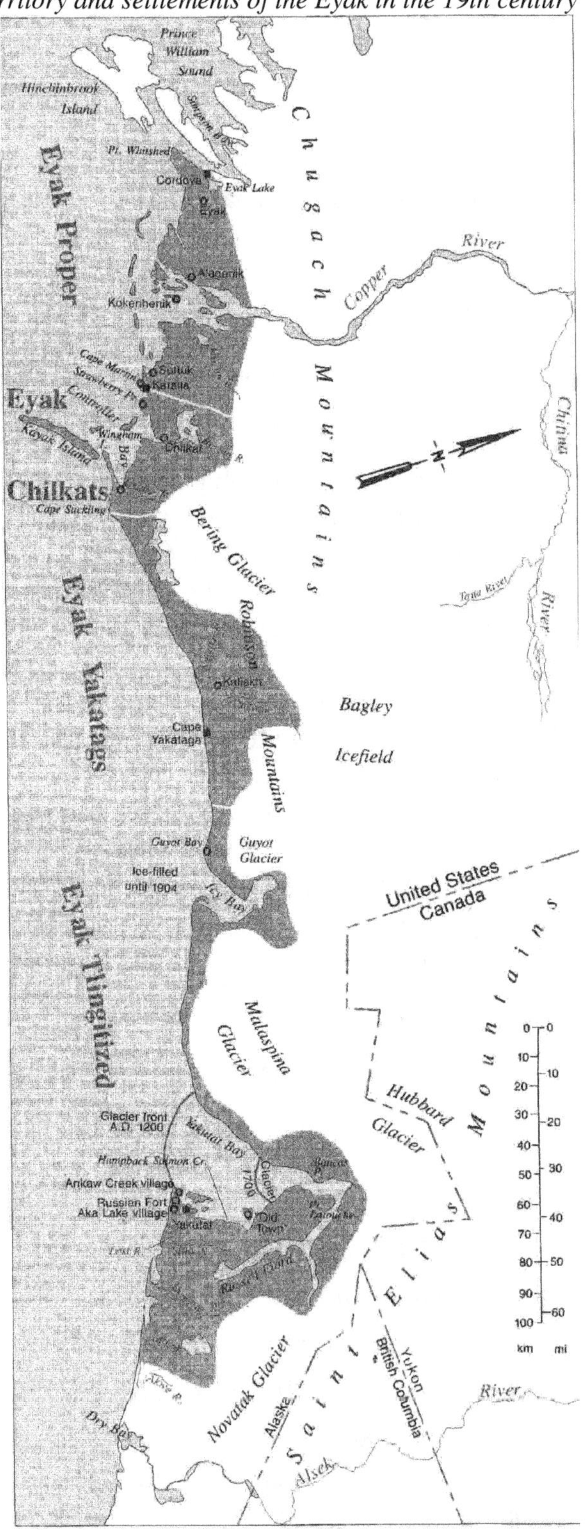

Fig. 1. Territory and settlements of the Eyak in the 19th century.

glaciers are said to have overwhelmed ancient villages or opened new bays; where the ice reached tidewater were ideal breeding grounds for seals. The many lakes and lagoons attracted the enormous flocks of the Pacific flyway; berries grew in profusion on the open gravel and sand; the tidal flats provided mollusks and seaweeds.

The only large rivers cutting through the mountain barrier are the Alsek, emptying into Dry Bay east of Eyak country, and the Copper River near its western boundary. The Alsek was used by Athapaskans and Tlingits traveling to and from the interior, and the Copper River was used by Ahtnas bringing native copper and fur to trade. An easier overland route from the Copper River valley across the Bagley Icefields to Eyak settlements on the Duktoth River was taken by Ahtna immigrants and traders, but these routes were seldom if ever attempted by the Eyak.

Culture

Annual Cycle

Beginning in February, eulachon were caught in traps under the ice; later, with dip net or multibarbed spears from lighted canoes. Seals were harpooned on the ice. Edible roots, wild celery, sweet inner bark of the hemlock were gathered, and probably spruce roots for baskets.

In spring and summer, herring were caught and dried, and herring spawn collected. Trout, whitefish, and cod were taken with hook and line. Bird eggs were collected and seaweed picked and dried for winter. During the salmon runs, from early May to the last stragglers in November, chinooks, sockeyes, cohoes, and pinks were taken with traps, harpoons (fig. 3), two-pronged fish spears, or dip nets from river bank or canoe. Most were split and smoked; some were buried to rot.

Summer berries were picked and dried into cakes or preserved in oil. Sea otter were shot with harpoon arrows from encircling canoes. Molting geese and ducks were clubbed. Bears and mountain goats were hunted with dogs and killed with spears and arrows.

Fig. 2. Copper River delta, covered by spruce, cottonwood, and willow. Mt. Eyak is in the distance. The house, used as a trading post 1898-1900, was built near Alaganik village, abandoned in 1892-1893 following an epidemic (Birket-Smith and De Laguna 1938: 21, 360-361) Photograph by Frederica De Laguna near present Alaganik, Alaska, 1930.

In the fall, Kamchatka lily roots and late berries were gathered. Clams, dried on strings, were put in boxes of oil. [191] Furbearers were trapped in fall and winter, with deadfall and snare; beaver could be taken only in fall and spring, not when protected by thick winter ice. Late fall, when larders were full, was potlatch time.

The poor snowshoes undoubtedly limited winter hunting, though young men attacked hibernating bears, fished for halibut, and snared ptarmigan and grouse. Most people remained home from December to early February, telling stories, making clothing and baskets, or doing other indoor chores.

Structures

The dwelling was a rectangular house of vertical planks, with a gable roof. A movable windscreen was hinged on the single ridgepole that crossed the smokehole. Sleeping rooms across the back and sides were roofed and floored with planks, entered by sliding doors, and illuminated by shell or cobblestone lamps. Bedding consisted of grass mats, pelts, twined goat wool blankets, and a sloping plank as the family pillow. Some Controller Bay houses in the nineteenth century had shedlike additions. There were also houses for single families, smokehouses for fish and meat in the villages and camps, and boxlike caches on tall posts.

Each village had a fort or palisaded enclosure around some or all the houses. Every important village also had a potlatch house for each moiety, with carved post (of Eagle or Raven moiety) in front. High benches around the walls served for sitting and sleeping; below were lockers with crest designs on the doors. These houses were equivalent to the Tlingit lineage or chiefs' houses, and like those were named; for example, Raven House, Goose House, and Bark House of the Raven moiety; Eagle House, (Eagle?) Skeleton House, Bed (Platform?) House, Beaver House, Beaver Dam House, Wolf House, Wolf Den House, and Wolf Bath House of the Eagle moiety. One built at Katalla about 1870 had two posts inside, carved with the Eagle, Beaver, and Beaver Dam crests (Barbeau 1950, 2: fig.376 top; Keithan 1963: 57).

Graveyards, as well as individual graves or grave houses, were surrounded by fences and also had crest memorials.

Transportation

The Eyak had a variety of wooden and skin boats. These included: a small cleft-prow dugout (fig. 4) for open water hunting, a small heavy-prowed canoe with a ram for sealing in the icy waters ofYakutat and Icy bays, a larger Tlingit-type dugout for 10-16 persons, sometimes with a European mast and sail, a larger war canoe with Raven or Eagle carved on the prow, slender dugouts for racing, Eskimo kayaks and two-hole bidarkas for sea otter hunting, and large canoes like umiaks of goat or sealskin.

Snowshoes webbed only under the feet were aboriginal from Cordova to Yakutat (fig. 6). Sleds were hand-drawn, for dogs were used only for hunting.

Fig. 3. Fish harpoon with detachable barbed iron head and cotton cord line. The iron head is 14cm long; the shaft, 356cm long and 3cm in diameter at the middle. The slotted end of the shaft is wrapped with cotton cord to prevent splitting, as the wedge-shaped tang of the barbed head would ram back and twist into the wood at every successive thrust. Abercrombie (1900: 397) reported that most of the salmon supply was taken with this implement. Collected by Frederica De Laguna, 1933. U. of Pa, U. Mus., Philadelphia; 33-29-1.

Fig. 4. Yakutat-type canoe, partly finished. Made by Gus Nelson, with an ad?., it was thought to be the more traditional shape (Birket-Smith and De Laguna 1938: 45). The man beside it is the canoe maker's brother, Galushia Nelson, one of Frederica De Laguna's major informants. Photograph by De Laguna, Old Town, Cordova, Alaska, 1933

Clothing and Adornment

Men wore their hair tied in a bunch, women in a braid, while the shaman's hung long and loose. Both sexes painted the face and wore earrings, nose ornaments, finger rings, and bracelets of native copper. Women, who tattooed their wrists, did not wear labrets except under Tlingit influence at Yakutat. No labrets were found in prehistoric sites.

The Eyak dressed like the Eskimo with trousers, boots, mittens, and a summer shirt with fur inside, over which was worn a hooded shirt in winter. For rain a hooded gutskin parka was donned. In summer men went barefoot and practically naked, for only a breechclout was noted in 1884 (Birket-Smith and De Laguna 1938: 70). An apron was worn to war. Men and women wore robes of small furs (preferably ground squirrel) or of twined goat wool. It was taboo for women to dress in fresh sealskins or to sew together land and sea mammal skins in one garment.

left, Naiionalmuseet, Copenhagen: H-2966; right, U. of Pa., U. Mus., Philadelphia: 3,1-29.3.

Fig. 6. Showshoes of the traditional type, with a 2-piece frame made from spruce; a pointed heel; a rounded, spliced, upturned toe; 2 or 3 crossbars; and webbing of seal thong (Birket-Smith and De Laguna 1938:56, 384). Photograph by Frederica De Laguna, Cordova, Alaska, 1933.

Technology

Tools, utensils, and weapons were like those of the Northern Tlingit or Chugach Eskimo except for the greater use of native copper for knives, ulu blades, scrapers, pins, harpoon heads for arrows, or sharp arrowheads. Eyak boxes, though decorated in Northern Northwest Coast style, were made of four separate pieces for the sides, morticed into the bottom. Abercrombie (1900) reported pipes with crude pottery bowls, the only mention of pottery. Bows were sinew-backed except the automatic bow set in a bear trail. Blunt arrows were used only at Yakutat. Fine spruce root baskets were decorated with false embroidery.

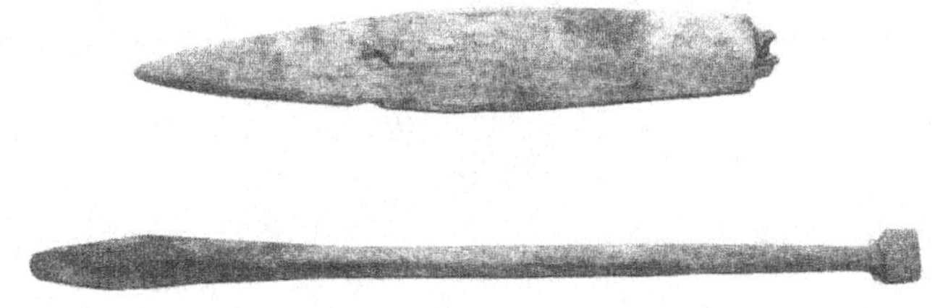

U. of Pa., U. Mus., Philadelphia; 33-29-2.

Fig. 5. Broken canoe paddle of characteristic Eyak form. with a crutch handle and an elongate, pointed blade. The handle has been reshaped as an ax handle. According to Birket-Smilh and De Laguna (1938:50) it was common for paddles to wear through at the handle from friction with the gunwale of the canoe. Collected by Frederica De Laguna, 1933. Length, 175 cm.

Social and Political Organization

Three classes were distinguished: chiefs and their families, commoners, and slaves. There was no tribal or village government; the moiety (or clan) chief in any village was leader only of his own people, although one chief was likely to be preeminent. Chiefs owned slaves, led war and hunting expeditions, and dressed themselves and their close kin in dentalia and fine clothing. Succession went to a younger brother or maternal nephew. Slaves (war [193] captives and their children) might be killed at the funeral of a chief or his relative.

The Eyak were divided into exogamous matrilineal moieties, Raven (or "Crow") (*či•lehyu•*) and Eagle (*gu•ʒgalagyu•*), equated with Tlingit Raven and Wolf-Eagle and with Ahtna Crow and Sea Gull moieties. Birket-Smith and De Laguna (1938: 447) believed that the Eyak lacked true clans and that even their moieties were recent, but Yakutat informants named their clans, and De Laguna (1975) has argued that matrilineal clans and moieties were ancient and widespread in northwestern North America. Krauss (1974) doubts their importance among the Eyak and points out that the moiety word for 'eagle' is of recent Chugach Eskimo derivation.

Eyak clans were semi-localized, while local groups tended to be identified as clans. Villages might be said to "belong" to a certain clan, probably because its chief was the most prominent or his clansmen most numerous, although both moieties were represented in each settlement. While Cordova Eyak denied that hunting areas were controlled by clans, this was the case from Controller Bay southward (Goldschmidt and Haas 1946; De Laguna 1972), although any relative of the owners might utilize their resources. The clans were the political and legal units.

According to Yakutat tradition, much Tlingit influence, probably including potlatch ceremonial and crests, was spread westward by *xatga•we•t,* a wealthy Tlingit chief and shaman of the te•q^we•dí (a Wolf clan), who was born near Dry Bay in the eighteenth century. He is said to have "organized" for trade the backward Eyak speakers of Yakutat, among whom he settled, but he also traveled all over, taking Eyak wives from places as far west as Cordova, bestowing Tlingit clan names on his wives' kinsmen, and introducing Tlingit ceremonial gift exchange (a familiar ploy for acquiring wealth from unsophisticated brothers-in-law). Stories about *xatga•we•t* belong among the many traditions documenting the northwestward movement of Tlingit into Dry Bay Athapaskan and Eyak territories, through trade, intermarriage, purchase of lands, or conquest (Swanton 1909: 154-165, 326-346; De Laguna 1972: 242-247).

Eyak clans are known chiefly by their Tlingit names (given in the following list unless otherwise indicated).

Clans of the Raven moiety were: 1. *ğa•'naxte•di',* 2. *qu•sk'e•di'* (Eyak *qu•sk'e•d),*
3. *łuk^wa•x?adi,* 4. *qahλayahd-dat'a•x-dalahğayu•* 'bark house people' (Eyak name), 5. *k^wa•šk'-q^wa•n* 'pink salmon people', 6. *hiny•di,* 7. *slax?adi or sdaxedi.*

Clans of the Eagle moiety were: 8. *ž̌i•šq^we•di* (Eyak *ž̌i•šq^we•t-yu'),* 9. *ğu•žihyu•* 'wolf people' (Eyak name), 10. *ğałyax-ka•g^wanta n,* 11. *ła•xa•yik-te•q^we•di,* 12. *ł'ux'^we•di'* 'muddy water people', 13. *y'any•di.*

Clans 1, 2, and 3 were in the Cordova-Copper River area, while 4 and 9 were "adopted Tlingit" who moved there from Controller Bay. Clan 8 was at Controller Bay, while 9, 10, and 11 were at both Controller Bay and the coast to the east. Clans 5, 6, 7, 11, 12, and 13 were in the Yakutat area, 7 and 13 at Arhnklin River, and 12 at Situk River.

Of clans 3, 6, 7, and 13, nothing more is known. Clans 1 and 5 are said to be branches of an Ahtna Raven clan who emigrated to the coast across the icefields. Those going west were named *ga'naxte'di* for the famous Chilkat Tlingit clan by *xatga'we•l,* who also named clan 2; those who went to Yakutat acquired their name by purchasing Humpback Salmon Creek. Clan 8, considered a branch of 10, is clearly equivalent to the Red Paint People of the Sea Gull moiety of the Ahtna, Upper Tanana, and Tanaina. Clans 11 and 12 were considered eastern branches of 10. Other clans at Yakutat are either Tlingit or of mixed Tlingit-Athapaskan origin.

Ambilateral cross-cousin marriage was preferred, with bride-service, and avunculocal residence. There was polygyny, the sororate, junior levirate (with access to the elder brother's wife during his lifetime), wife exchange, and even wife hospitality. There was avoidance between mother- and son-in-law; father- and daughter-in-law (?), grown brother and sister; but free joking between brother-and sister-in-law.

Killing or even accidental injury to someone in the opposite moiety or in another house (lineage or clan) necessitated payment of damages; grievances were aired in insulting songs.

Life Cycle

Fresh meat or fish were taboo to menstruants or pregnant women, for fear of offending the animals. All men left the house during childbirth; after 10 days of seclusion and taboos, the new parents purified themselves.

A girl's puberty seclusion lasted several months, involving special dishes, sucking tube, and bone scratcher. A boy's first kill was presented with gifts to members of the opposite moiety.

A dead body was laid out in the house for four days, watched by members of the opposite moiety, who tried to cheer the bereaved, then removed the corpse through a hole in the wall to be cremated or interred, according to the relatives' wishes. Slaves, witches, or evil taboo-breakers were always burned. Most of the deceased's property was burned or buried with him; some was saved to be burned or given away at his death potlatch. At this ceremony, the chief of the deceased's moiety acted as host to members of the opposite group, presenting food and gifts in order of rank, with special payments to the undertakers. Guests were addressed by their "potlatch names" (names of the dead in the hosts' moiety who were not yet reincarnated), but they accepted food and gifts on behalf of their own dead. Thus, all the deceased shared [194] what the living enjoyed. Potlatches were also held for building a new "potlatch house," or chiefs house.

Religion

All things, animate and inanimate, were believed to have spirit owners, or souls in anthropomorphic form. The human soul left the body temporarily in dreams, trances, or insanity. After death, it was supposed to enter the womb of a woman in the deceased's maternal line to be reincarnated, receiving again the same name and supposedly exhibiting the same personality and appearance.

Hunters cut the eyeballs of game, so that the animals could not see them, and put the heads, entrails, etc., in appropriate places to insure the animals' reincarnation. Bears were treated with respect, and there was a simple first-fish ceremony. Women were tabooed from touching or stepping over a man's weapons. A wife should remain quiet while her husband was hunting or chopping wood.

Cold water baths, use of a rubbing amulet (an incised pebble), sexual abstinence, fasting, bathing, or purging with devil's club infusion could bring good luck in a chancy undertaking or remove the contamination of childbirth or death.

Shamans (fig. 8) could be of either sex. The power was usually inherited though not manifested until after puberty when the spirit helpers appeared in dreams. The novice fasted, observed sexual continence, bathed in cold water, purged with devil's club infusion, and went alone into the woods, where spirits in animal or human form gave him power and taught him songs. Before practicing, the shaman observed the same regimen, put on bone and ivory necklaces, an apron with rattling fringe, a belt, and the special mask or face paint representing the spirit he invoked. Cures were effected by singing, laying on hands, and sucking out disease. Shamans could also prophesy, find lost persons or property, confer good or bad luck, walk on water, handle hot rocks or fire, free themselves from bonds, perform ventriloquist tricks, or make an image move (Birket-Smith and De Laguna 1938: 208-213). (Dolls were, therefore, taboo to girls.)

Witches of both sexes obtained evil power from dead dogs or human bones. They could fly, change shape, and bring misfortune or death. Shamans usually blamed sickness on witches, and those denounced might be fined or suffer death.

Prayers were addressed to the Sun. There was also belief in the Thunderbird, Property-Woman, monster animals, dwarfs, Tree People (giants that steal humans), man-eating Wolf-People, and Land Otter Men that transformed the drowned or lost into creatures like themselves. Northern Lights foretold death. Generosity to the poor or to starving animals was rewarded. Raven cycle myths are said to have been sung; other myths and tales resemble those of the Chugach Eskimo and Tlingit, some explaining the origin of crests.

left. Nalionalmimeet, Copenhagen; H-2966; right. U. of Pa., U. Mus., Philadelphia: 33-29-3.

Fig. 7. Ceremonial paddles used in potlatches like the dance paddles of the Tlingit, carried by song leaders 10 direct the singing and motions of their groups. Like Tlingh heirlooms, they could also be thrust between quarreling groups by a peacemaker lo end disputes. They are painted with commercial oil-based house paint, in black, red, and white. That on the left belonged lo the Raven moiety and was carved at the end lo represent the raven. On the sides were paintings probably representing an animal's face, two jumping salmon and a beaver lodge, The other paddle has a bear's head at the end and is painted with figures representing bugs with 6 legs, an anthropomorphic face, a jumping salmon, and beaver lodges. The owner said that the Raven paddle was carried into the potlatch house by the leader of the Raven guests to announce the coming of his group. The Bear paddle followed, and showed thai the Ravens were glad to come to the potlatch. Collected in 1933 by Frederica De Laguna; length of left 166 cm, other to same scale.

History

In 1783 Nagaiev (Zaikov 1979: 1-6) first learned from the Chugach Eskimo of the Eyak living "east of Kayak Island," but the Russians did not encounter any until [195] 1792, when Eyak from Cape Suckling and Tlingitized Yakutat Eyak attacked a party under Aleksandr Baranov in Prince William Sound (Baranov 1979: 27-37). In 1794 Purtov and Kulikalov (1979: 46-52) found no trace of habitation on the lower Copper River but discovered an Eyak village of 50 to 60 persons, at or near Kaliakh River, from which they took the chief and seven others as hostages, including two Yakutat men.

Fig. 8. Old Man Dude at his house on Simpson Bay, Alaska. He was a powerful shaman with a reputation among not only the Eyak but also the Chugach Eskimo (Birket-Smith and De Laguna 1938:10, 219-223). Photograph by Frederica De Laguna, 1933.

In 1796 Baranov himself supervised the establishment of a fort and agricultural colony at Yakutat, securing hostages from the Yakutat (Tlingit?) chief and from the Eyak-speakers of the vicinity. In the late eighteenth century, the

Yakutat people were still part Eyak, although the leading families were Tlingit or had adopted their speech and ways (Izmailov and Bocharov 1981; Beresford 1789; Colnett 1788; Malaspina 1885).

Native resentment of Russian tyranny and of poaching by their Aleut and Pacific Eskimo hunters led in 1799 to a massacre of a hunting party returning from Sitka by the Eyak at Cape Suckling; in reprisal an Eyak from Controller Bay was tortured to death by the Russians. The Yakutat people helped to plan the destruction of the Russian fort at Sitka in 1802 (rebuilt in 1804). In August 1805, the Russian post and colony at Yakutat were wiped out, the attack led by an Eyak of *the ła•'xa•yik-te'q^we•dí* clan; in commemoration the *te•q^we•dí* Bear crest was carved on a nearby rock.

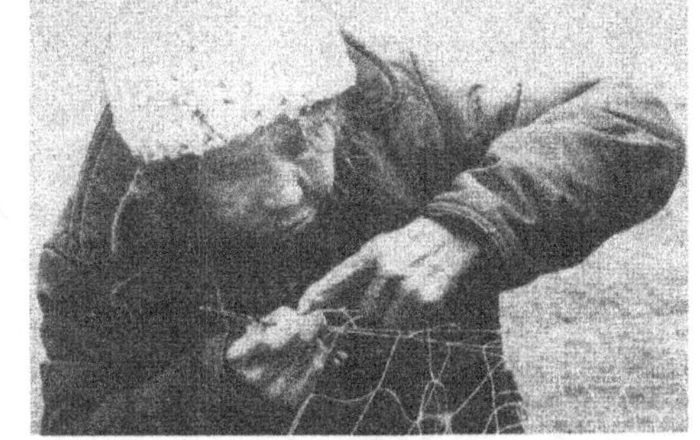

The *Fig. 9. Anna Nelson Harry mending a commercial gill net. She was an informant who gave valuable data on kinship terms and tales (Birket-Smith and De Laguna 1938:9-10), and on language (Krauss 1982: 17-18). Photograph by Martha Nelson. Yakutat, Alaska, about 1975.*
Russians never attempted to reestablish a post at Yakutat.

In the early nineteenth century, Tlingits from Dry Bay and southeastern Alaska, in part attracted by loot from the Russian post, completed their conquest of the Yakutat area, absorbing or enslaving the last Eyak people there. Smallpox in 1837-1838 wiped out about half the communities on the Gulf Coast.

From 1806 until about 1825, there were joint Eyak-Yakutat Tlingit attacks on the Chugach Eskimo and Chugach raids on the Eyak and Yakutat. Finally, the Chugach had to surrender Controller Bay, and the Eyak began to settle on the Copper River delta and the edge of Prince William Sound. Some Eyak were later involved in unsuccessful Russian attempts to explore the Copper River, apparently killing their masters. H.T. Allen (1887) used Eyak helpers on his 1885 expedition but could not induce them to venture into Ahtna territory beyond the first village.

Yakutat remained relatively isolated until visited by missionaries, prospectors, traders, and alpinists in the 1880s and 1890s. By 1900, practically all the natives from Dry Bay to Cape Suckling were concentrated at Yakutat, which was becoming a typical Tlingit cannery town, enjoying brief prosperity between 1910 and 1920.

In the Cordova-Controller Bay area the first cannery was built in 1889, but it offered little employment to the Eyak. After 1900 the Eyak found some work in the canneries. The discovery of oil near Katalla and the building of the Copper River and Northwestern Railroad, 1907-1910, forcing the natives from their homes, and the depletion of herring and salmon along the whole coast brought destitution to the remaining Eyak and their neighbors. This was the period in which the Cordova-Controller Bay Eyak were virtually destroyed. Debauched by alcohol, the native population was left to starve in winter or die from epidemics. Many children were shipped off to school at Chemawa, Oregon, from which few returned. By 1920 almost the only Eyak-speakers were those, fewer than 20, who lived at Old Town, Cordova. Population figures are given in table 1.

As a result of the Alaska Native Claims Settlement Act of 1971 (vol. 5: 657-661) the Eyak Corporation was established. In 1985, it included 319 Alaska Native shareholders [196] of which only two were Eyak. About one-third of the shareholders in the Eyak Corporation lived in the Cordova area (Lucas Borer, communication to editors 1985).

Table 1. Eyak Population, 1787-1985

Date	Population	Sources
1787	70-80[a] at most at Port Mulgrave	Beresford 1789: 87
1788	200[a] at most at Port Mulgrave	Colnett 1788
1791	1,000	Malaspina 1885: 345
1818-1819	117 in Controller Bay and Copper River delta	U.S. Census Office 1884: 33; Tikhmenev 1978-1979: 1: 161
1835	150[b] at Yakatut village	U.S. Census Office 1884: 35
1839	150[b] at most "near Mt. St. Elias"	U.S. Census Office 1884: 36
	38 families in Controller Bay area	Wrangell 1980: 49
1860	148 baptized	Tikhmenev 1978-1979, 1: 348
1874	300 in Controller Bay	Dall 1877: 23, 26-27
1880	444	U.S. Census Office 1884: 29
1890	236	U.S. Census Office 1893: 158
1899	59 Cordova area	Elliott 1900:739
1933	38 Cordova area	Birket-Smith and De Laguna 1938: 24
1973	30-40	Krauss 1974
1985	5	Michael E. Krauss, Personal communication 1986

[a] Includes Tlingit. [b] Mostly Tlingit.

Synonymy

The name Eyak, which is used in English as a self-designation, is taken from the name of the village Eyak near Cordova, where the last concentration of Eyaks lived. The Eyak name of this village is *ʔi•ya•g*, a borrowing from Chugach Eskimo *i'ɣya•q* 'outlet of a lake' (literally 'throat'). The spelling Eyak was first used by Abercrombie (1900: 384, 397) in 1884. Other spellings and variants include Ikhiak (Petroff 1884: 29), Eeak tella, for the Cordova-Copper River group (Emmons 1903), and perhaps Hyacks, 1869 (cited in Hodge 1907-1910, 1: 448).

The Eyak refer to themselves as *ʔi•ya•gdalahgayu•* (originally used in its literal meaning 'inhabitants of Eyak village') or simply as *daxyuyu•* 'human beings'.

The usual name for the Eyak in Tlingit *guté•x'qʷa•n*, but the Yakutat Tlingit use this or the variant k'*uté•x' qʷa•n* for 'Chugach Eskimo' (vol. 5: 7; Krauss 1970a: 280) and call the *Eyak yá•t qʷa•n* 'local inhabitants', because Eyak was the original language at Yakutat. The Ahtna, though farther up the Copper River, called the Eyak *dangene*, literally 'uplanders' (De Laguna and McClellan 1954-1968; Kari and Buck 1975: 59), perhaps because they most often reached them by going up the Chitina and Tana rivers and over the Bagley Icefield to the coast.

The Russians referred to the Eyak as Ugaliakhmiut-(with Russian inflections), variants having -la- for -lia- and -mu- for *miu*-, and by the Russianized form Ugalenfsy (Wrangell 1839: 51), names which appeared in German as Ugalachmut and Ugalenzen (Teben'kov 1981; Shelekov 1793, 1981; Radloff 1858; Wrangell 1839a, 1980: 49). This name is from Chugach Eskimo *uŋalaɣmiut* 'people of the southeast' according to Krauss (1970a: 654). Names that appear to be ultimately variants or corruptions of this include Wallamute (Portlock 1789), Lakhamutes (Petroff 1884), Lakhamit or Lakhamites (Bancroft 1886). Bancroft also applied Agelmute(s) to Eyak from the Copper and Kaliakh rivers. Elliott (1900) named Agahgniute the Indians at Eyak or "Odiak" Village.

The Russians recognized the Eyak as distinct from the Eskimo and as linguistically distinct from the Tlingit, yet they often called them Kolosh (Tlingit) because their culture was like that of the Yakutat Tlingit. Russian IAkutatskii 'the Yakutat language' sometimes refers specifically to Eyak (Davydov 1810-1812, 2: appendix).

It was Dall (1870, 1877) who introduced the erroneous notion that Eyak "Ugalakmiut" were really Eskimos transformed into Tlingits. This error was perpetuated by Petroff (1882, 1884), Emmons (1903), Swanton (1908a, 1952), Hodge (1907-1910), and Kroeber (1939). For a time Dall (1877) even confused the Eyak with the Ahtna, supposing that the "Ah-tena" or "Ugalentsi" had a colony on Controller Bay.

Sources

Aside from brief items in Shelekhov (1791, 1793, 1981), Coxe (1803), and in Wrangell (1839, 1970), or references in Tikhmenev (1861-1863, 1978-1979), the earliest ethnographic information on the Eyak is in Jacobsen (1884) and Abercrombie (1900). The major source on Eyak culture, problems of nomenclature, and territorial claims is Birket-Smith and De Laguna (1938), apart from the preliminary sketch of De Laguna (1937). The same problems have been discussed by Johansen (1963), without new data. Additional information obtained at Yakutat, including notes from Harrington and Krauss, is utilized in De Laguna (1972). Archeological data are found in De Laguna et al. (1964). The definitive works on Eyak linguistics are by Krauss (1970, 1970a), which include all information from previous sources.

Stories told in Eyak by Anna Nelson Harry, the last speaker of the language, translations, and a sketch of her life appear in Krauss (1982).

De Laguna

A History of Eyak Language Documentation and Study:
Fredericæ de Laguna in Memoriam

Michael E. Krauss

Abstract. Frederica de Laguna is generally considered the person who "discovered" Eyak. This paper chronicles a parade of characters who recorded Eyak in (over 9) vocabularies (1778-1862) and even phonographically (1899); more who defined or mapped it, even (1863) in color. Freddy's fieldwork of the 1930s is then discussed, and finally that of linguists after her (1940-2006). This is a history full of ironies that should entertain the reader appreciative of humanistics, human foibles, and the history of science.

Frederica de Laguna stumbled upon Eyak, i.e. (re-)"discovered" Eyak, in 1930. However, she was by no means the first to stumble upon Eyak. That honor goes to William Anderson, in 1778, the first person ever to write down an Eyak word. In fact, then from 1778 to 1885 there are over 20 written sources of various kinds, documenting or defining, or mapping the Eyak language. Of these sources, six are mere individual or a few words, identifed as Eyak or not, but six more are formal vocabularies of Eyak as such, ranging in length from 80 to 1,128 words transcribed during the Russian period. Of these formal vocabularies, one was published in English, and two more, including the 1,128 words, were published in German. Moreover, there are at least nine sources explicitly recognizing Eyak as a separate language. Two of those are well-known maps, dated 1796 and 1863, the latter published in color, no less! The other sources, no fewer than eight, are discussions of Eyak as such and its genetic relations. Six of these were published – mostly in German. Eyak was thus very well recognized and documented by the standards of the time, when Franz Boas arrived from Germany upon the American scene. Nevertheless, when in 1930 Frederica de Laguna, Boas's student, came to Cordova, Alaska, to outfit for Chugach Eskimo archeology, it was mere chance that she then first learned about Eyak. This is a history full of ironies. I hope to do justice to them for the reader appreciative of humanistics and the history of science. Given that even science is still done by human beings, in chronicling the remarkable parade of characters involved with Eyak, inevitably certain human traits that affect this history are too lively to conceal. I give up, and unapologetically hope that the result may be entertaining and instructive. For the Eyak contribution to this history we have not a single person's name, unfortunately, until all that changed with Freddy in 1930. A stylistic note: in his old age Krauss calls all females by their first name, and males, including himself, by their last.

The first part of this paper, the longest and most detailed, deals chronologically with the rich pre-1930 history of Eyak language work, completely unknown to Freddy, harping on that. The second section deals with the period of her Eyak work, and the last is a summary of work done after her. [173]

The Pre-Russian Period, 1778-1791

The Russians' first direct contact with Alaska Natives was Gvozdev at the Diomedes and

King Island in 1732; Bering's first landfall, Kayak Island, in 1741, without direct contact, was just offshore from Eyak territory. However, the Russians apparently did not approach Eyak territory again for another 40 years, until the 1780s, and did not establish installations near it until the 1790s. In the meanwhile, from 1778–1791, at least four foreign expeditions made significant contact at the extreme ends of Eyak territory, two English at the Prince William Sound end (Anderson and Walker-Strange), and one English (Colnett) and one Spanish (Malaspina) at the Yakutat end. This was enough to write down Native Alaskan words including some Eyak, or to notice Eyak as being different (Colnett). The Eyak words from Prince William Sound, collected in 1778 and 1786, were an admixture in formal Chugach vocabularies, not recognized as Eyak, as was the ethnonym collected at Yakutat as part of a formal Tlingit vocabulary. Here we shall deal only with those sources, not with those that may have had direct or indirect contact but show no evidence of Eyak language data or recognition of Eyak as a separate language from Chugach and/or Tlingit.

Anderson 1778

William Anderson (b. 1750, d. 1778) was James Cook's surgeon and naturalist on the *Resolution* in Alaska. This young Scot, not yet thirty and dying, was most certainly one of the very great lights on that momentous expedition. Modest, agreeable, diligent, Anderson was a most loved and esteemed member of that illustrious crew. His ethnographic and linguistic skills were outstanding, as were his medical and naturalistic. By the time the expedition reached Prince William Sound, mid-May 1778, Anderson knew he was near death from the tuberculosis that had consumed him for a year. His journals end two weeks after the expedition left Prince William Sound, and he died at sea, on August 3, 1778. The last of Anderson's three journal books from that expedition is lost, most unfortunately, and all we have left of it is what was taken from it by editor John Douglas for Volume II of the published *Voyage* (Cook 1784). This includes, pp. 375-376, a "Vocabulary of Prince William's Land," a list of 25 entries. Of these, the last 8 are numerals, not from Prince William Sound, however, but from Cook Inlet Tanaina Athabaskan – presumably unbeknownst to the editor. This short vocabulary thus has the first words ever written of Alaskan Athabaskan (as well as of Alutiiq and probably Eyak). The expedition reached Cook Inlet about one week before Anderson ceased to write, so this must be his very last work. Of the remaining 16 words on the list, 10 are identifiable uniquely as Chugach Yupik, 2 could be either Yupik or Eyak, and 3 are not identifiable as Yupik but could well be Eyak. The best example might be *Akashou*, 'What's the name of that?', possibly Eyak *'a:k'e:'sh ew* 'he/she/it maybe?' or *'anh k'e:'sh ew* 'he/she maybe?', meaning roughly 'Do you mean him/her?', hardly a poor response, given no common language. The year 1778 is rather early for Eyak to be in evidence in Prince William Sound, as the Eyak takeover of even the Copper River delta from the Chugach may not have begun until the early nineteenth century. If the words were not from Eyaks directly, it could be that the Chugach were using some Eyak words they knew, in order to communicate better with the English, especially since the Chugach must have known that the ships had come from the Eyak direction. The only manuscript source or version for this vocabulary is Admiralty ms. 55/113, f. 60, a clerk's copy of a comparative Eskimo-Aleut vocabulary, which for "Sandwich [Prince William] Sound" includes only the Tanaina numerals plus *Aa* for 'Yes, or Aye' (which could be Yupik or Eyak) and *Akashou*, here with a macron over the second *a* and an accent mark after it, glossed 'What call you that?' It is thus an independent source from that published, and is for some reason very partial. Of course it raises still further question as to what was in the lost Anderson journal, of which perhaps only this hodgepodge remains. It is thus quite unclear just how accidental the potential Eyak entries were.

Walker and Strange 1786

Eight years after Anderson sailed with Cook, two more enterprising Scots, now from the British military in India, sailed to Prince William Sound, where they also took down a Prince William Sound vocabulary. The expedition, private – though loosely associated with the British East India Company, was organized and led by James Strange (b. 1753, d. 1840) under the military command of Alexander Walker (b. 1764, d. 1831) in the *Experiment* and the *Captain Cook.* Inspired by Cook's *Voyage* (1784), their expedition, though basically commercial, also had scientific goals, and had also put in at Nootka, where they too collected a large Nootka vocabulary, before they sailed to Prince William Sound. They were in the sound from Au gust 29 to September 16, 1786. Both men kept journals, but neither of these was published until the twentieth century. Strange's appeared in 1928 (then again in 1929, reset, in Madras; Strange 1928 and 1929; the vocabulary is on pp. 54-57). Walker's was not published until 1982 (nicely, with informative apparatus and background; [174] Walker 1982, vocabulary on pp. 156-160). Unlike the unfortunate case of Anderson, we also have at least five manuscripts including the vocabulary, though still not the original. For Strange we have three manuscript copies in the Tamil Naidu Archives, Madras, number not given (from which the 1928-1929 publication presumably comes); British Library, India Office, Home Misc. 800, ff. 158r?- 160r (both are "true copy from the original" signed by Strange); and Archive of British Columbia, F8 St8, pp. 15-19. For Walker we have mss. 13776-13781 at the Scottish National Library, of which at least two include the vocabulary, ms. 13778, ff. 90v-92v, and ms. 13780, ff. 113r-114v. Walker himself states the original is lost. The 1982 publication is from the more fully prepared ms. 13780, but the vocabulary is from ms. 13778, presumably being closer to the original. It seems quite clear that the author of both the Nootka and Prince William Sound vocabularies was Walker, and not Strange. Strange was the businessman and entrepreneur, who evidently could see, however, the importance or desirability of including vocabularies in his report. The young Walker, on the other hand, savored contact with the Native Americans, took real interest in ethnology, and during his career in India became a prominent authority on Indian languages and culture. Most of the entries in the Prince William Sound vocabulary are of course clearly identifiable as Chugach, but there are eight which are much more probably Eyak, and not (or hardly) identifiable as Chugach. These entries are scattered in Strange (S), but – very significantly – six of them are clustered consecutively toward the end in Walker (W). An example of the non-clustered entries in Walker are (W) *Konee,* (S) *Hoonee* (Strange 1929, but Strange manuscript *Koonee*) 'to rain', modern Eyak *k'uleh*, from older Eyak **k'uneh* 'rain'; the closest possible Chugach would be *qaniq* 'snow'. An example of the clustered entries is (W) *Esh-est-esh*, 'No. you. do you hear.', cf., (S) *Esht-est-esh* 'No! you! do you hear? calling to one.' This cannot be read as Chugach at all, but as Eyak *'i:sh(d[uh]),'i:sh(d[uh]), 'i:sh*, where *'i:sh* is *'i:-sh* 'you (singular) (interrogative)', i.e., 'You?', cf., modern Eyak *'i:shuh* 'Hello', literally 'Is it you (sg.)?'; and the *'i:sh(d[uh])* is roughly 'I wonder if it's you (sg.), could it be you (sg.)?', probably truncated. They both also have *Kai* and *Agalshou* (Strange manuscript; but Strange 1928, 1929 *Agalchou*), for 'What is that?', probably in an attempt to reelicit Anderson's *Akashou* 'What call you that?', as they certainly had a copy of Cook 1784. The results were *k'e:'[-t]* and *' eg-, ' elsh ew* (where *-g-* is a spirant gamma about to become a *-w*), thus, roughly, 'How?/Wha-?' and '[You mean] tha-, this?', again with truncations, giving a pretty vivid picture of these attempts at communication. Without going further into linguistic detail, suffice it to say that possibly Anderson (in 1778) and even more possibly Walker-Strange (in 1786) had even an Eyak subsection in their lost manuscripts of original Prince William Sound vocabularies, though there is no evidence they knew they were getting more than one language there. However, if this were all we had, the forms are too few and the correspondence between the forms and meanings too vague for us so far to know, without the subsequent record, that there ever was an Eyak language – perhaps only that there was some strange admixture in Prince William Sound Yupik at the time. Also of course the spellings are far too deficient for us to discern phonetically whether the Eyak words were spoken by Eyaks or by the Chugach.

Colnett 1788

The last British source, of a new kind, is James Colnett (b. 1755?, d. 1806) in the *Prince of Wales*, who had been in Prince William Sound for a month, sailed thence to Yakutat, and stayed there a week, June 3-9, 1788. His journal from that voyage was only recently published (Colnett 2004). De Laguna (1972: 128-132) quotes from the manuscript, about Yakutat (here quoted from Colnett 2004: 225): "At this place appears to commence a different Nation from those residing to the North ... & I believe belong to different tribes, as there was a Variation also in their Language, several counting numbers not with the same name & when ask'd where resided pointed different ways." Colnett thus observes that there is more than one language at Yakutat. Moreover, he seems to imply, perhaps, that neither is the same as that he heard in Prince William Sound, of which he had even written a short vocabulary. Freddy adds: "Unfortunately no [Yakutat] vocabularies are given" (de Laguna 1972: 130). If there had been even a few numerals, we not only would have our first evidence that the other end of Eyak territory was Yakutat, but we already would also have had our first written direct proof that Eyak was different from both Tlingit and Chugach – though that might hardly have changed our history if it had been published.

Malaspina 1791

We do not know for certain that there were Eyaks near Prince William Sound before Russian penetration there, except insofar as we can tell from Anderson and Walker-Strange. At the other end of known Eyak territory, however, we have plentiful evidence that Yakutat Bay was still (partly) Eyak. Just before Russian penetration of Yakutat, we have one more "pre-Russian" contact and source for Eyak language there too, the major Spanish expedition [175] of the *Descubierta* and *Atrevida* led by Alessandro Malaspina. Malaspina (b. 1734, d. 1809) was a very able Sicilian, in Spanish service. His expedition, the most ambitious the Spanish ever sent to Alaska, was clearly meant to be the Spanish answer to Cook and his scientific accomplishments. Malaspina was in Yakutat Bay for ten days, June 27 to July 6, 1791. After his return to Spain he was working on the expedition results (1794-1795), but ran badly afoul of Spanish politics, was imprisoned (1795-1803), his papers were seized, and the results of his expedition were long mostly suppressed.

Finally in 1885 a report appeared including a Yakutat vocabulary, "Vocabulario del idioma [Puerto] Mulgrave," in *Viaje Político-científi co alrededor del Mundo ... desde 1789 a*

1794 (Malaspina 1885: 349-351). This turns out to be a nearly pure – except for one item – Tlingit wordlist, of 126 entries, in Spanish alphabetical order, plus 26 numerals. Of the 126 words, over 100 can be clearly identified as Tlingit, and almost none of the rest look like Eyak. One might wonder at this absence of Eyak admixture, given the still prominent presence of Eyak at Yakutat in 1791. However, the explanation is all too clear, from the introduction to the vocabulary. The 1885 version of that is as follows:

> En la formación del corto Diccionario que aquí se agrega, no nos hemos tampoco apartado del método lento y refl exivo, que nos habíamos propuesto: muchos Oficiales han formado por sí un Diccionario separado, y confrontados éstos no se ha admitido voz alguna, la cual no tuviese la sanción general ó no descubriese de dónde dimanaba una ú otra contradicción.
>
> [In compiling the short vocabulary added here, we still did not depart from the slow and thoughtful method we have intended; several officers compiled a separate vocabulary by themselves, and comparing those, not a single word was included which did not meet general approval or where the source of any remaining discrepancy could not be discovered.] (Malaspina 1885: 349-351)

This standardization surely was no trivial task in itself, if the officers were, indeed, working separately rather than looking very intently over each other's shoulder. The chance that any two would independently come up with the same words and even the same spelling of them had to be infinitesimal indeed, given no common language and the vast differences between Spanish and Tlingit or Eyak sound systems. They were in any case mightily striving that their collective result should be correct, authentic, official, standardized, pure Yakutat Tlingit language, cleansed of deviant impurities that they took such pains to reject. The probability that many or most of the rejected words were Eyak is of course very high – perhaps even whole lists of the greatest interest were thus lost.

It therefore became a high priority to search archives, to find any "pre-purified" Malaspina Yakutat wordlists. Krauss's search, mainly in 1978 and 1991-1993, revealed no fewer than nine manuscript versions of that Yakutat vocabulary (Spanish Naval Archives, Museo Naval, Madrid: mss. 95 ff. 118v-121v and 348-349v; 289 ff. 32-35v and 72-72v; 425 ff. 155v-157v; 633 ff. 82-83v; British Library, Bauzá Collection, ADD. 17.631, pp. 30-31, 32-33, and 34–35, copied at Bancroft Library, M-M 525, Microfilm 131). Sadly, these are all only the same "purified" vocabulary, with but minor variations, relevant only to the early documentation of Tlingit, not of Eyak. (Other much shorter vocabularies from that expedition at Yakutat have also been found so far, from Suria and Bauzá, at other repositories, but both these too are Tlingit only.)

The Malaspina expedition is not quite a total loss for Eyak, however. The captain of the *Atrevida*, Antonio de Tova Arrcdondo, reports that on approaching Yakutat again on July 25, from the West, they met and traded with a canoer headed toward Yakutat: "his language differed somewhat from that of the natives of Port Mulgrave" (Ortiz 1943: 161). Wallace Olson (personal communication, 2002) reports a Bauzá manuscript account of the same contact, more detailed about the canoer's language, as follows: "Era un joven de buena statura, y de fisionomia muy semejante a los de Mulgrave: el idioma parecia no ser el mismo; pues no contestaba a varias palabras que se le dijeron en aquel; parecia habíl, y manifestó muchas complascencias en los regales que se hicieron. [He was a young man of good stature, and his outward appearance was very similar to those of Mulgrave; his language did not appear to be the same, since he did not respond to the various words which were spoken to him in that (language); he seemed clever and showed much pleasure in the gifts that were given to him.]" Though we may never find record of any words written down from him, the accounts do indeed suggest his language may have been Eyak. It is of course unlikely that he knew no Tlingit, but, insofar as the Spanish were presumably reading off their Yakutat vocabulary we know, one can easily imagine their pronunciation from their woefully deficient transcription was so poor that the words could have been unrecognizable even to a Tlingit, let alone to an Eyak. For these and other accounts of that encounter, which vary in their characterization of the man's language from "the same as" or "similar to" that of Port Mulgrave, to "different," see Olson 2002: 371 (Malaspina, "same"), Olson 2002: 418-419 (Viana, "differed somewhat"), Olson 2002: 430-431 (Bauzá above), Olson 2002: 446 (Bustamente y Guerra, [176] "similar"), Olson 2002: 459-460 (Tova Arredondo above). No standardization here!

We do indeed have one Eyak word, nevertheless, from the Malaspina expedition, found frequently, routinely, throughout the Malaspina Yakutat journals, namely the ethnonym for the people themselves, *Tejunenses, Tejuneses, Tujuneses,* or *Tejunes.* With the Spanish endings removed, that clearly has to be the Eyak *dex. unh.* There the *d-* corresponds exactly to Spanish *T-,* - e- (Eyak indistinct short shwa) gets written, unsurprisingly, with an *-e-* or *-u-, -x.* - (Eyak voiceless back velar fricative) is very close to Spanish *-j-,* and *-unh* (nasalized *u,* followed by *h-* like aspiration) is fairly close to Spanish *-un.* In short, *Tejun* or *Tujun* is the very most likely result of any attempt to write *d ex. unh* in Spanish. That Eyak word means 'person, people' (as opposed to animals), or 'Eyak(s)' (as opposed to other peoples). The word *d ex. unh* is itself unanalyzable in Eyak; it is probably a diffusion from Yupik *taru* (where *-r-* is the voiced back velar fricative), meaning 'person,' usually used by shamans in rituals; that is relatable moreover to Eskimo forms which have an *-n-, tanru-, tarnu-,* hence probably the nasalization in Eyak; perhaps also thus relatable even to Aleut *tayaru-.* This word is also the only Eyak word – perhaps better, the only word of Eyak origin – in the entire "purified" Malaspina Yakutat Tlingit vocabulary. There it is listed, under *N-,* as *"Nombre de la Nación ó Tribú,"* and is spelled in the manuscripts *Tejunne* or *Tejunue,* usually with an accent, acute or grave, on the final *-e.* The variation between the second *-n-* and *-u-* is certainly from inversion of a letter, we cannot tell which, the segment *-ne* or *-ue* not being recognizable as either Eyak or Tlingit. It must derive from the Spanish versions of the ethnonym shown above, especially the *-ne.* The interpretation "[Chief] Juné's people" (cited in de Laguna 1972: 144) may well be inspired by Spanish *de*(!). It cannot be justified by any *Te*-like prefix in Eyak or Tlingit. It remains a mystery, though, how or why this one single basic Eyak word was given as the very definitive name of the people that the Spanish worked so unfortunately hard to get a "pure" Yakutat Tlingit vocabulary from!

The Russian Period, 1792–1867

Malaspina's 1791 expedition marks the end of the pre-Russian period of our history. By 1792 a Russian post was established at Nuchek in Prince William Sound, which lasted peacefully into the American period. At the other end of Eyak territory, at Yakutat in 1795, the Russians asserted their presence also much more ambitiously, establishing a veritable colony. The history of that colony was short (ten years) but nasty and for the Eyaks especially fateful. After 1791 information on Eyak and Eyak language is all of Russian origin, until well after the sale of Alaska. Moreover, all the rest of that documentation of Eyak seems to be from the Yakutat end, until about 1820, at which point Eyak was disappearing there.

Purtov and Kulikalov 1794

The year before the Russian colonization of Yakutat itself, Egor Purtov and Demid Kulikalov (d. 1806) – neither perhaps a very savory character – were leading a sea-otter hunting fleet of 500 baidarkas from Kodiak toward Yakutat. They stopped at Yakataga and made a personal visit, May 31 to June 5, to the nearby (Kaliakh River) village, then still all or mostly Eyak. There are published references to their stay and the fact that they made a census there (de Laguna 1972: 161-163; Grinev 1993: 75-76; Tikhmenev 1863: 82, 1979: 162-63), and at Yakutat, but the manuscript source, including the censuses themselves, not published, is at the Tentral'nyigosudarstvennyiarkhiv drevnikh aktov, (Fond 1605, Opis' 1, Delo 352, ff. 12-17v). The Kaliakh census (a "*Kopiia*") lists the names and ages of heads of families, their wives, their sons and daughters, and in some cases notes status as hostage or prisoner (slave). The Kaliakh list includes 83 such names, including 11 from "Yakutat Bay" (where "circumstances did not permit a full census"). The Yakutat (AkhoiRiver village) census itself lists 112. Personal names are very difficult to interpret to begin with, having no meaning shown, if any, being often of foreign origin (here especially Tlingit), and for this period being of course also very deficiently transcribed. Still, a few names from Kaliakh can be interpreted as Eyak with some confidence, e.g., *El'kunt* is ' *ełku:n't*, (where -*ł*- is the voiceless lateral fricative) 'grab it!' (a 25-year old man), *Shiia* is *shiyah* 'bad/cute' (a six-year-old girl), and *Kiin-ksh* is *k'i:nk'sh* 'dry salmonberries' (a 20-year-old wife). Many of the rest also look like they could well be Eyak names, but a good number look more like Tlingit or Chugach. Some Yakutat Bay and AkhoiRiver names look like they could be Eyak too, but far fewer in proportion, not surprisingly, than at Kaliakh. – In this connection, it should be noted that of the Eyak names remembered even from Cordova in the twentieth century, a fair proportion were opaque, or were of Tlingit or Chugach origin. – Thus our first Russian source of Eyak, the Purtov-Kulikalov 1794 Kaliakh census, from near the Yakutat end, is clearly recognizable as primarily Eyak, our first such source. But it is in the most problematical realm, of personal names, so that little Eyak linguistic information can be gathered from it so far, even from a list now of 72 or more entries. [177]

Figure 1. Right section of Shelikov's 1796 map. From Shelikhov and Pierce 1981. Endpaper.

Shelikhov 1796

We now come to a new and altogether different kind of contribution to the history of the study of Eyak, Shelikhov's 1796 map, the first (ethno-)linguistic map of Alaska we know of. Entrepreneur Grigorii Ivanovich Shelikhov or Shelekhov (b. 1748, d. 1795) was basically a founder of the Russian-American Company, though he spent only two years himself in Alaska, establishing the headquarters on Kodiak, 1784-1786. The year after his death in 1795, somehow this map, attributed to him, appeared (Fig. 1). We know of at least two basic versions of this map, one with eight small detail insets or cartouches along the bottom and a long legend set off by a scrollwork border, and a second without the cartouches and the same legend set off by a tree and vegetation figure. It is entitled *"Karta morskaia severo-vostochnoi Aziii, i severo-zapadnoi chasti Ameriki ...* [Maritime map of northeast Asia and the northwest part of America ...].*" This map is memorable for Alaska especially in two ways. It includes on Seward Peninsula and Norton Sound (and beyond) over 50 of the 80 Inupiaq place-names gathered by Kobelev from an elder on Diomede in 1779 and first published in 1783. Most originally, however, it includes ethnolinguistic borders along the Pacific coast, dividing that clearly into five sectors labeled vertically as follows: *KO-NIA-GI* across Central Yupik, Alaska Peninsula, and Kodiak, respectively (= Yupik); *KE-NAI-TSY* along the west side of Cook Inlet (= Tanaina); *CHU-GA-CHI* over Prince William Sound; *UGA-LAX-MIU-TY* right where it belongs, between Prince William Sound and Yakutat (= Eyak!); and *KO-LIU-ZHI* beyond (= Tlingit) (Fig. 2). The scrollwork version lacks the *Kenaitsy* label itself, and has Eyak as *UGALAX-MIUTY*. Aleut is not labeled on either map, the tree, or the scrollwork. It seems that Shelikhov was very naturally interested in producing for officialdom a map recognizing the distinct Native peoples of his colony, perhaps especially the newer part – Aleut, being a given, was not labeled. Shelikhov evidently assembled the map from information gathered especially during 1783-1788, including information from Nagaiev and Zaikov in 1783 and Izmailov and Bocharov in 1788 (for details see especially [178] de Laguna 1972: 112-138). Their reports must have made it clear to Shelikhov that *Ugalakhmiut* was a distinct group of some kind, though it is not so clear to what extent the distinction was based on language itself.

Figure 2. Detail from Shelikov map.

The name *Ugal(i)akhmiut* (with many variants) clearly comes from Chugach *Ungalarmiut* 'those who live to the East.' It means just that in the Chugach area, and could therefore refer to people of any language, including fellow Chugach who live, e.g., on Kayak Island, or of course to Eyak. The real Chugach name, at least in the twentieth century, for the Eyaks specifically was *Qiggwanat*, literally 'those to be raided, raidables' (personal communication, Jeff Leer), a name that never got into the literature. – *Ugal(i)akhmiut* with Russian plural *-y* often (redundantly!) added, became the standard "official" Russian name for Eyaks, along with also the Russified equivalent thereof, *Ugalentsy*. Chugach *Ungalarmiut* is accented on the second and third syllables, so allows for much variation in the transcriptions of the first, which often appears as *A-*, or as nothing. – The *A-* variants sometimes lead to confusion with *Aglurmiut* (*Aglegmiut* = *Agliogmiut*) of Bristol Bay, not related. With the initial syllable completely gone, the lip-rounding from the *-ng-* preceded by *U-* remains, with resulting "Wala-" (see especially Birket-Smith and de Laguna 1938: 328-340 in this connection).

Shelikhov's map shows conclusively that the Russians by 1796 had defined Eyak (language or not) quite clearly. His map itself though was not published until the twentieth century. The scrollwork variant was first published in Efimov (1964, map no. 184), but the tree variant was published before that, in Andreev (1948: 378-379); also the Alaskan part was published as an endpaper in Shelikhov and Pierce (1981). From the literature it appears, somewhat unclearly, that there are four versions of this map in Russian archives: 1) that in Efimov 1964, with scrollwork and cartouches, held in Moscow Tsentral'nyi (Gosudarstvennyi) Voenno-Istoricheskii Arkhiv (Fond VUA, Delo 23461); 2) that in Andreev 1948, with tree, no cartouches, in the same archive (no number given), but then Andreev 1948: 379 mentions another copy there "without cartouches;" 3) held in St. Petersburg, Tsentral'nyi Kartograficheskii Proizvodstva Voenno-Morskogo Flota (Fond Starinnykh Atlasov, Portfel' 4, No. 1301), possibly with scrollwork and cartouches; and 4) in St. Petersburg Public Library, Manuscript Division (Map No. 1406, a copy by Kozhavin). Krauss has seen only the last, not in color, but it is possible that any of the first three are in color. After Shelikhov all Russian maps that show Native groups clearly include Eyak as distinct. The first such may be from 1802, engraved, with the same group names and lines clearly shown (see e.g., Postnikov 2000: 197-200, 409; [179] used by A. von Humboldt 1811: 347-349). In 1821 Berkh published a map of

Alaska (and Canada), including those names, without the lines (see Efimov 1964, Map No. 190). After that there is a virtual profusion of such maps, even of all of North America, in French, German, and English, from 1822 at least to 1875. This includes an American one of 1867, very clearly showing "OOGALAKMUTE" along the Copper River to Yakutat stretch. Probably the first American version and a particularly important one was Albert Gallatin's color map of North America published in 1836 with his ground-breaking classification of Indian languages, certainly a hallmark in the history of American linguistics. Meanwhile, the Russian-American Company issued in annual reports (1844-1859) versions of a map of Alaska with those names, obviously still derived ultimately from Shelikhov 1796, e.g., in omitting Aleut. See also Verman in Tikhmenev (1863), listed separately below.

Tarkhanov 1796-1797

Our next known source after Purtov-Kulikalov of actual Eyak language data happens to come from the very same spot as theirs, Kaliakh, two years later. Geologist Dmitrii Tarkhanov, who had helped build the fort at Yakutat, started from the new colony October 7, 1796, on a journey on foot along the coast to and up the Copper River, through Eyak territory, with Native companions, including Eyak speakers. His journal lay long forgotten at the St. Petersburg Public Library (Manuscript Division, Sbornik Q.IV.311) until attention was drawn to it by Grinev (1987, 1997). It has not yet been published. Krauss examined it in 1988 and 1990, when he obtained a photocopy, with the help of NikolaiVakhtin. The part of its 67 pages that concerns us most here describes Tarkhanov's lengthy stay at Kaliakh, November 27, 1796 to February 4, 1797, including an exploration of the Kaliakh River January 3-18. On pages 28-30 of the journal Tarkhanov gives the names and description of five tributaries to the Kaliakh, four of which are easily enough identifiable as Eyak, especially because they are not proper names of specific tributaries, but in fact generic Eyak terms: 1. *Chakh* is *ch'a:x* 'muddy/silty water', 2. *Kats* is *q' ets'* 'slough', 3. *Lakh* is *l eq* 'ashore, up from shore', and 4. *Ikalaki* must be *'a:n-g el e-kih* 'small river,' where *-kala-* is the expected classmark *-g el e-* for anything liquid, *-kih* is 'small', and *I-* is a mistake for *A-*, for *'a:n-* (with long nasalized *a*) 'river', given that Cyrillic *i/I* and *a/A* are very easy to confuse in copying, much like English cursive *a* and *u* are, depending on how much the top is closed. Number 5. *Kastye* is not clearly identifiable. In addition, Tarkhanov adds one noun, *sak* for *sa:k* 'eulachon, candlefish,' which is the same in Eyak and Tlingit, and writes several times in various spellings the name of the Kaliakh itself, *Gełyex* (where *G* and *x* are back velars), literally "the lowermost of a vertical series." These seven forms from Tarkhanov are the last addition we have to the Eyak documentation of the eighteenth century – not too spectacular a contribution for the man who must have heard incomparably more Eyak than any other European of the time.

Davydov 1802-1806

Personable Gavriil Ivanovich Davydov (b. 1784, d. 1809) was an intrepid young naval officer and keen observer of Native life. He made two trips to Alaska in rapid succession, the first to Kodiak where he wintered November 1802 to June 1803, then traveled back to St. Petersburg. On his second trip, more adventurous, along with Rezanov (see below), by summer 1805 he was back in Kodiak for a month (July 21-August 20), then he traveled to Sitka (August 25-October 15), then to Kodiak again and back to Sitka (where he stayed November 7 to Feb ru ary 26, 1806). He accompanied Rezanov from Sitka on his famous trip to California, and was back in Sitka June 9-July 27. This shows that Davydov evidently never came near Yakutat or Eyak country on either trip. We have his journal for the first trip, but not for the second. Volume I of his publication (Davydov [1812] 1977) contains his journal for the first trip, and Volume II is all (very valuable) ethnography of Kodiak. Two vocabularies are most mysteriously appended to Volume II, without any information on date or place of collection. The first vocabulary is Yakutat Tlingit, the second is Tanaina Athabaskan, and there is no Kodiak! It appears certain that Davydov did this work with displaced speakers of these two languages at Kodiak or Sitka or both, as there could have been such speakers at either place. Rezanov definitely did his six vocabularies (see below), including these two languages, in Sitka, and Davydov too could have done his there on that second voyage, but he could have done them at Kodiak just as well, where he had more time, leisure, and perhaps inclination, than on the second. Perhaps favoring that possibility is the fact that his Tlingit vocabulary is clearly from Yakutat, entitled *"Slovar' nariechii narodov, nazyvaemykh* Kolozhami, *obitaiushchikh mezhdu zalivom Chugachoi i Iakutatom* [Vocabulary of the dialects of the peoples, called *Kolozh* (Tlingit), living between Chugach Bay and Yakutat]." Such a title appears to offer great promise of a bilingual Eyak- Tlingit vocabulary. Alas though, the vocabulary is merely bicolumnar, the first labeled *Ruskiia*, the second *Kaliuzhskiia*, not according to the promising title (including even different spelling for the ethnonym, *Kolozh-* and *Kaliuzh-*), and every single [180] entry of this substantial 317-word list is Tlingit. Finally, though, to the seventh-to-last entry, for 'dog,' Tlingit transcription *Ketl'*, is added in parentheses, *po Iakut. xauva* [in the Yakutat language *xauva*], i.e., that the specifically Yakutat [Eyak] word for 'dog' is x̱ewa:. This exceptional entry is made either because this Yakutat speaker was more or less monolingual or dominant in Tlingit, but added the Eyak in this case because it was one of the few Eyak words he knew, so could not resist adding, or that, with this exception, the bilingual intention promised by the title somehow got sadly changed. Krauss has not found reference to Davydov's manuscript papers. In any case, this 1812 publication gives us the first-ever printed Yakutat Eyak word we have. It is, though – very significantly – by no means the last.

Rezanov 1805

To set the stage for the magnificent contribution to our history made by Nikolai Petrovich Rezanov (1764-1807) we need now to provide some broader perspective on the five "official" Alaska languages as shown on Shelikhov's 1796 map. The Russians took Alaska's Native languages very seriously, not only as objects of scientific study, but also they recognized them quite naturally as a positive or at least practical asset to their colony. They were not something to be suppressed, but to be used, even cultivated. It is therefore not really so surprising that the Russians considered them important to define, even more or less officially. They knew Chugach and Kodiak were very similar; they may even have known that Kodiak and Chugach were more similar to each other than Kodiak was to the Central Yupik of the *KO-* part of the name on Shelikhov's map. Yet they still chose to divide what they knew of Yupik in this way, for some reason, probably geographical. A comparable case in today's Europe would be Norwegian and Swedish, which are really one language for practical speaking purposes (though different in spelling, and of course politically!), and if there are really two languages there, it is more because there are two main types of Norwegian. For Alaska, partly with the early help of the British, Spanish, and even French (for Tlingit), by the time Rezanov came to Alaska in 1805 there were already ten substantial wordlists for Aleut, another ten for Alutiiq (five for Chugach 1778-1791, then five more for Kodiak), and eight for Tlingit, so that for all three (or "four") of these languages there were explicitly hundreds of words written down. For Eyak, though, there was nearly nothing, only a few mostly accidental scraps or crumbs that it takes our sophisticated linguistic retrospect to identify. Perhaps with the one exceptional Davydov word, anything more than that had in fact been tossed by Malaspina, and maybe by Davydov too.

Between adventures in Japan, and later in California, enter the imperialist Rezanov, on an inspection tour of his (deceased) father-in-law Shelikhov's colony. *Kammerherr* (Chamberlain, Plenipotentiary) to the Emperor himself, Rezanov was obviously competent and ambitious. After visiting the Aleutians and Kodiak (see Davydov above), Rezanov spent an increasingly uncomfortable six months in Sitka, Au gust 25, 1805 to Feb ru ary 25, 1806, after which he left, understandably, for his California venture. It is clear that during his stay in Sitka he wrote his magnificent dictionary. The title here reads *"Slovar' unalaskinskago, kad'iakskago, kinaiskago, koliuzhskago, ugaliakhmutskago i chugatskago iazykov, po Rossiiskomu Alfavitu sobrannyi dvora EGO IMPERATORSKAGO VELICHESTVA dieistvitel'nym, Kamergerom, Sanktpeterburgskikh IMPERATORSKOI Akademii Nauk i vol'nago Ekonomicheskago obshchestva chlenom i kavalerom, Nikolaem Rezanovym, vo vremia puteshestviia ego po Aleutskoi griadie i Severo- Zapadnomu beregu Ameriki 1805go goda."* – A fair copy ends instead after his name *"v pol'zu v novoi Chasti sveta obitaiushchikh – 1805 Godu. Na Severo-Zapadnom beregu Ameriki, v porte Novo-Arkhangel'skom.* [Dictionary of the Unalaska (Aleut), Kodiak, Kenai (Tanaina), Koliuzh (Tlingit), Ugaliakhmut (Eyak) and Chugats languages, collected in the Russian alphabet by the true Chamberlain of the court of His Imperial Majesty, cavalier and member of the Saint-Petersburg Imperial Academy of Sciences and Free Economic Society, Nikolai Rezanov, at the time of his voyage along the Aleutian archipelago and Northwest coast of America of 1805. – (fair copy) for the use of the inhabitants of the new world. In 1805. On the Northwest coast of America, at Port New Archangel (Sitka)]."

In his letter of transmittal of this work to the officers and stockholders of the Company, dated November 6, 1805 and first published in Tikhmenev 1863: 215-216, Rezanov expresses his disgust that the priests (who had been sent to Kodiak since 1794) were neither learning the languages for their prayers and sermons, nor making a dictionary of them as they were supposed or even commissioned to do. He therefore took the burdensome task on himself, in hopes that it would be used in the American schools and by Company personnel, perhaps also in Russia for science.

In sheer size alone this is an amazing work, containing six parallel vocabularies averaging about 1,150 entries, approximately 7,000 items in all. Moreover, this was apparently done not during the six months Rezanov spent in Sitka, but entirely during the first two. The date of the letter of transmittal is November 6, 1805, but the date at the end of his introduction in the fair copy sent is October 29, and it must have taken some of that time for the scribe to make that copy. However, if Rezanov [181] had 50 days for the work, that would average 23 entries per day, times six for each column, ca. 140 words per day. If done very efficiently, five hours a day would have allowed over two minutes per word. It is certainly clear that Rezanov spent a good part of those first two months on his dictionary!

The appearance of the "rough" original or closest-to-original is quite puzzling. It is neat enough throughout, fully legible, but on close examination, there is a progression from very neat on the first pages to somewhat less neat towards the last, the parallel columns across the page quite uniformly following that progression. Thus the pages must have been written in that order, all six columns across, rather than each language separately down each column, no column being neater than another. Thus Rezanov must have worked with all six different language speakers together, lined up, working across the page for each entry, a spectacle that one should perhaps not put past Rezanov! Otherwise the original is not that, but a copy from earlier notes, working down the list with each speaker alone – which would seem a more reasonable procedure – and the results then copied, in Rezanov's own hand, it appears, into parallel columns across the page. Some doubt is cast on this latter explanation by two matters. One is the extra time the copying from the original field notes into the parallel columns would take, but another is that in each column there are corrections, on each page, revisions which Rezanov could have made only with the speaker present. Does this mean that Rezanov had time to check the whole recopied combined version over with the speakers to make corrections on it? Moreover, the fact that the fair copy dated October 29, 1805, has in it the corrected forms (and not the crossed-out ones) shows that the corrections had also been made before October 29, not at leisure after that.

The Eyak column will provide a good example for the phonological quality of Rezanov's transcriptions. These are woefully inadequate, yet rather good for their time on the part even of those persons who might be called linguists of those days in dealing with Native American languages. For example, the Eskimo-Aleut languages distinguish (only!) two *k*-like sounds, *k*, as opposed to uvular or back-velar *q*, which the writers of course failed to distinguish. However, Eyak distinguishes in fact not just two but six (!) *k*-like sounds (likewise Tlingit and Tanaina), in a perfectly structured system of front and back, plain or aspirated or glottalized (thus 2 x 3 = 6) *k*'s. In Eyak these are written here *g k k'*, *G q q'*. These are all, of course, written by Rezanov as *k*, lamentably. Eyak also has front and back versions of the *kh*-like sound in Russian and German (Tlingit has four), written only *x*. Eyak carefully distinguishes, as do also Tlingit and Tanaina, three varieties of all its stopconsonants: plain, aspirated, and glottalized. The Russians wrote these only as one: thus they wrote *d* and *t* and *t'* all alike as *t; dl, tl, tl'* all alike as *tl; dz, ts, ts'* all alike as *ts; dj, ch, ch'* all alike *ch; g, k, k'*, and, still more lamentably, as noted above not only those but also *G, q, q'*, all alike as *k*, thus only one symbol for six different *k*-like sounds! Eyak further has vowel length, extremely frequent voiceless barred-*l*'s, *h*'s, and glottal stops, which never get distinguished or shown, simply because the Russian sound system lacks them altogether and therefore its writing system has no means to handle them. Eyak nasalized vowels are written very erratically. All this of course makes Rezanov's Eyak (and Tlingit and Tanaina) very hard to interpret even where the translations are reasonably accurate – Eskimo-Aleut somewhat less hard.

Nevertheless, Rezanov's transcriptions, within these very serious limitations, are still rather good for their time. At least for the Eyak he comes about as close as he can, within those limits. Here are a very few examples. The very first two entries are Russian *babka* 'old lady, grandmother,' Eyak *kaaken* for *qa:-k'inh* 'our (paternal) grandmother,' and Russian *babka povival'naia* 'midwife,' Eyak *xukukhteiash*, for *xu: qu'xdəyahsh*, which in fact means 'I [not someone else] am going to have a baby,' relatable perhaps to the Russian, but not so closely as the preceding entry. There are many entries just as problematic as 'midwife,' some worse. Another type of pitfall is the speaker's hearing of the Russian, e.g., for Russian *liud* 'people' the Eyak transcribed was *tyts*, for *t'əts'* 'ice,' which in Russian is *liod*, the vowel misheard. Still, taking *Shchekotno* 'it tickles, tickly' as perhaps a nice example of an item not easy for a non-Eyak ear to hear clearly, Rezanov's Eyak *khuil'khakhchi* is not a bad effort for *xuyəɬxa'xch'inh*, which means 'he is tickling my hand.' Rezanov's form not only gives a vivid picture of exactly how the work was being done with gestures, but his precise spelling also may even represent a perfectly plausible nice archaism, for "generic" tickling – unless Rezanov has failed here to hear yet another consonant, between the *-ch'-* and the *-inh*, either *-x̱-* for 'around, here and there,' or *-g-* for 'repeatedly, in the same spot,' a distinction which seems to be required in the more recent stages of Eyak.

While Rezanov's vocabulary is perhaps not very rich particularly in local fl ora-fauna, or in items and concepts special to Native culture, it is rich in Russian items such as muskets, musketballs, canons, anvils, pieces of eighteenth-century clothing, or vodka (*kakh"al'tseiats"-kaia*, for *qa:x̱a'łts'iya'ts' giyah*, approximately 'water at the ultimate stage of decomposition on us, utterly decomposed/ rotted water'). It is of course hard to tell in some cases whether the responses are *ad hoc* [182] spontaneous descriptions, or established usages. Though there is often more than one form of a verb, there are no conjugations, and though often there are phrases, e.g., the "vodka" case, from which a little syntax could be deduced or recognized, there are no running texts of any kind. From Rezanov alone we could have little idea of Eyak grammar, but we would certainly have, in a sense, a very significant part of the Eyak lexicon, more than enough for a good philologist to determine not only the distinctness of Eyak from any other language, but also its genetic position as not itself Athabaskan, but a separate branch coordinate with Athabaskan, and perhaps distantly related to Tlingit.

Rezanov appends to the rougher copy a draft introduction to the dictionary, addressed to the officers and stockholders of the company. Then (Krauss's translation): "Aside from the usual labor of composing any dictionary, I also had to explain to those uneducated peoples the meaning of each word, adapt to their concepts, listen carefully to the pronunciations, and finally to check several times. Many things unknown to them before the coming of the Russians they have adopted generally from our language, others they have deformed by endings [not Eyak, but Eskimo-Aleut], but the Kolyuzh or Kolosh have a language fuller than the others and their own names for all European things, which their trade with the English and the Americans has permitted them to see." Rezanov thus emphasizes the care he took, and takes special interest in the practical need for developing new terminology, even revealing, in a nice diplomatic way, some of his frustration that the Tlingits quite decisively were much more receptive to Anglo-American culture than to Russian. He then goes on to give a brief statement about each language. (He recognizes that Chugach and Kodiak are very similar.) About the *Ugaliakhmut* he writes that they "constitute a small nation living near Yakutat or Bering Bay. Their language is entirely different from others, though they have borrowed some words from the Koliuzh contiguous with them," a statement not implying anything about genetic relationships. He firmly places the Eyak he got at the Yakutat (= Bering Bay) end. He closes with the hope that the originality of the work will merit the attention of the learned, but even more that it will be of practical educational benefit to the colony and its clergy, to the honor of the Russian Company.

Rezanov's placement of Eyak at Yakutat or nearby (possibly then Kaliakh) virtually proves that the speaker at Sitka was not from the Copper River end, else the placement would presumably have at least to include refl ection of that. It therewith also proves abundantly to us that Eyak dialect variation, at least that surviving to 1805, was minuscule indeed. What differences there are between Rezanov's 1805 Yakutat and twentiethcentury Cordova can almost all be attributed to the passage of time as well as, or rather than geographical difference in dialect. In fact some of those phonological differences are also attested in early transcriptions from the Cordova area a few decades later. One lexical item comes to notice, however: *Briukho* 'belly, paunch' *kagott* for *qa:wət'*, as a possessed anatomical noun, ancient cognate to Athabaskan *-wət'* with the same meaning. However, no Cordova speakers could remember it that way, knowing the stem only as unpossessed *wet'* meaning only 'vomit,' thus perhaps a (rare) example of a difference that could not be explained by time.

The autumn of 1805 was fateful for the history of Eyak language work. Rezanov's dictionary put Eyak documentation at the same level as the other "official" Alaska languages, whether or not its small population justified the work also for practical or enlightenment purposes. Rezanov's dictionary of course far surpassed all the previous lexical work in any of those languages, and was not in turn itself to be surpassed, except by Veniaminov for Aleut and Tlingit only, until well into the twentieth century.

That same autumn of 1805 was also fateful for the history of Eyak. About the very same time in August as Rezanov was arriving in Sitka, the Natives of Yakutat destroyed the Russian fort and colony there, pillaged it, and massacred the colonists. The Yakutat Eyaks clearly played a prominent role in the event. Not long after, probably while Rezanov was still at Sitka, maybe still doing the language work – the news did not reach Sitka until February 1806, by which time that work was long done – the Yakutat and perhaps other Tlingits, believing that the Eyaks had gained the better part of the booty, proceeded in turn to massacre the Eyaks there (see de Laguna 1972: 173-176; Grinev 1988, 1989). In any case, the Eyak language was not to survive much longer at Yakutat itself. We still have two more vocabularies from Yakutat a few years later (see below), but by 1820 our Eyak documentation comes from the Copper River end only.

Rezanov died in Krasnoiarsk in March 1807 on his way back from California and Alaska. His rough dictionary manuscript very fortunately survived, and is now at the St. Petersburg Public Library, Manuscript division (Fond 7 [Adelunga], Opis' 1, Delo 139), 67 six-column-wide pages or spreads. In that same file is the fair copy probably sent October 6, 1805 from Sitka to St. Petersburg, and another fair copy. Some explanation of the fact that this stunning work was never published as such is called for in this history.

For all his strengths Rezanov was certainly also, as noted, an effete and devious man, not to mention arrogant and imperious, so he has had his [183] share of detractors. A contemporary instance is the Russian-Alaskan scholar Lydia Black (1989: 100-101), who does not believe Rezanov personally could have done the work, in spite of the rough manuscript and introduction in his handwriting, and other evidence, but rather that he must have gotten someone like Monk Gideon, priest and educator at Kodiak, whom Rezanov could not persuade to visit Sitka and whose handwriting is unmistakably different, to do the work and then appropriated it to himself. Far more consequential, outliving Rezanov, was the enmity, abhorrence, and even cruelty he inspired in his shipmates and officers on the ill-fated Japan adventure on the way to Alaska. Those so inspired with enmity included the captain, Kruzenshtern. After the voyage, this able, affable, and increasingly influential officer published an important account of the voyage, discreet about Rezanov, and also a compilation of vocabularies, which minimizes or hardly includes Rezanov's work (Kruzenshtern or Krusenstern 1813, in German). Kruzenshtern was an admirer of Davydov; the compendium is, in part, a tribute to and lament for his friend, not for the despised Rezanov. So it is hardly a surprise that the Alaskan vocabularies are based on Davydov's and include from Rezanov only the equivalents thereto, namely 171 Tlingit items and 218 Tanaina. Rezanov's dictionary was (and is still) in the Adelung collection (now Fond Adelunga at the St. Petersburg Public Library; see *Mithridates* 1816 below). Kruzenshtern does include a comment made by Adelunga on Rezanov's dictionary, calling it "an extremely valuable collection of about 1,200 words in the six so far known major languages of the inhabitants of New-Russia, viz. Unalaska, Kenai, Chugaz, Ugalächmut, and Koliusch ... still unpublished ... " (Krusenstern 1813: x). Nothing of the Eyak is included, presumably because Davydov did not include such. With Rezanov dead and practical or educational Native language policy in the colony at a low ebb (until the arrival of Veniaminov in 1823), Rezanov's dictionary was virtually forgotten or ignored. True, it is hard to say whether the published book could have been realistically useful or practical, especially for the three Indian languages for which the spelling itself is so woefully deficient. In any case, of the six vocabularies, only two were ever published as such, but in German by academics, the Eyak (see Radloff 1857, below) and the Tanaina (by Radloff and Schiefner in 1874).

In 1954 Knut Bergsland, distinguished scholar of Aleut in Norway, managed to get a microfilm copy of the rough version. About 99% of Rezanov's Aleut forms can be accounted for in Bergsland's 1994 Aleut dictionary. The Alutiiq dictionary soon to be published by Jeff Leer in Fairbanks can account for something approaching Bergsland's success now for the Kodiak and Chugach, and Leer's ongoing work with Tlingit may approach the level with Alutiiq. Krauss can interpret or at least partly interpret up to 97% of the Eyak, and James Kari is currently working on the Tanaina. A complete publication of the whole work, with the appropriate interpretations, explanation, and apparatus, long envisioned by the Alaska Native Language Center remains too much of a luxury for the Center to allow itself under present conditions.

Anonymous 1810

We can only date this vocabulary to within the range of late 1808 to late 1811. Because we know it preceded Baranov 1812 below, the cover letter for which is dated February 20, 1812, the latest date for this vocabulary would probably have to be late 1811. The list includes Bodega Miwok of California. We know that the earliest major contact with Bodega Miwok was by Kuskov from December 15, 1808 to August 2, 1809. He was back in Bodega Bay in No vem ber 1811, but not for long, as he soon established Fort Ross slightly north of Bodega, in Kashaya Pomo territory. That makes 1809 the likeliest year by far for Bodega Miwok. The Eyak list itself would therefore have to be done between late 1809 and late 1811, so we arbitrarily pick 1810. Ivan Aleksandrovich Kuskov (1765-1823), a long-time and important Company official, was the leader of the California expeditions, and may be the author of the Bodega vocabulary and one or more of the Alaskan vocabularies in the compendium, but the handwriting, uniform throughout, is in a hand different from Kuskov's and not signed by Kuskov (or dated), so it is safest to leave the authorship anonymous – the only instance of that in this history.

This never-published manuscript is at the St. Petersburg Public Library (Fond 7 [Adelunga], Opis' 1, Delo 146), where it was unexpectedly discovered by Krauss in 1990. The title page reads *"Slovar' obitaiushchikh narodov v vedenii Ameriko-rossiiskikh Kompaniiskikh Zaniatii Sostoiashchikh* [(approximately:) Dictionary of the resident peoples under the authority of Russian- American Company business]." It is on 34 pages, with Russian plus three languages on the left and three more on the right, very much in the same format as Rezanov 1805, in parallel columns and about half as long, with 481 numbered Russian entries plus 161 unnumbered (= 642), in an order not alphabetical, but vaguely topical. The columns are not as uniformly or equally well filled in for the different languages, unlike Rezanov's work, nor is the same ink or quill used throughout. Down through the pages it is quite uniform and neat, with relatively few corrections, spottily distributed, so is unproblematically a copy of earlier [184] manuscripts. Though similar in format to Rezanov's work, it is not derivative thereof, but presents primary data throughout. The first column is the Bodega Miwok, the next Fox Island

Aleut, then Kodiak Alutiiq, then Sitka Tlingit, then "*Slova zhitelei Beringova zaliva* [Words of the residents of Bering Bay]," i.e., Yakutat Eyak, then Kenai Tanaina. Here again are the "official" languages, now including Californian Bodega Miwok, and not the (redundant?) Chugach. The Bodega Miwok has (470 + 28 =) 498 items, the fullest for the numbered part, in the first column, showing the rest were probably done after that. Aleut has 560 items and Kodiak 555, i.e., much more past the numbered part, while Tlingit has about 450, Tanaina 318, and Eyak only 285. Presumably, the work was started in California, then the rest was done in Sitka, first with Aleut and Kodiak, then Eyak, and Tanaina last. In some ways it complements Rezanov, e.g., it is richer in fauna-fl ora terms, having around 140 such items.

Most interestingly, not only the label but also the content of the Eyak column clearly shows it is from Yakutat. One sign of that is that it too has 'belly' as *kavvat* (cf., Rezanov *kagott)* for *qa:wət'*, the one item that is specifically Yakutat and not Cordova Eyak. More interestingly, it shows that Yakutat Eyak, at least for this speaker – and by then there may not have been many such left – was in a far more advanced state of assimilation to Tlingit than it had been in 1805 (Rezanov), perhaps only five years earlier. This is especially evident in the fact that of the 285 words in that list, at least 41 are new Tlingit loanwords. These include not only new items or concepts, which, if present in Rezanov 1805 are Eyak neologisms, replaced by Tlingit (e.g., for brass, rigging, mast, cannon, pistol, gunpowder, bullet-lead, cloth, tobacco, smokingpipe, cloth blanket, mirror, scissors, paper), but, even words for traditional Native items for which we naturally have good Eyak words (e.g., trout, octopus, clam species, fl ea, crane, loon, owl species, two berry species, hemlock, shield-fern, bracket fungus, mountain-goat or sheep fat, whale blubber, birch-fungus punk, seine, dip net, deer or caribou fat, arrow, quiver, comb, earthquake). This is an obvious sign that Eyak was rapidly giving way to Tlingit at Yakutat in 1810.

Baranov 1812

The preceding was still not the end of Yakutat Eyak documentation – quite. At the same time Krauss unexpectedly found the anonymous multiple vocabulary, he also found at the St. Petersburg Public Library, Manuscript Division (Fond 7 [Adelunga], Delo 143), a document closely related to Delo 146, but later and shorter, with the library title "*Sitkhinskii Iazyk, materialy sobrannye A.A. Baranovym 1812* [Sitka language, material collected by A.A. Baranov, 1812]," and on the document itself a title and transmittal page in German, to the effect "Language of Sitka, Ben[jamin] Cramer has the Honor to deliver the word[list]s ordered for State Councillor von Adelung from Sitka Island. The contributions have not yet been delivered from Kodiak, but as soon as they arrive[?], i.e. not before October or November, B.C. will have the Honor of presenting them to Herr Councillor. February 20, 1812." It is six leaves long, and deals with three languages; the last half is for Alutiiq, the first for Tlingit and Eyak combined. The first two pages are a printed form, first for the Lord's Prayer and the second with 70 numbered Russian words, plus 16 numerals, with space to fill in the target-language equivalent. The Lord's Prayer is filled out for the Tlingit but not for the Eyak. The wordlist is filled out with both Tlingit and Eyak squeezed in the space, in the same handwriting, different from that for Alutiiq. The numerals are on an attached tab, evidently because some of them are too long to fit on the form. The close relationship of this work and that of Anonymous 1810 is obvious, in that for Eyak, 38 of the 70 numbered words and 6 of the 16 numerals are identical to those in the anonymous 1810 document, identically spelled, but 32 are different in having a variant spelling for the same word, and 6 have an altogether different or partly different word. The words that show the great increase in Tlingit loans in 1810 are not the types that come into play in this, much shorter, basic vocabulary.

We do know that there is a Tlingit Lord's Prayer attributed to Baranov in *Mithridates* 1816 (see below); the handwriting could be Baranov's and the collection title attributes the document to him, so the label here accepts that attribution. This work, like that of 1810, now involves resident Company officialdom. Especially interesting in this connection also is the reference to Adelung in the cover page and the printed questionnaire form itself, certainly connected with the 1816 publication, and the beginning of published academic literature explicitly including Eyak words, and showing Eyak as a separate language (see *Mithridates* 1816 below).

Mithridates 1816

This source is named here for the title of the publication rather than the authors, because it is not clear which of the authors is/are responsible for the inclusion and treatment of Eyak from Rezanov's data, the first publication of any of that. The authors are leading men of the time, Johann Christoph von Adelung (b. 1732, d. 1806), and Johann Severin Vater (b. 1771, d. 1826); also involved are Johann Christoph's nephew Friedrich von Adelung (b. 1768, d. 1843), and both brothers [185] Wilhelm (b. 1767, d. 1835) and Alexander von Humboldt (b. 1769, d. 1859). King Mithridates VI of Pontus (b. 132, d. 63 B.C.) was famed, among other things, for speaking twenty-some languages, and this was not the first or last time a book meant to be a kind of encyclopedia of all the world's known languages was named after him. This one though is by far the largest, some 3,000 pages, published in German in Berlin, 1806-1817, in four volumes. Volume III is itself issued in two volumes and three parts. Parts 1 and 2 are in the first volume, published in 1813, and Part 3, that for North American languages, is in the second volume of Volume III, published 1816.

This whole compendium was truly a great and famous work for its time. The elder Adelung had already died in 1806, and Vater finished writing Volumes II-IV, with input from the Humboldts. Some of the older Alaskan material had been collected by the elder Adelung, but more, including presumably the Rezanov material, must have been collected by his nephew Friedrich, who also spent his later years at St. Petersburg, and must have had good access to manuscripts on the languages of Russia's dominions. Hence also the name of the collection in which it is found, Fond Adelunga, at the St. Petersburg Public Library.

Mithridates III (3: 218-229) has a goodly section on Tlingit, comparing vocabularies, including Rezanov's, and then on pages 228-238 there is a section on Eyak and Tanaina quoting Rezanov's short statement about the separate identity of Eyak – now in print, in German – on p. 229, "*dass seine Sprache eine, von den übrigen durchaus verschiedene sey* [that their language is one altogether different from others]." On pages 230-238, 30 words of *Ugaljachmutzi nach Resanoff,* all now of course written in German transliteration of Rezanov's Russian are compared with Tanaina, followed by grammatical comments exemplified by 25 more Eyak words, then a comparison of 14 Tanaina, Tlingit, and Eyak pronouns, then of 21 Tlingit and Eyak nouns. These are then followed by comments on Eskimo-Tanaina contact, including two more Eyak forms, 117 or 10% of Rezanov's Eyak list in all. Of course the transcriptions are inadequate to begin with, and the grammatical and comparative work is primitive indeed. Nevertheless, we have a crucial statement and some evidence of the status of Eyak now in print in German in 1816 in a very well known and prestigious work.

The Swiss-American Gallatin, friend of Alexander von Humboldt as well as of Thomas Jefferson, in his classification of American languages (1836) begun in 1823, of course uses *Mithridates* and Rezanov's Tanaina and Tlingit, but not his Eyak, so only mentions Eyak (Gallatin 1836: 14). Gallatin (1836: 14) also has Eyak (Ugaljachmutzi) on his map (see Shelikhov 1796 above), but has no comment on its separateness. (See Wrangell 1839 below for the next and greatly amplified stage of this public information in German.)

Khromchenko 1823

We now come to the period when new Eyak information comes from Russians at the Copper River end of Eyak territory, as the Yakutat end is disappearing or gone. The first such word list was the third unexpectedly found in 1990 by Krauss in the Adelung collection, St. Petersburg Library, Manuscript Division (Fond 7 [Adelunga], Opis' 1, Delo 145). The manuscript is the work of Vassilii Stepanovich Khromchenko, or Khramchenko (d. 1849). He was in Alaska as a naval officer in the Russian-American Company 1820-1825 and took down five Eskimo vocabularies in 1821-1822. Since partial parallel copies of these are included in this work, the earliest date for the rest is probably 1823 and the latest 1825. The manuscript is undated, but is clearly a copy of Khromchenko's work in a disciplined scribal hand, not Khromchenko's. We have copies of Khromchenko's Eskimo manuscript from the Perm' library, but not the rest. This manuscript is in two sections, each in parallel columns; with Russian plus five Eskimo languages in one, and then Russian plus the four Indian languages in the other: *Tynsnakoan* (Ahtna), *Ugalents, Sitka-Khan*, and *Innon* (Indians of Rumiantsev Bay, i.e., Bodega Miwok). The attribution is "*Sobran Leitenantom Khramchenko, byvshim 5 liet v Kolonii Rossiisko-Amerikanskoi Kompaniii* [Collected by Lieutenant Khramchenko, having been five years in the colony of the Russian- American Company]."

The Ahtna and Eyak columns are intimately related, in fact jumbled together in such a way as to suggest that they are from one and the same speaker, whose stronger native language is Eyak and second, weaker is Ahtna. The parallel columns have 102 Russian words, 71 of which are filled out for the Ahtna and 91 for Eyak. A careful check shows, however, that when Eyak duplicates for Ahtna (29 cases) and switches are sorted out, there are 96 Eyak items and only about 42 Ahtna. The speaker(s) knew the 12 numerals asked for in Eyak but not in Ahtna. There are no Tlingit loans. Obviously the Eyak is Copper River dialect, even though the title page might imply the Eyaks live "near Bering [Yakutat] Bay." This first Copper River Eyak list is adequate to confirm that that dialect shows no surprising features different from what we expect for the time and place.

Wrangell 1839

Ferdinand Petrovich von Wrangell (b. 1796, d. 1870), of Baltic nobility and a distinguished naval officer who had already traveled extensively [186] also in the Arctic, served as governor of Alaska in 1830-1835. As a man of letters and science he wrote invaluable reports on Alaska and its peoples, which were published in Russian and German; the German edited and published by his friend von Baer in 1839. This date is taken for this entry, but almost certainly the language work was done in 1830-1835. No manuscript of the language work has so far been located. We have a statement about Eyak from Wrangell himself, that they are a small tribe of

38 families, living in a bay east of Kayak Island in winter, and in summer at the east of Copper River delta. They are similar and related to the Tlingits; their language is different, but genetically related. In the immediately following statement on the Ahtna, Wrangell includes a comparative table of 11 words to show genetic relationship between Ahtna, Eyak, and Tlingit. Two of these are in fact perfectly valid cognates for Ahtna and Eyak: 'sky' *Ja-at* and *Ja-a* (*ya:-t* and *ya:-* [*q'-t*]), and 'blood' *Tell* and *Tedlch* (*del* and *d eł*), the first such ever shown for Athabaskan-Eyak (Wrangell 1839: 96-99). The book also includes a fold-out table, facing page 258, entitled "*Vergleichende Wörter-Sammlung aus 8 Sprachen der Bewohner von Nordwest-Amerika, von dem Contre- Admiral von Wrangel* [Comparative Table of Eight Languages of the Inhabitants of Northwest America, by Vice-Admiral von Wrangel]." The table lists, in parallel columns, Aleut, Kodiak Alutiiq, Chugach Alutiiq, Eyak, Tanaina, Ahtna, Copper River Kolchan [Tanacross!], and Sitka Tlingit, altogether 97 items, with 81 filled out for Eyak. The statement and Ahtna-Eyak-Tlingit comparison part was also published in the original Russian in 1839 – and in 1853 also in French – but the big table was published only in the von Baer 1839 book, though in the original Russian transcription for all the languages. That was the first Eyak vocabulary ever printed.

Wrangell's Eyak vocabulary was also included in Radloff 1857 (see below). Editor von Baer discusses the Gallatin 1836 work and map extensively, including a discussion of genetic relations (Wrangell 1839: 283-289), albeit vaguely, with Gallatin's newly defined [Northern] Athabaskan and Tlingit-Eyak-Ahtna-Tanaina-Ingalik-Kolchane [Tanacross].

Veniaminov 1840

Ioann (Ivan) Evseevich Veniaminov (b. 1797, d. 1871), later (St.) Innokentii, had spent ten years in the Aleutians, when in 1834 Wrangell called him to Sitka, where he remained until 1838. It was probably during that period that Veniaminov formed his ideas about Alaska's languages generally. He was no doubt the most remarkable European – in good company – who ever set foot in the colony. Language was by no means the least of his many interests and accomplishments, so his statements on that certainly were not liable to escape notice. He came to St. Petersburg in 1839 to oversee publication of a number of his works, written in Alaska.

Two publications with overviews of Alaskan languages, including Eyak of course, were printed in 1840 (Veniaminov 1840a, 1840b), and one more in 1846. *Zapiski ob ostrovakh Unalashkinskago otdiela* [Notes on the Islands of the Unalaska District] (Veniaminov 1840a) is three volumes of "notes" on the Aleutians etc. In Volume III: v, the *Ugalentsy* are recorded as living near Mt. St. Elias (Yakutat), and number no more than 150 persons, as of 1834. On page 139 Veniaminov says Alaska has 6 languages: Unalaska, Kad'iak, Kenai, Yakutat, Sitkha, and Kaigan, i.e., Aleut, Yupik, Athabaskan, Eyak, Tlingit, and Haida, a sophisticated breakdown. "Yakutat speakers are no more than 300 souls, and they too [like Aleut] have two dialects." We have no evidence that Vcniaminov was ever near Eyak territory, and his knowledge of it is a bit vague. It does not appear that Veniaminov had seen Wrangell's 1839 publication or other such literature, but reflects rather his own Alaskan knowledge and contacts. Here, clearly enough, he is referring to Eyak in two names, "Yakutat" and Ugalents, as two dialects of one language, each group of 150 souls. He is aware that the community of Yakutat had two languages, Tlingit and "Yakutat" [Eyak], but his information there is badly out of date in that the Eyak language at Yakutat was no longer spoken by 150 souls, half the population there as he guessed, but rather by 1840 was very possibly quite extinct. These statements are exactly repeated in Veniaminov

1846. In Veniaminov 1840a: 143, the above outdated interpretation is clearly confirmed: "The Yakutat language is spoken by [some of] the inhabitants of Yakutat and further to the West, and it is divided into two dialects, Yakutat and Ugalents, the number of speakers of both dialects is not more than 300 souls." In *Sostoianie pravoslavnoi tserkvi v russkoi Ameriki* [The State of the Orthodox Church in Russian America] (Veniaminov1840b: 44-45) Veniaminov points out that of the six Alaskan languages, "Yakutat" is the smallest, specifying or guessing 150 speakers each for the "Yakutat" and Ugalents (dialects). These sources were then published in German in 1842 and 1849, in French in 1853, and republished in Russian in 1857 and 1887. Veniaminov thus does not add to the linguistic data on Eyak, but adds significantly, in three languages, to the published literature on the separate identity of Eyak.

In 1841 Sir George Simpson was in Sitka, where he learned that Tlingits lived "near Mount St. Elias; thence to Prince William Sound is another [187] language;" (Simpson 1847: 89), demonstrating that we have this information, common knowledge, printed also even in English, indirectly from Veniaminov or before.

Radloff 1857

Leopold Radloff (Lev Fedorovich Radlov; b. 1818, d. 1865) was a Russian working in St. Petersburg and publishing there, but who wrote and published in German, hence the spelling of the name. He was a *gimnaziia* Latin and Greek teacher, administrator, and museum curator. In the last decade of his short life, he worked extensively on Tlingit (including a year, 1862-1863, with an elderly native speaker brought from Alaska for the purpose), published on Haida, Tanaina (from Rezanov), and published *Über die Sprache der Ugalachmut* [On the Language of the Ugalachmut] (Radloff 1857). This is a 57-page monograph, the first publication ever entirely about Eyak. The first 20 pages are Radloff's introduction, and the rest is Rezanov's Eyak, alphabetized by the German translations, though (wisely) keeping the original Cyrillic Eyak transcription. The work is done rather carefully and accurately, except that for some reason 60 of the original entries are missing. It includes not only most of Rezanov, but also Wrangell's material, which after all was the only explicitly Eyak material thitherto in print – not counting Davydov's 'dog.' Thenceforth no one could say that primary Eyak data were lacking, as there were over 1,000 words of Eyak in print as of 1857, in German, the main European language of science.

The first 20 pages are Radloff's introduction. The first four pages of that give his discussion of the position of Eyak, i.e., its genetic and diffusional relationships to other languages. He concludes clearly that the Eyak language is not genetically related to Eskimo, but it is to Kenai in the narrow sense (Tanaina) though indirectly, with Atna and Kolchane (Tanacross, from Wrangell) as intermediate languages, and somehow perhaps related also to other Alaskan Athabaskan (Kenaiin the broader sense) and (the rest of) Athabaskan itself. He also concludes that Eyak is genetically related to Tlingit, but also diffusionally, just as Wrangell had said. Radloff attempts to fine-tune these relationships, but cannot add significantly to previous understanding of the position of Eyak.

The remaining 16 pages of Radloff's introduction are poor discussions of Eyak sounds and grammar. It does not appear that the man has any idea that the transcriptions he is dealing with are so woefully inadequate. This was perforce the case with any transcriptions of these languages made by Europeans. The sound systems are so profoundly different from European ones, and have so many distinctions that escape European ears. The mid-nineteenth century was an exciting period for a thriving new linguistics, centering on Indo-European and on the precise and regular system of sound-correspondences between its different branches and different languages. Linguistics was therewith developing into a precise science, and was discovering the relationship between languages, some over surprising distances, e.g., between English or Latin and Sanskrit. It was therefore quite natural, that the same ideas should be aspired to with Native American languages. However, because these languages were not written down by native speakers, but rather by Europeans who could not hear or transcribe accurately the complex Native American sound systems so different from European, transcriptions then available were vastly inferior to the European ones. They were underdifferentiated, overdifferentiated, inconsistent, too vague and impressionistic for the kind of rigor achievable in Indo-European studies. Therefore progress in determining relationships between American languages lagged decades behind the achievements in Indo-European. Radloff's attempts at extracting any Eyak grammar from the material he had of course had paltry results. Radloff did manage to recognize the nounprefix for 'my,' and even for 'our/human' *ka-* (i.e., *qa:-*), but even the 'I' subject of a verb (usually *-x-*) was beyond Radloff to identify. In the end, one has to say that Radloff's main contribution to Eyak was merely to make Rezanov's vocabulary available in print in German, the first publication ever on Eyak itself.

Buschmann 1855-1863

Radloff was not the only man of his time publishing in German on Eyak. Johann Karl Eduard Buschmann (b. 1805, d. 1880) was a Berlin librarian, friend of the von Humboldts, who worked with them in Mexico on Aztec. At the same time, he made a "hobby" of Athabaskan, and his publications of the period 1854-1863 included five discussions of Eyak. Two of these are before Radloff 1857, and since he was in touch with Radloff, the three after 1857 show the difference.

In his first publication Buschmann cites *Mithridates* 1816, Gallatin 1836, Wrangell 1839, and Veniaminov 1840a, but cannot add to those (Buschmann 1855: 233-235). The second publication (Buschmann 1856: 253, 260-319) repeats the previous statement, citing the same authors, and adds a major comparative table of 260 items as (insofar as) found in Athabaskan languages (narrower sense): Chepewyan, Tahkali(Carrier), Kutchin, Sussee (Sarsi), Dogrib, Tlatskanai, Umpqua, Navajo, T[J]icorilla; the "Kinai" (broader sense, i.e., Alaskan Athabaskan, minus Kutchin): Kinai, Atnah, [188] Ugalenzen, Inkilik (Koyukon), Inkalit (Ingalik), Koltschanen (Tanacross); and Koloschen (Tlingit). Hence Eyak belongs somewhere in the "Kinai" branch of this three-branched family.

In his third publication Buschmann summarizes the history of Eyak language studies up to then, adds Radloff's Rezanov – received April 22, 1858, but does not do much with it, critiques *Mithridates*, suggests comparisons between Athabaskan-Kinai-Tlingit and Aztecan, and compares Rezanov from *Mithridates* and from Radloff (Buschmann 1859: 683-689). Such unproductive enterprises as comparing Aztecan with Athabaskan- Eyak-Tlingit were attractive not only because Buschmann had been in Mexico and studied Aztec, but because phonological precision was so lacking that any languages that had, for example, frequent "*tl*"'s at the end of words, as did Eyak and Aztec, were fair game for comparison, and if proven to be related language families, especially at so long a distance, would be exciting, and a feather in the linguist's cap. In fact, W.W. Turner of the Smithsonian had done just that in 1852, by showing Apache-Navajo related to Athabaskan languages far to the North.

In the fourth treatise Buschmann has had time to appreciate Rezanov for what he adds to the available data, and even goes so far as to say that Eyak shows *"erstaunlich Fremdkeit* [astounding foreignness]" to all Athabaskan languages, without going so far as to conclude that Eyak is a separate coordinate branch with the Athabaskan family (Buschmann 1860: 513-515, 541-581). A "systematic" comparative table follows, including perhaps 600 Eyak items. Regular sound correspondences or gain in rigor are not refl ected therein.

In his fifth and last discussion of Eyak, using Rezanov from Radloff, Buschmann reasserts the specialness of Eyak and tries naively to fine-tune more exactly its position by showing: I (17 cases) where Eyak has a comparable word to that in Athabaskan generally, II (22 cases) where Eyak has a comparable word to one or more in Athabaskan, and III (27 cases) where Eyak has one or more words for an item that has nothing comparable to it/them in Athabaskan (Buschmann 1863: 232-235).

Beyond Buschmann, the Englishman Robert Gordon Latham (b. 1812, d. 1888) might be mentioned. He is an example of several Europeans outside Germany as derivative sources, who discussed the linguistic position of Eyak, often with data, in well-known publications in English – the American Gallatin and the the British Latham.

Furuhjelm 1862

We now come to the sixth and last Russian Eyak vocabulary, this one being transitional to the American. In fact it was requested by an American and appeared only in American publications. Johan Hampus Furuhjelm (b. 1821, d. 1909) was the second-last governor of Russian America, 1859-64. George Gibbs (b. 1815, d. 1873) was an American lawyer, geologist, naturalist, ardent philologist, and Smithsonian Institution officer, who had spent the years 1848 to 1860 in Oregon and Washington, collected Indian vocabularies there, and worked with vocabularies at the Smithsonian. He had already corresponded with Furuhjelm's predecessor Voevodskiisince 1856 and with Furuhjelm since 1859, especially about Alaskan languages and vocabularies of them. Furuhjelm showed a lively interest himself in that subject. On June 30, 1861, Gibbs wrote Furuhjelm that he now needed especially "a vocabulary of the Iacoutat, one which you mention as differing from the Kolosh, but which I had confounded with it" (National Anthropological Archives [NAA] ms. 371). Furuhjelm received that request March 30, 1862 and replied April 23, 1862, "I send you annexed vocabularies of Iacoutat and an Indian language. The last one [the latter] was spoken by an Indian tribe inhabiting 20-30 years ago the country round about Ross, California. The words have been written down after the dictation of two old Indian women, who, married to Russians, followed their husbands to Sitka, when Ross was evacuated [1841]" (NAA ms. 528). Krauss had earlier thought that this Eyak vocabulary must have been done by Abbot Nikolai Militov during one of his summer missionary visits of that period from Kenai to Copper River. However, unless such a thing had been at hand in Sitka, given the dates of the letters, Furuhjelm's obvious personal interest in the subject itself, and the story of the California vocabulary, it appears most likely after all that the Eyak vocabulary too was done in April 1862 at Sitka, indeed perhaps by Furuhjelm himself.

The vocabulary is on a 6-page Smithsonian "Comparative Vocabulary" form of the time, 180 (182) words, sent by Gibbs, with 161 words filled in (NAA ms. 527). Just as those letters from the Russian Governor are written in an elegant English language and hand, the Eyak vocabulary is written on the form in an elegant Latin alphabet transliteration of a Cyrillic original that has not come down to us, as seen, for example, in the first entry 'man' *Lilia* for *łila:'*, where the -*ia*- reflects the original Russian vowel. A nostalgic entry is 'thou' *Ishu*, for *'i:shuh* 'is it you (sg.)?' (also 'Hello,' cf., Walker and Strange 1786). Aside from the improbability that there were any Yakutat Eyak speakers still left at Yakutat in 1862, let alone at Sitka, there is further suggestion that the Eyak speaker was from Copper River in the entry for 'town, village', *Tchiishk*, which is clearly *chi:shk* meaning 'gravel,' probably a reference to the site at the Cordova end of Eyak Lake, in fact, as in the placename *chi:shk qi' k'u:łeh* ('where there is gravel'). [189]

On February 17, 1868, President Andrew Johnson called for information about what was still called "Russian America," and on May 27 a suggestion was made to send an expedition including Gibbs for the ethnology. "As language remains one of the readiest, and perhaps the most certain mode of tracing affinity among the races of men, it is particularly desired to collect accurate vocabularies of a sufficient number of words in common use ... The most important tribes remaining are those extending from Copper River along the coast to Cape Fairweather, especially those known as Ugalentses ... " (Henry 1868: 193) – prose surely from Gibbs. Already having a "Yacoutat" vocabulary since 1862, Gibbs still considered Eyak an especially important language for further investigation.

Gibbs was in touch with William Healy Dall (b. 1845, d. 1927), a very major U.S. specialist in Alaska. In his tome *Alaska and Its Resources* (Dall 1870: 550-551), Dall presents a short 37-word comparative table of Alaskan languages, presenting as one of the Tlingit dialects a column for Yakutat, and next to that, as one of the Athabaskan ("Tinneh") languages or dialects, a column for "Ugalentsi." The "Tinneh" column is Eyak from Wrangell 1839. The "Yakutat" one is said to be from Gibbs, but it is in fact, deplorably, a mixture of Tlingit and Eyak, with 25 items of the 36 filled in from a Taku Tlingit vocabulary gathered by William Fraser Tolmie in 1836 on a Smithsonian 60-word form of the time. For the items not on the Tolmie list, Dall fills in with 11 words from the Furuhjelm-Gibbs Eyak list. One can only guess what possessed him to do that. Unfortunately, between the 11 Eyak words in that mixed "Tlingit" column and the Wrangell 1839 Eyak under "Tinneh" in the next, there are only two words even partly the same, here with Dall's respelling of Wrangell, *Yakulkutzku* and *Yakutschk* for 'small' (Eyak *ya:kuts'k*), and *Khutak* and *Hoo-oo* for 'I' (Eyak *xu:[-d ek]*) for 'I (too).' This is surely not enough left for Dall to notice that his "Yakutat Tlingit" and "Ugalentsi Tinne" are – or were – the same language. On January 20, 1873, Gibbs writes Dall, "I have your book on Alaska [1870], but had not read it carefully ... As you do not expect to meet with the Kutchin and Tinne again, will you endeavor to enlist some of your friends out there in the making additional vocabularies of the tribes you have not heretofore reached, as also of the northern tribes of the Thlinkitt family. The vocabularies published in your work do not fill the Smithsonian blank and consequently are not entirely suitable for comparison with the others, though they establish the relationship ... " (Smithsonian Institution Archives, Record Unit 7073, Dall papers, Box 10, Folder 41; Dall had been to interior Alaska on a telegraph line expedition 1865-1867 and gotten several Athabaskan vocabularies himself). Here Gibbs is obviously responding in a very diplomatic way to his friend ("My Dear Dall,") about his dissatisfaction with Dall's treatment of the vocabularies. In his last letter to Dall, February 26, 1873, by now quite ill, Gibbs writes "I should be very glad however to do up the North West Coast tribes of Indians proper, and any vocabularies of the northern tribes of the Thlinkits, such as the Chilkat, I should like." This no doubt includes the Yakutat and Ugalents just beyond. Six weeks later Gibbs was dead.

Gibbs's list of Eyak words, sent by Furuhjelm 1862, was first fully printed, finally, four years after Gibbs's death (Dall 1877: 122-133). It was presented as the first "Tlingit" dialect in a sort of comparative Tlingit vocabulary of five parallel columns, without question or comment concerning the Yakutat that invariably sticks out like a sore thumb as different from the rest, e.g., item one, 'Man' *lilia - ka - kah - kah - kha*, i.e., Eyak *ɫila:'*, Tlingit *qa:*. It would seem unlikely that Gibbs, after all the trouble he had taken, would have allowed Eyak to be dealt with so shoddily, but by then it was too late. The American confusion over Eyak and the loss of all information about the position of the language for 60 years, until 1930, was well under way. Dall is much to blame for that.

Verman 1863

Fedor Karlovich Verman (Wehrmann) was in Alaska 1854-1861 as a naval officer. Petr Aleksandrovich Tikhmenev (b. 1820s, d. 1888) worked in St. Petersburg as the Company historian from 1857 to 1863, when he published a two-volume definitive history of its affairs (Tikhmenev 1861-1863). In that is published a most remarkable color map entitled *Karta tuzemnykh nariechii na Aleutskikh ostrovakh i severozapadnom beregu Ameriki, s karty, sostavlennoi sostoiashchim na sluzhbie Rossiissko- Amerikanskoi Ko. Kapitan-leitenant Vermanom 1863g.* [Map of native languages on the Aleutian Islands and northwest coast of America, from a map compiled by Russian-American Co. servant Captain-Lt. Verman, 1863] (Fig. 3). (An original, not seen by Krauss, is reported in the Archive of the Russian Geographical Society, St. Petersburg, Razryad III, Opis' 1, No. 232.) It was clearly Verman, not Tikhmenev, who compiled the information, so this last Russian statement on the position of Eyak belongs to Verman. Aleut is shown in blue, Eskimo in red-pink, Tlingit in brown, with a lighter brown used for the Yakutat dialect thereof. The fourth category, "separate languages" – in fact Athabaskan-Eyak – are Kolchan (far interior Athabaskan) in yellow, Ahtna in light green, Kenai (all around Cook Inlet) in purple, thus showing more than the modest title promises by including two varieties of interior Athabaskan. Eyak (Ugalenskoe) itself is colored gray and placed geographically right where it belonged in [190] 1863, along the coast, no longer from Yakutat (Z. Mul'grav), but now from about Kaliakh to about the mouth of the Copper River with division lines as well as shown with color. This map is far from alone at the time in showing Ugalents as a separate entity, this having been done ever since Shelikhov 1796. Still, in view of the originality, language boundary lines, and color of this map explicitly of Alaskan *languages*, it is here treated separately. It is not only the Russian-America Company's final statement on languages, but also draws as dramatically clear a picture as can be of the exact 1863 position of the Eyak language.

Summation of Russian Period

Maps from 1796 to 1863 invariably showed Ugalents as a separate group or language, with geographic accuracy, as one of the "official" or "major" languages of Alaska, even though they recognized Eyak also as the smallest such group by far. From the beginning all Russian statements recognize Eyak as being not Eskimo and not Athabaskan or Tlingit, but as related to Tlingit and Athabaskan and this with increasing accuracy of detail, especially in later years in German publications. Maps and such statements were spilling over also into English. Of the six formal Russian vocabularies of Eyak, two appeared in German publications (Rezanov, with about 1,100 words, and Wrangell with 97 words) and the last (Furuhjelm, 161 words) appeared in American publications (1870, 1877), where it was sadly misrepresented.

Figure 3. Detail from the Verman map. From Tikhmenev 1863, original in color.
This may also be the best place to mention that in the Russian Orthodox Church records there are many Eyak personal names, starting in the Kodiak records for 1843 and 1844 (including a total of 14 Ugalents names). From 1846 to 1870 these names come from the Kenaivital statistics records (about 300 instances, of about 180 different Ugalents names). There then seems to be a gap, and another group appears, from Nuchek, 1894 to 1907, containing both vital statistics and confessional records (total about 380 instances of about 150 different "Agalents" names from Eyak and Odiak and a few from Katalla). This corpus of course spans the Russian and American periods, as the Orthodox Church by no means abandoned Alaska in 1867. Note that these sources cover only the western end of Eyak, basically Eyak only, very marginally Katalla, and nothing towards Yakutat, which was never missionized by the Russians; [191] but of course the western end had become home to most or all of what remained of Eyak speakers. As mentioned in connection with Purtov and Kulikalov 1794, Eyak personal names in inadequate orthography are very difficult to identify, let alone interpret. However, copies of all this material are also included in the Alaska Native Language Center Archive (ANLC) for Eyak, with excerpting of the names by Krauss and identification of perhaps a quarter of them. Their ultimate historical value for Eyak is of course yet another matter. Finally, the *Index to Baptisms, Marriages, and Deaths in the Archive of the Russian Orthodox Greek Catholic Church in Alaska* (1964-1973) includes Eyak personal names from 1845 to 1893 under Kenai, which may help fill in the gaps, and from 1894 to 1907 under Nuchek.

The American Period,
1867 to Present

The very first American mentions of Eyak after the purchase of Alaska were not wrong about the language, for example distinguished geodesist and astronomer George Davidson (b. 1825, d. 1911), writing November 30, 1867 (Davidson 1868: 293) stated: "The natives inhabiting the coast between Yakootat and Prince William Sound are called Oogalentz, and number about thirteen [!] hundred souls [which sounds like Veniaminov, and thirteen for three]. They have their own language ..." By 1870, however, Dall was already confusing matters, ignoring or forgetting that the Eyaks had their own language increasingly through 1885 giving the impression that they were some kind of Eskimo- Tlingit mixture. Dall was joined in this mistaken assumption by several others, such as Petroff, Abercrombie, Emmons, and Swanton – though not by Bancroft and Powell, who, like Gallatin, mention Eyak and quoted sources, but did not make misleading speculations or conclusions. Unfortunately, the first – and for 96 years the only American ethnolinguistic map of Alaska in color – was that dated 1875 and published with the 1880 Census Report by Petroff, showing Oogalakmute as a mixture of green-red for Eskimo-Thlinkit, now restricted to the Cordova area. For this confusion, much of which is painfully chronicled by Frederica de Laguna, see Birket-Smith and de Laguna (1938: 327-337). For further reading on that see Pinnow (1976: 31-40) and Johannsen (1963), which indiscriminately list derivative sources, including even opinion statistics. Finally, see the Hodge *Handbook* (1910: 862-863), for an eloquent epitome of the confusion. Rather than repeat or elaborate that mess here, we shall confine ourselves to the two major exceptions which are, in fact, holdovers from the previous "German" period.

Jacobsen 1883

Johan Adrian Jacobsen (b. 1853, d. 1947) was a Norwegian seaman and entrepreneur, who spent the period 1881 to 1883 traveling widely in Alaska and collecting artifacts for the Berlin Ethnology Museum. He spent July 28 to August 11, 1883 in Eyak country, at Eyak, Alaganik, and Cape Martin, buying artifacts and making observations. His artifact-acquisitions lists contain some Native words for the artifacts, e.g., seven Eyak words from Eyak village, but those from Alaganik and especially Cape Martin are Tlingit instead. Thus Jacobsen is a minor source of Eyak language data. His journals, however, written in a sort of German heavily influenced by and mixed with Dano-Norwegian and English, are of significant interest for language also. For instance, of Eyak village he writes, inimitably, "*in Iggiak* Villag, *zwischen das Kopfer* River *und Prinz Williams* Sound *am ein* Lake *beliend – sprechen ein eigne Sprache sollen von ein Inlands* treib *sein – sind jetzt mit Eskimo und auch Thlinket* intermarried *und die meisten verstehen die beide Sprachen* [in Eyak Village, between the Copper River and Prince William Sound, situated on a lake – speak a language of their own, must be from an inland tribe – are now intermarried with the Eskimo and also Tlingit, and most understand both languages (Eyak and Tlingit?)]." This accords with his comment on Alaganik, where the people "*sind verwandt mit die Indianer aus Iggiak – sprechen das Iggiak und Thlinket Sprache – scheint aber mehr zu der letztere Stam gehörend* [are related to the Indians from Iggiak, speak Iggiak (Eyak) and Tlingit – but seem to belong more to the latter tribe]." These statements imply that at Eyak they were already Eyak-Tlingit bilingual, likewise at Alaganik, but there Tlingit was already dominating, as the words in his artifact lists show. This is good evidence of how far assimilation to Tlingit was progressing in 1883. However, six years later, after the establishment of the canneries in that last Eyak stronghold and in spite of the resulting disorder and its disastrous effect on the Eyaks, the assimilation to Tlingit was evidently arrested and even reversed. The last speakers of Eyak in the twentieth century in Cordova did not speak Tlingit, only Eyak and English. Ironically, that tragic disorder thus might well have prolonged the survival of the Eyak language enough to have made a crucial difference for the last-minute academic salvage of Eyak culture and language.

In his journal for July 28, 1883, upon arriving at Eyak, Jacobsen writes, "These people must speak an entirely different language [from the Chugach] ... Their language is the most incomprehensible gibberish [*unbegraifbare Gibbel*] I have ever heard." Jacobsen was no academic, but a well traveled man, who had heard many languages, and [192] who was making only first-hand observations. His journals were edited and published first in German (Jacobsen 1884), then in Norwegian (1887), and finally in English, a good summary quote from which (1977: 207) is "... these people are of another type, different from the Eskimo and the Tlingit, and their language also differed to such a degree that my interpreter could not understand a word of it. I also realized that I had never heard a language so unintelligible ...." Jacobsen's journals and lists remain at the Hamburg Ethnology Museum. Obviously, published or not, Jacobsen's information on Eyak had no effect on the reverse progress of Eyak studies.

Krause 1885

Aurel Krause (b. 1848, d. 1908) and his brother Arthur (b. 1851, d. 1920), on an expedition for the Bremen Geographical Society, spent some five months in Tlingit country De cem ber 12, 1881 to May 14, 1882, especially in the Sitka and Chilkoot-Klukwan areas. The results were published by Aurel Krause in Jena, 1885, in what is widely considered an irreplaceable classic on Tlingit (Krause 1885). It takes serious account of the preceding academic literature, of course, including that on groups neighboring Tlingit. In that (1885: 323-325, here from the English translation, Krause 1956: 218-219), Krause reviews the literature on Eyak, noting from Wrangell that "their language is supposed to differ from the Kolushan but to have the same roots," and

> Dall's opinion that the Ugalenzen belong to the Innuit not only contradicts Wrangell and Veniaminov, but also disagrees with the linguistic research of Radloff, whose results cannot be doubted. He claims that the Ugalenzen are actually an independent people, however related to the Tlingit. "Even though the Ugalachmut," says Radloff, "through their geographical location and the description of their customs by Wrangell, show themselves to be related to tribes which belong to three different linguistic groups, namely the Kadjaken and the Tschugatschen (Eskimos), the Atnahs, and Athapascan people belonging to the Kinai, and finally the Kolushans, their languages shows little relationship to the first two. It can be stated with certainty that there is no relationship between the Eskimo dialect and Ugalachmut." (Krause 1956: 218-219)

However Radloff found among the 1,100 recorded words of Ugalachmut from the vocabularies of Resanov about 40 which bear phonetic and structural resemblance to Tlingit words. This information published in German in 1885 should certainly have caught the notice of American scholars, most of whom were supposed to read German in those days.

Franz Boas was right then spending his last year in Germany, 1885-1886, redefining himself as an anthropologist. He was even spending time in Berlin helping Captain Adrian Jacobsen with his Alaska collection! It is even more ironic that Boas, who was soon to make his first field trip to the Northwest Coast in 1886, and was to study Tlingit first in Victoria in 1888, evidently did not then notice, or perhaps never noticed, that clear statement of Krause 1885 or any of the literature leading to it. In spite of Boas's extended career with Tlingit, including a remarkable grammar published in 1916-1917, there is no record of Boas's ever taking note of Eyak. Did he doze through those pages of Krause? – This fateful lapse is especially surprising, considering that Boas placed very high value on salvage fieldwork on languages nearing extinction and considering for example, his own heroic work on Tsetsaut in 1894 and on Chemakum in 1890. During the Jesup Expedition years, 1897–1902, one might especially have expected some such attention, but in fact Alaska was basically skipped, supposedly on the grounds that it had been relatively well covered by Nelson in Beringia and Krause in the Southeast. So Eyak was ignored for 60 years.

Harriman 1899

The next episode in this ironic history is in an entirely different category, the "Harriman cylinder." In summer of 1899 Edward Henry Harriman (b. 1848, d. 1909), powerful railroad magnate and financier, chartered a luxury ship, the *George W. Elder*, for a vacation and "scientific" cruise to Alaska. This crass tycoon invited along family members, including young Averill plus a couple dozen of America's scientific and artistic elite including the naturalist-conservationist writers John Burroughs, John Muir, and George Bird Grinnell – Grinnell being the closest to an ethnologist of the group, as well as C. Hart Merriam and our major Alaska expert Dall. Both Merriam and Dall were vocabulary-writers, but not on this trip. Young Edward S. Curtis also graced the group but was a vocabulary-writer only later. In short, although the luxury cruise produced a remarkable wealth of published scientific data, Alaska Native languages were evidently beneath the dignity of any of this crew, with the notable – but forgotten – exception of the tycoon himself. Harriman had bought the most expensive and spectacular phonograph of the time, a Columbia Graphophone Grand, with a six-foot horn and outsized cylinders five-inches in diameter. Those did not play any longer than the usual 2½ minute ones, but played louder. As the ship approached a landing Harriman would blare rousing music on his toy to entertain and impress the assembled. What is less well known is that [193] Harriman used the machine also to record Alaska Native song and speech.

At a meeting on cylinder restoration at Sapporo, Japan, in 1985, Anthony Seeger, then of the Indiana University Archive of Traditional Music, brought along a Harriman cylinder especially to find if anyone could identify its language. Krauss is very proud to have guessed that it sounded like Tlingit played backward. Seeger reversed the cylinder on the mandrel (not tapered), and the cylinder indeed proved to be Tlingit, one of those made, as described in Goetzmann and Sloan (1982: 92), in the Governor's Mansion at Sitka, June 17, 1899, at a formal reception by Governor Brady. There is one cylinder of song, and one of speech by two Tlingit men (followed by one by Brady). The two Tlingit speeches are routine fine specimens of proud Tlingit oratory. The sound quality is such that they were perfectly easy to transcribe (transcription by Dauenhauer and Dauenhauer 1990: 156-181, 325-327). The ship stopped at Yakutat for some time. "North of Yakutat Bay no Indians were met with, all the natives seen from that point onward being Aleuts or Eskimo" (says our ethnographer Grinnell 1901: 185). June 24-28, 1899 the ship was at Orca cannery near the present Cordova, for repairs.

In 2001 Krauss's enquiry at the Indiana archive revealed that in the box in which the Tlingit speech was found was the typewritten label: "COLUMBIA GRAPHOPHONE RECORD. Made in Orca, Alaska, June 27, 1899 – Story by two Indians of a man drowned from Steamer Wildcat. Gift of Estate of Mrs. Mary E. Harriman, May 1934." Also on a slip in the box is typewritten "Record No. 11. Made in the Dining Saloon of the George W. Elder at Orca Station, Alaska. In the Eyak language. This is a speech by two Eyak Indians who give a vivid description of a white man drowning from the Steamer 'Wildcat' at Orca, Alaska, about 4 month previous. The man, who was cleaning fish, fell overboard head first and during the interval in which they were putting a boat over for him he threw up his hands in despair and sunk. His body has not been recovered." The typewriting in both is clearly later copy from what must have been Harriman's own hand, at least the latter slip. There are expressions such as "4 month previous" and "and sunk," possibly also "Dining Saloon," which reflect more the language of the tycoon than of the elite. The use of the phrases "Eyak Indian" and especially "Eyak language" is, it must be realized, probably the first ever in the history of written English, 31 years ahead of its time. Harriman was just spontaneously using those phrases to label Indians he knew were from the village of Eyak, and their language.

Krauss made additional efforts to locate more of the Harriman cylinders (for example, at the University of Indiana archive, Heye Foundation National Museum of the American Indian, and at Arden House). There must have been ten cylinders before Eyak, No. 11, and an unknown number after it – the cruise was less than half over at Orca – and those outsize cylinders would be quite noticeable in any collection. Krauss's efforts have so far met with failure. The centennial of the expedition was well observed, with much publicity. There was even a reenactment. No attention whatever was given to the matter of cylinder recordings. Harriman's great-grandson David H. Mortimer, Harriman family historian, very kindly checked his contacts (personal communication September 2005), even asking his aged mother, but no trace or memory of the missing cylinders has yet been found.

Frederica de Laguna

Frederica de Laguna had been a Ph.D. student under Boas at Columbia since 1927, went to Greenland the summer of 1929, and was finishing her dissertation that year on Eskimo and paleolithic art (published 1932-33). Her Greenland trip put her especially in touch with Danish ethnographers. In 1930 she was planning to go to Alaska as an archeological assistant to Kaj Birket-Smith, originally to the Shumagins, but they changed their plans and went instead to Prince William Sound, the southeastern limit of Alaskan Eskimo territory. It is not clear that they knew anything at all about Eyak at that point. At most they might have been familiar with the confused garble in the 1910 *Handbook*. Boas himself was presumably no better informed on Eyak than that either, in spite of all the preceding publications so pointedly chronicled here. Freddy further notes (de Laguna 1996: 68): "My own professor, Franz Boas, who had heartily approved my trip to Greenland, was less enthusiastic when Iinformed him of my plans for Alaska and warned me, on the basis of his own [?] experience, that I would have to move a lot of shelly midden material to find only a few specimens." Obviously, the plan was strictly for Alaskan Eskimo archeology, and about even that Boas was unenthusiastic.

Expedition of 1930

At the last minute, ill health forced Birket-Smith to cancel, but Freddy went anyway, with her brother Wallace, a geology student, to survey for Eskimo archeological sites in Prince William Sound and Cook Inlet. They arrived at Cordova June 27, 1930.

> I learned from Mr. H. C. Cloes, the U.S. deputy marshal in Cordova, that there were members of four linguistic groups (or tribes) in Cordova: the Chugach of Prince William Sound, Atna Athabaskan from the Copper River, Tlingits from Southeastern Alaska, and the Eyak. [194]

> "Those Eyaks are altogether a different breed of cat from the others," Mr. Cloes said, "Don't let anybody tell you different."

Did Mr. Cloes's vehement statement refer to the "official" opinion expressed in the *Handbook of North American Indians North of Mexico* (Anonymous 1910, vol. 2: 862) that the Eyak were a small group of Chugach who had been so strongly infl uenced by the Tlingits as to be recognized as part of that nation? This information was based on information furnished by William H. Dall in the 1870s.

My curiosity was aroused, although I did not fully understand the implications of this emphatic statement. Few people outside this part of Alaska had ever heard of the Eyak, but Birket-Smith and the Russians, who zealously collected vocabularies from all the tribes that they encountered, were well aware that these natives formed a distinct group.... (de Laguna 2000: 36-37)

Since this disclosure was news to Freddy in 1930, and there had been no mention of Eyak in their plans, it is doubtful that Birket-Smith should be cited as being as well-informed as the Russians had been on Eyak, and even Freddy's mention of the Russian awareness in this connection is obviously from her much later (2000) retrospective point of view. It is a nice coincidence, however, that she likewise now blames Dall for much of the confusion, a point probably never discussed with her by Krauss.

The de Lagunas must immediately have followed Cloes up and met the key figure Galushia Nelson, who was to be their chief guide and interpreter – also in 1933 – to take them on a tour July 1-2 to Alaganik, then old Eyak Village, and Eyak Lake, looking for house sites. Concerning this, Krauss has copies of twelve small notebook pages from 1930 and one page of Eyak vocabulary possibly from that summer. The de Lagunas left for Prince William Sound on July 5 and may have been back to Cordova for as much as a week before leaving for Cook Inlet August 20. They apparently tried to make a bit more contact with Eyak before Au gust 20, finding Old Chief Joe "aloof." They realized that the remaining Eyaks were few and deserved further investigation. Not the least reason for this was the understanding that Eyak culture and *language* were distinct from any other (Chugach, Tlingit, Ahtna). In fact Freddy thereupon came to the hypothesis that Eyak was an Athabaskan group from the interior which had come down the Copper River to its mouth. This hypothesis was evidently first published in the *Cordova Daily Times* of September 9, 1933, in a report she sent the local newspaper at the end of the major 1933 return expedition and then in *The Archaeology of Cook Inlet* (1934b: 156): "I reached the conclusion that the Eyak are an Athabaskanspeaking people who have pushed down the Copper River to its mouth ... This hypothesis, formulated in 1930, has been supported by the results of our ethnological studies in 1933." In other words, it was not until some time *after* the 1933 expedition that Freddy explicitly understands the real position of Eyak, that it was not what might be called "just another" Athabaskan language. We have a letter from Freddy to Boas, September 19, 1930, at the end of her Cook Inlet survey.

... I am very anxious to do some linguistic work with you. I did not know how little I knew until I tried to write down the names of old places. I would like to devote a lot of time to taking dictation if there is to be any Indian around the University. I would like of course to make the work have a particular bearing on the various languages which I have encountered here: Prince William Sound Eskimo, "Eyak", which sounds something like the little Tlingit which I hear[d] on the way up, and Cook Inlet Athabascan. The Museum will probably send me back here next summer and I was thinking of staying longer and trying to do so[m]e ethnological work among the Eyak or "Egiaq" as they call themselves. There are only five women and seven men left, and they all live in Cordova. The oldest man, Chief Joe, is said to know many stories, but so far I have not won his confidence. One of the other men [Galushia Nelson], who speaks English well, but his own language rather poorly, has promised to help me, so I have no doubt I could learn a lot from the old man.

We do not have Boas's response, but from this it is clear Freddy had a strong interest in following up the Eyak, and doing a decent job with the language.

"Aloof" Old Chief Joe, oldest of the Eyaks and said to know many stories, died that next winter. We have the good fortune, however, that young Annie Nelson, Galushia's wife, had learned a lot of his stories, some of which we have in English in Birket-Smith and de Laguna

1938. We moreover have several hours of tape recordings of Annie telling those stories much later to Krauss in Eyak (see Krauss 1970a, 1982).

Expedition of 1933

Whatever her intentions or priorities, during the summers of 1931 and 1932 Freddy returned only to Cook Inlet for further archeology there, without Birket-Smith, who remained ill. In any case, her primary purpose was still Eskimo archeology, even in summer 1933, when she finally returned to Cordova. Birket-Smith had published a "plan for an archeological expedition to Alaska for the summer of 1933" in the Danish geographical journal for that year (Birket-Smith 1933), involving Freddy, with no mention whatever of Eyak. Birket- Smith had recovered, and the expedition now also [195] included a graduate student from the University of Washington, Norman Reynolds, along with Freddy's brother Wallace, and her mother Grace. The 1933 priorities remain clear at least from Birket- Smith's reports: *"Da vi den 27. April kam til Cordova, var det endnu halvt vinter, og det var alt for tidligt at tage fat paa udgravningerne. Vi benyttede da den første tid til studiet af de saakaldte Eyak-indianere ... Det 11.Mai fl yttede vi ud ...* [When we came to Cordova April 27, it was still half winter, and much too soon to undertake excavations. So we used that first period to study the so-called Eyak Indians ... May 11 we moved on ...]" (Birket-Smith 1935a: 191, 192; also similarly in German, Birket-Smith 1934: 284-285), and "On April 27th we arrived in Cordova in Prince William Sound and immediately started an ethnological investigation of the few surviving Eyak Indians. As soon as the weather permitted, however, we left for the shell heap Palugvik ... " (Birket-Smith 1953: 1). Freddy dates that departure May 14 (1956: ix), but the *Cordova Daily Times* reports it on May 11. Thus their main session with Eyak lasted at most 15 days – and subtracted from that must be the time during that period spent on outfitting and arranging for Prince William Sound Eskimo archeology. According to the *Times*: "The party outfitted in Cordova after spending some time here in preliminary work. Five tents, camp stoves, several hundred pounds of food, cataloguing books and personal effects comprised the equipment for a month or more of work which Miss de Laguna and her companions expect to put in on Hawkins Island." The lack of any mention of the Eyak work may reflect the expedition priorities or the *Times*'s perennial silence on Eyak, or both.

The amount of time spent with Eyak after that in the summer of 1933 is still less clear. Birket-Smith returned to Cordova first, August 6, and left August 14 (*Cordova Daily Times*, Au gust 7 and 14). All we know is that his week included a jaunt up the railroad to Chitina and back. The rest of the party returned from Prince William Sound to Cordova on Au gust 25; Frederica de Laguna and Norman Reynolds did some more Eyak ethnography there and left Sep tem ber 9, but that period included a boat trip along the east shore of Prince William Sound "exploring several sites and collecting Eskimo and Eyak folk tales" (de Laguna 1956: x). Therefore, aside from the Eyak tales on the boat, the sum total time for Eyak was less than three weeks.

Throughout, their main informant and interpreter was Galushia Nelson (b. 1889, d. 1939) (Fig. 4). As a boy, he had been taken (abducted) to Chemawa boarding school in Oregon, from 1902 to 1912. For more on him see Birket-Smith 1935b: 89-94, Birket-Smith and de Laguna 1938: 8-10, and Krauss 1982: 15-17. Given his personality and love of his people, he was an ideal interpreter in both senses of the word, but at the same time, because of his absence between the age of 12 and 22, his active command of the Eyak language was somewhat limited or faulty, according to later memory. Galushia's wife Annie also played a crucial role in 1933, as well as in this entire history since (Krauss 1982). Others were Old Man Dude and Johnny Stevens.

Published and Archival Results

The published 1933 expedition results for Eyak were the following. First was Frederica de Laguna's report to the *Cordova Daily Times*, printed the day of her departure, a good column and a half long, about a quarter of which is about Eyak: " ... It has always [!] been believed that they were originally an offshoot of the Chugach Eskimo, who became absorbed by the Tlingits ... Their language is certainly neither Eskimo nor Tlingit. Though it is too soon for us to make a definite statement, we think that the Eyak are a branch of the great Athabaskan nation of the interior ...." Next Freddy published two pages about Eyak ceremonial paddles she had gotten for the University of Pennsylvania Museum (de Laguna 1934a: 57-59). There she remarks, in connection with her Athabaskan hypothesis, that "they do speak Athabaskan, but theirs is a very divergent dialect" – a key point, to which we shall return. The next publication was Birket-Smith's "preliminary report on the Danish- American expedition to Alaska," in Danish (Birket-Smith 1935a), 50 pages, about five of which are about Eyak: " ... there are now only 11-12 adults left in the tribe, and if anything was to be salvaged of their past, we had arrived at the very last minute ... The language is a kind of Athabaskan." Also in 1935, Birket-Smith published his *Guld og Grønne Skove* [Gold and Green Forests] (Birket-Smith 1935b) for Danish popular consumption about the expedition. About one-tenth of the book gives an account of their findings on Eyak, and also some revelations about the situation and treatment of the Eyaks in Cordova in 1933, giving a much more intimate glimpse of that than the main joint publication. Krauss has translated that subsection, with the feeling that it deserves to be more widely known. The chapter ends with a crucial new understanding of the position of the Eyak language, to which we shall return below. This new understanding is likewise included in Freddy's 13- page "Preliminary Sketch of the Eyak Indians ... " (de Laguna 1937).

In all fairness, even though it is abundantly clear that Birket-Smith himself before the 1933 expedition showed not the least enthusiasm for the Eyak part of the expedition, one might wonder in the first place why he then came to the area two [196] weeks before weather was to allow the Chugach archeology. More important still is that he not only went along with the Eyak phase, and made a major contribution to the 1938 book, but also in his reports afterward, shows a real personal enthusiasm for what was accomplished. At the very least it must be acknowledged that Birket-Smith was a very "good sport" about the Eyak, and no impediment to it. Still, one might wonder what this history would have been if Birket-Smith instead of Freddy had gone to Cordova in 1930. The archival results are very disappointing, in that most of the field notes or papers of Birket- Smith, Norman Reynolds, and Frederica de Laguna herself, it seems, have been lost. From Birket- Smith all we have are two pages of 30 Eyak words and names copied by L.L Hammerich out of an original text of 20 pages, probably in the 1950s. It was sadly confirmed by the Ethnographic Museum in Copenhagen and by his son to Krauss that Birket-Smith had destroyed all his ethnographic notes in his old age. Krauss was also in touch with Norman Reynolds's widow in 1985, and ascertained that his boxes from his ethnography days in Alaska contained only books and no papers. All that is left from him is a total of 24 pages in his hand among the six small notebooks from the de Laguna collection. In the mid-1960s Freddy kindly sent Krauss Xerox copies of all the notebooks that contained Eyak linguistic material, even bits thereof. That collection consists of 12 pages from the 1930 Alaganik trip, no language, except perhaps one loose page; six small notebooks from 1933, 122 pages in her hand plus, interspersed, the 24 mentioned in Reynolds's; and 5 larger notebooks, 83 pages, all in her hand. Though there must have been more, neither the materials in possession of Freddy's literary executrix [197] Marie-Françoise Guédon, nor the materials taken to the Smithsonian National Anthropological Archives by Robert Leopold, reportedly contain any Eyak notebooks whatever, not even the originals of those Xeroxed for Krauss. Apparently there had never been any field journals or diaries kept during the 1930 or 1933 expeditions by Freddy either, or those too have disappeared.

Figure 4. Members of the expedition with Galushia Nelson's family, Cordova, 1933. Left to right: Galushia Nelson, Johnny Nelson, Anna Nelson, Norman Reynolds, Kaj Birket-Smith, and Frederica de Laguna. Photograph courtesy of Michael E. Krauss.

The major result of the Eyak part of the expedition is Birket-Smith and de Laguna's joint work *The Eyak Indians of Copper River Delta, Alaska* (1938). Of its 591 pages, 80 are folktales, 36 are "Critical Analysis of Previous Writers on the Eyak," 101 are a comparative "Analysis of Eyak Ethnology" (mostly by Birket-Smith), leaving exactly half the book, pages 17-242, for "Description of Eyak Ethnology." Given the format of the pages, at roughly a 1,700 character-count, that might not be more than 65 pages in the format of this journal. It is also virtually the last work ever done on Eyak ethnography. Not so for Eyak language, fortunately.

Linguistic Results

The 1938 book does include, however, aside from words and phrases throughout, an appendix on the language. That appendix played a crucial role in this history. It contains some phonetics on two pages, then an Eyak vocabulary of not much more than 500 entries, nine pages of grammar and phrases, and seven pages on kin terms (from Annie Nelson). Not all, but most, of the remaining archival material in Freddy's hand or in Reynolds's is here, but there is more here than in the notebooks too. We also have a 41-page typescript version of that appendix, very much refined from the notebooks, preparatory to the printing, probably datable to 1934, prepared by Freddy. "All words were obtained from Galushia Nelson, except those [31 in number] marked 'Dude,' which were obtained from Old Man Dude." The published texts are all in English, but even the phrases and titles of the texts in Eyak provide the very first samples of the language more than a word or two in length. (The notebooks include one short text in Reynolds's hand, the very first written down in the language, later edited by Krauss in 1966.) The appendix also presents the very first attempts at Eyak verb paradigms, possessive prefixes, etc. The transcriptions are significantly better than those of the previous century. Freddy had training from Boas, and Reynolds had training from Boas's student Melville Jacobs. Written in a phonetic script for the first time, as anthropologists were taught to do in those days, the 1933 transcriptions – using barred *l*'s, *q*'s, *x*'s, an apostrophe for both glottal stop and glottalization, *c* for *sh*, and the like – gave the impression of much greater accuracy and credibility than they truly deserve, however, as they may be wrongly heard as often as right. Noting the inconsistent or variable results in their "scientific" transcription, between speakers and between transcribers, led them to believe in far greater variability than the language truly had, even to the point of believing they were dealing with more than one dialect. There were at least two things Krauss was never able to convince Freddy about. First, that her own transcriptions were fully as good as Norman Reynolds's (though Krauss had a clear basis for comparison from those pages of field notes), and second, that a "phonemic" transcription could be of as much value as a phonetic one, and could even demand a greater degree of understanding and rigor. Possibly also, that attested dialectal variation within Eyak was minimal, even considering Yakutat, which she only became aware of later, after 1949. It seems doubtful that she had by then also been aware of and misled by the Veniaminov statement, of a "Yakutat" and Ugalents dialect, discussed above.

We have an undated letter from Freddy to Boas evidently April or May, 1935: "Here are the Eyak notes and vocabulary [probably the typescript]. You may keep them all summer ... We will publish the vocabulary as an appendix to this report [eventually 1938]." She continues with recommending Reynolds for a follow-up investigation. We also have a crucial letter from Sapir to Boas, April 26, 1935:

> Enclosed is Miss de Laguna's manuscript on Eyak. Please return it when you are through with it as I have promised to give her a statement about it. I think you will find it interesting.
>
> As far as I can make it out it is nearer to Tlingit than to Athabaskan though it has quite a number of words and forms that are reminiscent of Athabaskan. It may turn out to be either a very divergent Tlingit dialect which has been infl uenced by Athabaskan or else an independent division of a linguistic group that includes Tlingit, Athabaskan and itself. It would be an important language to investigate in either case. ... (Boas 1972: 745)

Sapir then wonders where money might come from, and prefers it should be for someone "who already knows something of Tlingit and Athabaskan".

It is thus difficult to determine whether Freddy had first addressed Boas or Sapir about Eyak. Birket-Smith's *Guld og Grønne Skove* (1935b) has a foreword dated April 1935, and on p. 102 concludes the Eyak section:

> This, one is tempted to say "microscopic", tribe of eleven twelve persons speak their own language, which is so different from the neighboring tribes' that it is altogether unintelligible to them. Never in all my days have I heard such a fireworks of fourfive hissing, spluttering, lisping and exploding consonants piled tight together as in the Eyak [198] language, and it was not therefore without difficulty that we managed to write down a vocabulary. But it paid off! After our return we showed it to two men whom one might well call the most expert on North American Native languages, Professors Boas and Sapir, and both decided unanimously that we are dealing not just with a new language, but an altogether new language branch, possibly distantly related to Athabaskan and Tlingit. It seems so interesting to them that now they want to send an American expedition to study the Eyak language itself, before it is too late. Our discovery really opens whole new perspectives for the ethnography of that region.

Birket-Smith's report had been very swift, the same month as Sapir's letter. Freddy's appears in her 1937 "Preliminary Report," much less dramatically. "The vocabulary which Norman Reynolds and I collected has been examined by Dr. Boas and Dr. Sapir. The latter reports that the phonetic system is suggestive of Tlingit, and the language itself may be a new dialect [*sic*, i.e. branch] of the Na-Dene group, coordinate with Athabaskan on the one hand and Tlingit on the other." Sapir may have gotten or given this impression because he was intimately expert in some Athabaskan, far less so with Tlingit, so that he was more deeply struck by its difference from the Athabaskan he knew than by its difference from Tlingit.

Finally, in the chronology of this revelation, one is left wondering about Freddy's use of the phrase in her much earlier note about the paddles, published Janu ary 1934, that Eyaks "do speak Athabaskan, but theirs is a very divergent dialect," which foreshadows the 1935 Sapir revelation, without explanation, considering that her hypothesis at that time was that Eyak was (part of?) Athabaskan. In fact, taken at face value, Freddy's statement is more correct than Sapir's. In any case, however ironically, American scholarship was finally catching up with the Russian, at least at the Copper River end – not that anyone was seeing it that way, of course.

We have good student notes by both Stanley Newman and Mary Haas from Sapir's course on Comparative Athabaskan at Yale, starting January 28, 1936. From these it is possible to reconstruct Sapir's lectures in some detail. The initial lecture, including of course mention or listing of the relevant languages, seems to include no mention of Eyak (or Tlingit) at all. By then, near the end of his life and energies, far from the loftier interests of the beginning of his career, e.g., Na-Dene, even that with Sino-Tibetan, Sapir was far more preoccupied with Comparative Athabaskan at most, more in fact just with Navajo itself. At the 1984 Sapir Centenary Conference in Ottawa, Krauss remembers Freddy's surprise that he had nothing to say about Sapir and Eyak. By that time, Mary Haas had explained to Krauss, it was hard to get Sapir to teach a course even in Comparative Athabaskan itself, let alone anything beyond that. "His heart wasn't in it" (see Krauss 1986, for more on Sapir in this respect).

Ironically also, the *magnum opus* on Eyak, the joint 1938 book, came out with no mention whatever about any revelations on the genetic position of the Eyak language, from Sapir or anyone else. It also showed no awareness that Eyak was or had been spoken much east of Copper River or Comptroller Bay. That latter ignorance shows that the authors had still not acquired any real knowledge of what the Russians had published on the Eyak language, in spite of the historical section of the book. Possibly the printing chronology of the 1938 book was such that the 1935 Sapir revelation came too late, though not too late to be included in the 1937 "preliminary" report.

Nothing came of the proposed follow-up. Freddy continued to recommend Reynolds to do the work. Boas and Sapir were polite, but they kept stipulating that the work be done by someone trained in Athabaskan and the like. Mary Haas (Swadesh), then a student of Sapir's at Yale, was nominated. In the ACLS Bulletin No. 25, July 1936 (courtesy of Victor Golla) Boas's "Progress Report" for 1935 notes:

> One very urgent piece of new field work has turned up that ought to be tended to. It is an investigation of the Eyak, a tribe which seems to be intermediate between Tlingit and Athapascan, the knowledge of which would be of the greatest importance for an understanding of the relation between these languages. If this can be done, we should entrust Mrs. Swadesh with the work. The amount needed for the field work is estimated at $1000 to $1500. (Boas 1936: 745)

But it was the Depression, and Mary Haas told Krauss furthermore that she was advised that "Cordova was no place for an unaccompanied lady to go." Sincere attempts to have Reynolds go as her assistant came, unfortunately, to nothing.

Much then intervened, including Sapir's death, Boas's death, and World War II. Though Freddy did not directly return to Eyak, she evidently soon found she could not get away from it. As soon as she began her work on Tlingit at Yakutat in 1949, she discovered that Eyak had been there too, before Tlingit. She therewith began to develop a far broader perspective on Eyak geography and prehistory. This comes to light in her three volume 1972 masterpiece on Yakutat, and is made very clear in her 1990 *Handbook* chapter on Eyak. Thus, finally, Russian knowledge is regained, though still without the full realization that the Russians had all this clearly figured out in black and white, and even in color. [199]

Freddy's thinking was never static; it was always in motion. This certainly was no less true of her thoughts about Eyak. As of April 1930, what little she knew was at most (1) the Americans were confused by and mistaken about Eyak, believing it some kind of mixture at Cordova, then 2) that Eyak was a separate Athabaskan language that had come downriver to Cordova, or somehow that Eyak was a specially divergent Athabaskan language, then 3) from Sapir that Eyak was an intermediate branch of Na-Dene between Tlingit and Athabaskan; then, in a new direction, 4) that Eyak had been the language of the coast at least as far as Yakutat. A few months before her death, Krauss visited Freddy for the last time, and she alluded to new ideas, 5) that Eyak was once a far more widespread language still, of a once far more powerful people. During the very last weeks of her long life, she spoke extensively to Marie-Françoise Guédon of these ideas. It now remains for Marie-Françoise to pass Freddy's last thoughts on Eyak on to us.

Note on the Name Eyak

It is altogether clear that the origin of the name "Eyak" is the local Chugach Eskimo name of the Eyak village site near the mouth of the Eyak River on Eyak Lake at Mile 6, in Chugach *Igya'aq*. In this the initial *I-* is pronounced as the *-i-* in *sing*, the *-g-* as a voiced fricative gamma, and the *-ya'aq* has not the vowel of *yak* as in the English pronunciation of the name, but rhymes more or less rather with *hawk*, except that the final consonant is of course the Eskimo-Aleut back velar *-q*, not midmouth English *-k*. Both syllables are accented, the first with a vowel of short duration, and the second is of quite long duration, because the *-a'a-* is in fact the result of the dropping of an old back velar voiced fricative Eskimo-Aleut *-r-* (as e.g., Parisian "*r*") in an older form of the word still widely found as such in Yup'ik, *igyaraq*. The word *igyaraq* or *igya'aq* has the basic meaning 'throat, gullet,' and also very commonly, 'outlet of a lake into a river.' Not surprisingly, it is therefore also commonly found as a place-name elsewhere in Alaska, e.g., *Igiugik* in that very position on Lake Iliamna, where the *-u-* represents the *-u-* of English *dug* and the second *-g-* represents the *-r-*.

The first non-Russian spellings of the name were written *Ihiak* (Petroff in 1880 [1884]), *Iggiak* (Jacobsen 1883 ms.), but by the time Americans were on the scene, it was already *Eyak* (Abercrombie in 1884 [1900]; Allen in 1885 [1887]). Harriman, as we have seen, wrote *Eyak*. Probably because it was never spelled **Eyawk* or the like, the local English became *Eyak* with the second syllable vowel as in *yak*, a "spelling pronunciation." That has remained also the "standard" [!] academic pronunciation, though Krauss often heard it pronounced with the first syllable as in *eye*, as that "spelling pronunciation" evidently had some currency in "outside" academe. Krauss heard that for example from Harry Hoijer in the 1960's, who may have gotten it from Sapir, for all we know.

Obviously, the original name *Igya'aq* was given to the village site because it was first occupied by Chugach. When that site was taken over by the Eyak Indians, possibly as early as some point in the eighteenth century, the Chugach name was retained by them, adapted as *'i:ya:q*, somewhat predictably. The gamma is gone, into the lengthening of the first vowel, since the Eyak language has no gamma. The English spelling Eyak could perhaps come equally well from the Eyak *'i:ya:q* or Chugach *Igya'aq*. Harriman's "Eyak Indians" may only have been his spontaneous phrase and/or it might, by 1899, already reflect some established local English usage. Certainly, that latter was so by 1930 and by that time Cordova was also the only place left where the Eyak language was spoken. It was therefore entirely natural and logical that, through Frederica de Laguna, "Eyak" became the American name for the people and language.

There is some irony in this history too, that it is the Chugach village name that became the definitive academic name for the Eyak Indian people who made their "last stand" at that site, to be (re-) "discovered" there by Freddy as such – at such a late point in their history, and at such an extreme point in their distribution.

Currently, the "Eyak (Village) Corporation" is over 90% Chugach, for two reasons. First is the near-disappearance of Eyak Indians, and second, the partial depopulation of the Chugach Prince William Sound villages, with urbanization of those people at Cordova. By now there is a new, real question locally of who the "Eyaks" really are. "Eyak (Village) Corporation members" is factually definable, but "Eyaks" is now a name becoming ambiguous with an irony that is painful.

Eyak Language Work
after de Laguna

Given the preceding history, clearly no modern linguistic fieldwork was done on Eyak until after Frederica de Laguna did her work of the 1930s. Beginning in 1940, however, there have been four significant contributions. The first three involved brief periods of a month or so of fieldwork: Harrington in 1940, Liin 1952, and Austerlitz in 1961, all of whom produced documentation of much better quality and greater quantity than their predecessors. Harrington's work with Eyak was done quite "independently," i.e., in no collegial sense, so is motivated rather exclusively by whatever moved Harrington (see below). Li's and Austerlitz's [200] work is part of the larger (pre-Chomskyan!) academic perspective. Krauss's is in a different class altogether, being a long-term commitment, and the only such. This last phase of our history will be dealt with in less detail, in part because there is so much more of it, but also in part because it is anticlimactic, after Freddy's work.

Harrington 1940

John Peabody Harrington (b. 1884, d. 1961) worked for the Smithsonian. This man very probably was the last to write down more dying languages than any other individual in linguistic history. He certainly must be given credit for being early to recognize the enormity of the American language extinction tragedy, and for doing something about it. Not a nice man, he is reputed, for instance, to have made a habit of instructing his language consultants never to work with other linguists after him. He had a paranoid streak and was quite secretive with his work. Anti-Semitic as well, he was predictably resentful of Boas and Sapir. At the same time, he evidently felt a need to publish on comparative issues, including Athabaskan and Tlingit, in order to make his mark, in his own way, in that arena also. Fortunately, his publications are a very minor part of his accomplishments, which must be recognized for what they truly are, namely an incomparable corpus of terminal or near-terminal documentation of American languages. Eyak became one of those languages. Harrington must certainly have heard of Eyak through Freddy, though no acknowledgement of that is evident. He did his work on it in 1940 without her knowledge. Harrington had already spent 33 years recording Native languages of the American West, including extensive work in Athabaskan, by the time he came to Yakutat to work with

George Johnson, and was already familiar with Tlingit since 1939, having worked with two speakers in Seattle.

George Johnson (Fig. 5) was born 1892 probably at Bering River Village and came to Katalla as a child. Eyak presumably was his first language, but Tlingit surely was a close second. We do not have the date of his moving to Yakutat, but Johnson told Krauss he had probably not spoken Eyak for 30 years (i.e., since 1910) before Harrington came to work with him. One can easily see from the Harrington material that Tlingit was Johnson's dominant [201] language in 1940, much steadier than his Eyak.

We have a good account of Harrington's work with Johnson in Elaine L. Mills's guide to the Harrington papers at the NAA (Mills 1981, Volume I: 8-14). She notes that Harrington wanted to bring Johnson to Seattle, but ended up instead having to go to Yakutat to work with him. He stayed there from May 12 to June 14, 1940, working "eight hours a day" with Johnson (Johnson told Krauss "about six hours."). There is no question of Harrington's interest in Tlingit. In fact he ended up writing a paper on comparative Athabaskan and Tlingit, his so-called "Phonematic Daylight in Lhiinkit, Navajo of the North" (Harrington 1945) – in which Eyak does not figure. The article is a competent enough presentation of Tlingit phonemes. However, that had already been done remarkably well by Boas in 1917 – ignored by Harrington. What few comparative remarks Harrington makes in the article show he has no idea whatever of real comparative method, the rigorous process that had become so well established by then in linguistics to show genetic relationship, e.g., through regular sound correspondences, as opposed to vague surface resemblances. It seems certain that Harrington's reason, at least his original reason, for working with Johnson was that Johnson was bilingual with Eyak. (Perhaps, very secondarily, it might also have been that Johnson represented the Yakutat dialect of Tlingit, but not that Johnson was known for being an exceptional font of Tlingit knowledge.) Clearly, the material Harrington got from Johnson is predominantly Tlingit, the Tlingit normally given first, ("Y." [Yakutat]), then the Eyak equivalent, if any ("C." [Cordova]). The latter is often missing, or merely noted or dismissed as "= Y.", while the former is perhaps never missing. One cannot tell, however, that Harrington was disappointed or frustrated that he was getting less Eyak, and less good Eyak, than Tlingit, or, from this material, just what the nature of Harrington's interest in Eyak, as such, was. Here Eyak seems to be, after all, just an accompaniment, where available, to the Tlingit. It is obviously dangerous to play guessing games on a psyche like Harrington's, but apparently he lost interest in or gave up plans for using the Eyak comparatively. Hence Harrington never published on it. Harrington was of course a good sleuth for finding last speakers, but never seems to have considered going to Cordova, where he had to know there were of course several more speakers, or working with Annie Nelson (Harry), who had recently moved to Yakutat.

The only printed mention of Eyak we have from Harrington is in the *Smithsonian Annual Report* for 1941 (1942 51-52):

Dr. Harrington then proceeded in May to the study of the Atchat, or Eyak, Tribe, which was found to have occupied the entire eastern half of the Gulf of Alaska, a stretch of coast 350 miles long, extending from Prince William Sound in the west to Lituya Bay in the east. This tribe has earlier been called Ugalenz and Eyak, but the real name of the tribe has never been known, Atchat, meaning 'on this side' or 'opposite,' referring to location on the Gulf of Alaska and opposite the islands. This language also proved to be closely related to the Navaho, and, as might be expected, more closely related to the languages of British Columbia and the Navaho than is the island language.

There is no Eyak ethnonym remotely resembling *Atchat*. Rather, that must be the Eyak demonstrative *'a:nch'aht* 'from here, hence', or possibly, from Johnson's Eyak, *'a:nch'a:t* 'this side'. Freddy might, in the end, have agreed that Eyaks once lived as far south as Lituya Bay, but not on the evidence Harrington could have had. Harrington is, of course, right that Eyak is related to Canadian Athabaskan and Navajo more closely than is Tlingit ("the island language"?), but this is hardly new.

Definitely, Harrington's interest was overwhelmingly lexicon. He transcribed no texts and got very little into the grammar. He did, though, take a very broad interest in the natural history, especially flora and fauna, and place names. His notes are full of local lore of many kinds, including current salmon prices, but they could hardly be considered either disciplined linguistics or ethnography. Harrington did have an excellent ear, however, and from the first he was transcribing both the Tlingit and the Eyak in his own idiosyncratic but essentially adequate writing system. He was far from infallible, so made frequent mistakes, but his writing performance is good enough that the mistakes are at least definable. The Harrington transcriptions are thus in fact the first essentially adequate ones for Eyak ever. If they were the last we had, we could at least verify with them what we had hypothesized philologically from the earlier transcriptions we have of Eyak.

In terms of quantity, there may be some 1,500 Eyak items in the corpus, so in this respect too, Harrington surpasses all previous Eyak work. In terms of sheer paper bulk, it should be added, since Harrington had the habit of taking a new sheet of paper, often foolscap size, for each new word, the number of microfilm frames listed for the collection by Mills is for at least 3,547 sheets of paper, a good hundred sheets a day. One section, of 221 pages, is quite different from the rest, being a rough typescript draft, with the title "Southern Peripheral Athapaskawan in Alaska and Canada," "By John P. Harrington and Robert W. Young." Late in 1939, Harrington had traveled in Canada with Young, working on Sarcee, Carrier, [202] Sekani, Beaver, and Chipewyan, with a view towards comparative Athabaskan. The Tlingit and Eyak were certainly to be connected with that, but the 221 pages we have show no sign of that or of Robert W. Young. All that is present is the Yakutat fauna and flora information, including terminology from Tlingit and Eyak. By far the longest part is a disquisition on salmon, most of that with no Tlingit or Eyak at all – 89 pages, other fauna an additional 89 pages, flora 41 pages. Throughout there are about 374 Tlingit and 238 Eyak terms. Harrington's Eyak from George Johnson must, moreover, be used with care, as Johnson's Eyak was so rusty, and Harrington's approach and judgment such that the Eyak forms are too often contrived or forced translations of the Tlingit.

Harrington was not any kind of "mainstream" linguist, needless to say, and his career was such that his work or data were hardly shared with his contemporaries. Freddy became aware of it only when George Johnson told her about it in 1949. She never saw it until Krauss sent her copies, as it was being prepared in the 1960s for microfilming.

Fang-Kuei Li 1952

Fang-KueiLi(LiFang Kuei, LiFanggui; b. 1902, d. 1987) came first to the U.S. in 1924. As a student of Sapir's at Chicago, his 1927 M.A. thesis was a study of Sarcee verb stems from Sapir's 1922 field notes. (The Sarcee had made Sapir tone-happy, and Sapir was pleased to have a tone-sensitive bright young "Chinaman" working for him.) In summer 1928, while Sapir was working on Hupa in California ("no tones!"), Li worked nearby on Wailaki and Mattole (no tones either). His Ph.D. dissertation (1930) was the Mattole. In 1929, looking especially for more Athabaskan tone, and of course counting on Li's ear, Sapir sent Linorth to Chipewyan and Hare. Li came back with data showing tone alright, but the reverse of what Sapir expected from what he had found in Sarcee (1922), Kutchin (1923), and Navajo (1926). Krauss believes that the result, between the already revered Sapir and the deferent discreet young "Chinaman" was the opposite of fruitful, but rather that the study of Athabaskan syllable nuclei became taboo, and, in any case, Li returned to China in 1929. Li's last Athabaskan paper (brilliant), was "Chipewyan Consonants" – not vowels! (Li 1930). That was the end of Li's Athabaskan career. After that Limade an enormous lifetime contribution to the study and classification of Chinese and Tai languages. He returned to the U.S. in 1949, and remained in Seattle until his retirement in 1969, when he went to Hawaii {then to his daughter in San Francisco}.

After Freddy's first summer at Yakutat in 1949, realizing that Eyak had been there – and was still there in the sense that two Eyak speakers originally from Katalla (George Johnson) and Cordova (Anna Nelson Harry) lived there – and in preparation for a much wider investigation there in 1952, she took the brilliant initiative to enlist Fang-Kuei Li from Seattle to work on Eyak language. She got a grant from Wenner-Gren to support Lifor that, separately, but in connection of course with her larger project.

Li spent about six weeks in Yakutat and then Cordova, June-July 1952. In 1965 Li kindly allowed Krauss to make Xerox copies of all his Eyak notes. We have two notebooks from George Johnson, 41 pp. and 22 pp., then one from Anna Nelson Harry, of 42 pp., and then one from Minnie and Scar Stevens in Cordova, 24 pp. The Johnson notebooks contain about 750 words and phrases, and six texts, the Anna one about 700 words and phrases and one text, and the Stevens one about 480 words and phrases. The Li materials thus then constituted not only the most extensive Eyak lexicon, but also included seven texts, the first (not counting the few brief attempts by Reynolds in 1933) we have for Eyak. Throughout, especially with Anna, there are, moreover, the beginnings of verb conjugations, going at least a step beyond Harrington and Rezanov in the direction of exploring Eyak grammar. The transcription throughout is fairly good, at the level of Harrington, but using a system obviously from Sapir.

The Johnson texts are extremely halting or "stiff," especially at first, but limber up somewhat in the later ones. The notebook from Anna is the first work with her, not counting her 1933 kin terms and "background" contribution, prompting her first husband. Li's work with Minnie and Scar Stevens, mother and father of Sophie and Marie – the last two speakers of Eyak, is the only documentation we have directly from them.

In addition to the notebooks, we also have from Li his file-slips. These are about 1,200 three-by-five-inch slips that have been Xeroxed and shingled onto about 140 pages, containing about 2,000 Eyak words and phrases. These are largely, but not entirely, copied from his notebooks, the contents thereof organized alphabetically by the stem of the word. This thus begins to be an organization of his data into an inventory, or dictionary of Eyak, and is something of a standard part of the results of good linguistic fieldwork in the best tradition.

Li's only publication from this work is the four-page article (Li 1956) comparing the -ł instrumental noun suffix in Athabaskan and Eyak. Liconcentrated rigorously on the suffix, but treats us to a number of insightful comments: "a few words may be said about the relationship of Eyak to Athabaskan, as their relationship has not yet been clearly stated. In vocabulary, Eyak differs tremendously from Athabaskan in general ... A fair number of words can be directly compared with the Athabaskan ... Regular phonological correspondences can be obtained from such comparisons." [203] Li does not, however, take the time to make them explicit. "Eyak is not a tonal language." On the top of his first page of notes from Johnson Lihas marked "1. check tones." He then proceeds dutifully to write tone-marks throughout all his Eyak notes, in spite of the obvious conclusion he must soon have come to that Eyak has no distinctive tones. He must have taken the trouble out of extreme caution for his debt to posterity, especially in view of Sapir's enthusiasm for tone in this language family.

"On the whole it seems to me that while Eyak is definitely related to Athabaskan, it cannot be considered as one of the Athabaskan languages. Perhaps Sapir's Na-Dene group may be said to have definitely two members, Athabaskan and Eyak, what other members may eventually be included will remain to be worked out." Here Li is distancing himself from Sapir in questioning whether even Tlingit is genetically related to Athabaskan-Eyak, let alone Haida. Further, any question whether it was Krauss or Li who finally made clear the position of Eyak with regard to Athabaskan should herewith be definitively answered – unless of course it was Freddy: Eyaks "do speak Athabaskan, but theirs is a very divergent dialect."

This brief Eyak interlude was the only time Licame back to, or near, the Athabaskan phase of his distinguished linguistic career. Here too, we have Freddy to thank for getting Li to do it.

Austerlitz 1961

Robert Paul Austerlitz (b. 1923, d. 1994) had a multilingual childhood in Hungarian-Romanian Transylvania and came to New York in 1938. His training and career were at Columbia University, but his interest and experience were very broad in real languages, most especially Finno-Ugric-Uralic, and in Giliak (or Nivx) from Sakhalin, which work he did in Japan in the 1950s. Eyak was to be documented by yet another distinguished linguist, this time on something of a "lark," by Austerlitz, who, unlike Li, had no particular experience in any languages related to Eyak.

Krauss had come to the University of Alaska, Fairbanks, in the fall of 1960, and promptly began efforts to establish work with Alaska Native languages. By spring of 1961, he had obtained funding for basic survey and documentary work from the National Science Foundation, with a generous grant of $38,000 (in 1961 dollars). Krauss circulated a poster, featuring a woodcut of an Eskimo fishing through the ice, to recruit fieldworkers for the program, expenses paid plus $60 a week (token) salary. In April 1961 Austerlitz responded, thinking of Aleut. By May Krauss and Austerlitz were corresponding about Athabaskan; in July Catharine McClellan, a major disciple and colleague of Freddy's, who had worked with her in Yakutat, strongly suggested Eyak to Austerlitz and by the end of that month he wrote Krauss he was "sold on Eyak." Reviewing that correspondence, Krauss is reminded that he was merely happy to have Austerlitz to do anything, and cannot take the credit for the decision that Austerlitz work on Eyak.

Krauss insisted that Austerlitz get immediately in touch with Li, who responded helpfully and, on his way to Alaska, Austerlitz spent from August 17th to the 20th in Seattle, conferring with Li. Au gust 20th to the 22nd Austerlitz was in Yakutat, August 22nd to September 19th he spent in Cordova, then September 19th to the 22nd he was again in Yakutat, so he really had about one month in all for the study of Eyak. He managed to work briefl y with Anna Nelson Harry in Yakutat at both ends of his trip, but most of his time was spent in Cordova, with Lena Saska

Nacktan (Fig. 6) and Marie Smith (Fig. 7). Lena Saska Nacktan (b. 1902, d. 1971) had been married, for the last time, to a Chugach man, but was by this time divorced. She enjoyed speaking Eyak. In the last few years before 1961, she had spent a lot of time talking and refreshing her Eyak with Minnie Stevens. Li had worked briefly with Minnie and her husband Scar Stevens in 1952. Minnie was the last of the "old [204] generation," born perhaps before 1880, and certainly the last person who routinely spoke Eyak. So it is correct to say that the era of routine or traditional conversation in Eyak ended when she died in March 1961, a few months before Austerlitz's arrival. However, not only was Lena's Eyak still "refreshed", but "Grandma Stevens" had continued to speak Eyak with her daughters Sophie (b. 1911, d. 1992) and Marie (b. 1918), who thereby became the last two speakers of Eyak.

Figure 6. Lena Saska Nacktan, around 1960.
Photograph courtesy of Michael E. Krauss.

From Austerlitz's work with Anna Nelson Harry, Marie, and Lena, we have about 600 notebook pages with perhaps 4,000 elicitations, including a fair amount of duplication. The largest part is vocabulary, and for this Austerlitz included special effort on systematic fl ora-fauna work, which is perhaps his most important contribution. Austerlitz also attempted to go into the grammar to an extent, perhaps a bit more than did Li, but with less background for it. He also got a small amount of text, but it is rather artificial as it consists mostly of translation from English. The quality of Austerlitz's transcription is perhaps not quite so good as Li's, again because he had not had the previous experience with Athabaskan that contributed to Li's accuracy.

Finally, we also have a six-page, dittoed handout from a linguistics class taught by Austerlitz at Columbia, dated Oct. 10 1961, consisting of a phoneme inventory, basic verb conjugations, a three-line text, a list of 48 animal names (mostly mammals), and statistical analysis of biota terms (monosyllabic, polysyllabic, loans; 173 fauna, 68 flora). Austerlitz recognized that Anna Nelson Harry had outstanding talents, and for a while entertained hopes to return to Yakutat at Christmastime 1961, but other priorities intervened, and Austerlitz could not continue with Eyak.

Summary of Work before Krauss

Here we pause to take stock of the totality of the work on Eyak through Austerlitz. The period 1778-1867 is quite remarkable both for the number of primary and secondary sources. The primary include six formal vocabularies, one of which is 1,128 words long, and the secondary sources, including important maps, statements, and studies of the data, are adequate to show the geographical distribution of Eyak, its dialectal uniformity, its genetic position and, in woefully inadequate transcription, a very poor picture of perhaps 15% of its vocabulary, and practically no grammar. Frederica de Laguna essentially began the resumption of Eyak language work. Harrington, Li, and Austerlitz all finally transcribed better, but still with many mistakes since none worked long enough to start learning the language or its system to hear it with consistent accuracy, to make much headway into Eyak grammar, or to get any quantity of text in it. There had been no steady progress, nothing building on previous work. Thus, even the accumulated lexicon is heavily duplicated, such that a skillful collation of the total, if any heroic philologist were to attempt that, might at best be found to represent somehow 25% percent of the vocabulary of the language. Only a small fraction of that could be considered clearly represented, given the variation or fuzziness from the frequency of mishearing. That problem, especially with verbs, which are highly infl ected and derived, would have been exacerbated by the opacity necessarily resulting from near total lack of grammatical analysis.

Krauss 1961 to Present

Michael Krauss (b. 1934) has always gravitated toward the cause of minority and endangered languages. His training in linguistics, 1953-1958, perhaps most influenced by André Martinet at Columbia and Paris, was at the very end of a "classical period," when Indo-European and the description (documentation) of American languages as Boas, Sapir, and Bloomfield had done, were still important, before all of that was eclipsed by the Chomskyan redefinition of linguistics. Inspired by Edouard Bachellery at Paris, Krauss took to Celtic, [205] and spent 1956-1957 with Gaelic on Inis Meáin, Ireland. A fellowship at Harvard followed, where there was significant Gaelic expertise in the custodial staff, and also a Celtic department that did two good things: it rubberstamped Krauss's dissertation, and prevented him from straying down the street too much to MIT. Krauss then spent two postdoctoral years, 1958-1960 on Iceland and the Faeroe Islands. The marginal survival of Gaelic and the spectacular strength of both Icelandic and Faeroese had a profoundly formative effect on Krauss's approach to language. The University of Alaska hired him from the Faeroes to come to Fairbanks, as a Visiting Professor on Carnegie Foundation money to establish new disciplines, in this case linguistics. The offer was irresistible to Krauss, given his experience and agenda. His "bread and butter," however, he found was teaching French and heading a department newly organized as Linguistics and Foreign Languages. Alaska Native language work was to be supported by NSF grants, and NSF indeed came through. During the 1960s, it was still too early to agitate with any success for Native language rights, bilingual education, or for any but subterranean work to alleviate the suppression of Alaska Native languages in school or society. At the same time, though, the need to document those languages before they – necessarily – disappeared was obvious and recognized.

Figure 7. Marie-Smith Jones. Photograph by Kiyoshi Yagi, 1992.
Courtesy of Michael E. Krauss.

Under those clear conditions, given both that Eyak was much closer to extinction than any other Alaskan language, and given its key genetic position between Athabaskan and Tlingit, Eyak was of the highest academic priority, by far. It was of course at the other end of the scale socially, except in the all-important symbolic sense that even the smallest of nations matters (or, if not, where do we draw the line?).

Krauss had Austerlitz doing the Eyak work on the 1961 grant, and among others, two very competent workers, Irene Reed and Martha Teeluk, working with Yupik, Alaska's largest and strongest language group, while he himself began his career with Athabaskan at Minto, near Fairbanks. He also visited the fieldworkers, including Austerlitz in Cordova, where he met Marie Smith and Lena Saska Nacktan, and made his first few Eyak transcriptions, especially to establish or confirm some basic sound correspondences between Eyak and Athabaskan. In 1962 Krauss continued his Athabaskan fieldwork, a statewide survey to begin to define Alaskan Athabaskan languages. By 1963, however, Krauss realized that the urgent [206] Eyak work was not going to be done by Austerlitz or anyone else with the experience Krauss by then had with Athabaskan, so he determined to commit himself to Eyak – on a long-term basis.

Figure 8. Sophie Borodkin and Michael Krauss in 1987.
Photograph courtesy of Michael E. Krauss.

Krauss's primary Eyak data, in the form of field notes, so far span the period 1961 to 2006, 45 years. These need, however, to be classed into three phases: 1) Intensive – 1963-1965, 2) occasional or intermittent – 1971, 1972, 1980, 1987, and 3) epilogue 1993-. We shall return to the chronology after an account of the Eyak speakers then still alive. Needless to say, Krauss investigated as thoroughly as possible to find all remaining speakers of Eyak, following all leads, not only in Cordova and Yakutat, of course, but also in Anchorage, Fairbanks, Juneau, and Seattle. In the 1960s there were still in fact six, as follows: Anna Nelson Harry and George Johnson at Yakutat; and Lena Saska Nacktan, Marie Smith, Sophie Borodkin (Fig. 8), and Mike Sewak (Fig. 9) at Cordova. All but the last two have been mentioned as having worked already with previous contributors. Sophie, again, was the older sister of Marie, and Mike Sewak (pronounced "Sea-walk") (b. ca. 1880, d. ca. 1966) was from Bering River Village-Katalla. By 1963 he was blind and mostly deaf, living in the Cordova hospital, speaking mostly Tlingit and English, with very partial recall of Eyak.

Here Krauss has the pleasure to say that every one of these persons sympathetically understood the purpose of preserving as good as possible a record of the Eyak language and worked obligingly to the very best of their ability with Krauss to that end. Looking back at that record, Krauss considers himself exceedingly fortunate in that regard, among others, to have been in the right place at the right time in order to preserve as much has proved possible at such a late date, thanks of course to the good will of every single person who remembered any of the Eyak language. As a result, Krauss was able carry out his fieldwork with extreme efficiency and luck (Fig. 10).

Eyak Speakers 1961 to Present

Here follows an account of the Eyak speakers still alive as of 1961, and of Krauss's work with each.

Figure 9. Mike Sewak, around 1964. Photograph by Michael E. Krauss.
Figure 10. Michael Krauss and colleagues in Cordova, in 1961.
Left to right, clockwise: Michael Krauss, Lena Saska Nacktan,
Jane Krauss, Robert Austerlitz, and Irene Reed.
Photograph courtesy of Michael E. Krauss.

Anna Nelson Harry

Anna Nelson Harry, then of Yakutat, was the most fluent still, the only one who seemed truly most comfortable speaking Eyak. In fact, she took the most initiative to speak Eyak conversationally with Krauss, who remembers with great pleasure getting over the hump of beginning to converse and work in Eyak with her. She also had a highly creative personality, and spoke with verve and "creativity" [207] in Eyak. That creativity included an ability to take something like poetic liberty with Eyak, to etymologize imaginatively, or even answer questions that way when Krauss pushed the edge, for instance giving 'hot cocoa' glibly as 'eagle soup' (see *In Honor of Eyak: The Art of Anna Nelson Harry* [Krauss 1982] for more about her and her profound literary art). Because she was full of such vitality, and also because she had become rather deaf (and would not accept a hearing aid, so that one had to shout), it was difficult to get her to sit still for long or go over grammatical questions. At the same time, Krauss could ask her to tell a particular story, and perhaps the next day she would sit down and thoughtfully tell it, with a far-away look, yet onto a tape recorder, being the only one who was comfortable doing that. It is from her that we have perhaps 90% of the connected text preserved in Eyak. As noted above, she had worked with the 1933 group, Li, and Austerlitz. Krauss worked directly with her in 1963, 1965, 1971, and 1972. In 1971, as Krauss was walking out of her house for the last time, she muttered to herself – as if to teach him a lesson – *"te'ya' x. esiyah,"* which caused Krauss to wheel about. *Te'ya' x. esiyahł* would mean 'I ate a fish,' but this sounded odd, and lacked that final consonant, so could not be accounted for by the Eyak grammar, all of which Krauss thought he knew by then. He double- checked and, as she took out a frying-pan, Anna confirmed that he had heard aright, saying that the phrase spoken in exactly that way meant something like 'I think I'll (cook myself and) eat a fish.' Lena in Cordova later confirmed that she had heard such speech, some old people used to talk that way, and cautiously came up with some further examples of that type of verb conjugation, confirming a whole "new" obsolescent Eyak conjugation, named now the *"s*-optative," which is starting to turn up now also, marginally, in Athabaskan as well.

George Johnson

George Johnson, of Yakutat, though quite rusty in Eyak, not having spoken it regularly since before he was twenty, or for 50 years as of 1961, was already a grizzled veteran of linguistic work with Harrington and Li. A highly practical and modern man, with a toy-breed dog in his lap, not one to be preoccupied looking backwards; it is remarkable that he was as obliging as he was, during fishing season, to sit with Krauss. Krauss does remember Johnson protesting that he had "taught Harrington all he knew." Krauss should have asked Liand Austerlitz if he said the same thing to them. Krauss worked with Johnson only in 1963.

Lena Saska Nacktan

Lena Saska Nacktan was probably the most important of all the Eyak speakers for Krauss during the intensive fieldwork phase. Though still babysitting grandchildren, she seemed to have the most time and above all the most inexhaustible patience. It seems she had taken deliberate pains to keep up or refresh her Eyak, as noted above, with Minnie Stevens, sharing a certain kind of interest in or value for the language, even for its actual structure. There were many special rewards in working with her. For example, it was she who told Krauss, when he must have slacked off momentarily and asked a question that could be considered redundant: *"dik'sh d etli: ' ew 'u:la'yiłga:q q'ah* [shouldn't you already be able to figure that one out by yourself by now]?" At the same time, after a whole day of conjugating verbs or the like: "When I was a kid learning this language, I certainly never thought some day I'd be sitting in a hotel room all day long going over this stuff." But with her it was possible to go over the long lists of questions that Krauss had prepared during the intervening academic year, e.g., checking derivational possibilities of verbs.

Lena could be perfectly objective or detached. "I died yesterday" would be no problem. There was one lapse, when Krauss was uncertain about vowel length in negative future forms, and "I won't bring you water" came up, and she replied that one could not say that in Eyak as "we Eyaks would never refuse to bring someone water." When Lena got peeved, which had to have been often, even that was productive as she would come up with relevant and colorful Eyak remarks such as *"'a't sil eqahy eq't ' esh k'ułe'kkga' ' edu'xd eg ewih* [I sure feel like someone's reaching all the way across the inside of my head (with probing questions)]." She was meticulous about authenticity: "Now put that down with a question mark because I'm not sure it's right," and would glance at the paper to make sure the question mark was there. She was the perfect partner and counterbalance to Anna: "Yes, Anna might say that, but I wouldn't." With her Krauss went over all but the latest of Anna's taped texts, with great care and objectivity, e.g., even helping to explain with truncated sentences or words what a momentary abandoned intention had been on the tape.

At first, sometimes Lena could not remember even a relatively basic word, such as "navel," and would feel bad about it: "I'll think about it and it might come to me," and the next day, "All night I couldn't sleep and finally it came to me, *k'uji'tl'k.*" Later on, as her recall deepened, profoundly, with reference to some kind of white sheet fungus found in rotting trees: "When I was a little girl, I remember that stuff, and I didn't know the name of it, maybe could use it for doll-clothes. There was this old man, used to sit on the pier. I was afraid of him, but I asked him about it, and he told me 'The old people used to call that ___.' It'll come to me," and next day, "All night I couldn't sleep, but then [208] I remember what he called it: *ła:* or *ła:n,*" – something that might not have been heard for a century already in 1963.

At one point Krauss observed that there seemed to be no Eyak equivalent to the plentiful supply of auxiliary verbs in English indicating unexplained obligation, such as "I must/should/oughta/gotta/hafta/better go," which Lena agreed Eyak seemed to lack. When Krauss pressed her on this, she answered, "Well, I guess then you'd have to say what'll happen if you don't go."

Toward the end of the intensive fieldwork period, Krauss was calculating that he had salvaged or resurrected a very large proportion of the Eyak vocabulary left in living memory. He had tried his best to not only to write down what was offered, e.g., randomly in texts, but also, of course, to get as much as possible through guided elicitation, of two types. First, semantically guided elicitation, by subject, for example asking systematically for all body-parts, bird species, or sewing-stitches, at least as a stimulus, allowing for freer associations and tangents, but eventually working back to the list. A second type is elicitation guided both semantically and phonologically. A first and most obvious subtype of that is checking previous Eyak data. By 1963 Krauss had a copy of all the data noted above in this long history, including by 1964 also Li's and Austerlitz's. The earlier materials, poorly transcribed, that had not been accounted for, could be re-elicited by "can you think of anything that means something like X, that sounds anything like Y?", so that by suggesting both a meaning and sounds somehow resembling the word, one might be able to reconstruct what had been faultily transcribed in the earlier efforts. In this way, especially with Lena, given her patience and her discipline, it was possible to resurrect 97% of Rezanov, and, of course, achieve a still better percentage than that with the more modern sources where unclear. A second subtype of such elicitation was from lists in cognate languages, i.e., Athabaskan, by going through a Chipewyan or Hupa or Navajo stem-list or dictionary, making the expected changes via the known sound-correspondences and asking if Eyak had anything sounding like the result, meaning anything like what was shown in Athabaskan. Again, especially with Lena, since about one-third of Athabaskan stems have cognates in Eyak, often that was a relatively efficient way to find new Eyak vocabulary. – The point that Eyak is not Athabaskan, but coordinate with it, means that Alaskan Athabaskan is, in principle, no closer to Eyak than Navajo is. It is a pity, however, that in the 1960s we had no full list or dictionary for Alaskan Athabaskan we could use, especially that of Ahtna, against which to test that conclusion.

Finally, one last method of elicitation had not been tried, a kind of desperate method, guided purely by sound, i.e., systematically going through all potential "words" by the permissible order of permissible sounds that the language might allow: "do you have any word that sounds like X (meaning anything)?" – in order to look for allowable sequences not yet attested as words or parts thereof. This of course involves many thousands of possibilities, as if systematically going through English, getting to *g-d* (*god, good, goad, guide, gad; gooed? gowd?, gid?, geed??, ged??, gud??* ....), in Eyak necessarily adding some very versatile affixes to help the many thousands of forms being tested to sound more like real nouns or verbs. With Lena, whose integrity was absolute, Krauss offered a bonus for each new stem so discovered, and with a week of such tedious work, Lena came up with about 50 new Eyak stems, all of very low frequency. Only with Lena could this have been attempted! It is certainly fair to say that the largest part of the grammar and vocabulary, and verification, came from Lena.

Marie Smith Jones

Marie Smith Jones (née Stevens) was the youngest Eyak speaker and is now, age 88, the last speaker of Eyak. The first to work with her was Austerlitz – as Liwas able to work with her mother and father. In some ways, in part because her English was the best of all the living Eyak speakers, she was the best to work with for anyone beginning to study Eyak. By her own account, however, her Eyak is more limited to household conversation, which she kept up with her mother until her death in 1961. She considers what is conventionally referred to as "deep talk" beyond her. Since 1961 she has used or spoken Eyak mainly with Austerlitz and Krauss, as she did not speak that frequently with her older sister Sophie. Since Sophie's death in 1992 Marie has worn the mantle of "last speaker" with grace and dignity. Krauss worked with her in 1963 especially, also in 1964 and 1965, then again in 1980 to do some belated checking of verb classes (by checking what conjugations can be used with them), which she helped greatly with. She continues to help to the best of her ability with remaining questions which occur to Krauss.

Sophie Borodkin

Sophie Borodkin (née Stevens) was largely bypassed by both Austerlitz and Krauss, in part because there were speakers easier to work with in Cordova in the 1960s. Austerlitz advised Krauss that because of her situation at the time it was hopeless to try to work with her. However, much later, in 1987, Krauss found her to be in substan tially [209] better condition and spent a very productive week working with her in Cordova. She had a certain amount of new vocabulary, and perhaps most important, she was able to use and explain some very important absolutely basic, but infrequently used (or infrequently elicited!), forms of verbs. Finally, working with Sophie, Krauss learned also, or rather confirmed for himself, that every remaining speaker of a language in a situation like that of Eyak is potentially the source of important new information and insight.

Mike Sewak

Mike Sewak's name came up only when, after considerable insistent inquiry, Lena was moved to say, "maybe Mike Sewak still knows some Eyak." Sewak, too, was glad to be approached, and tried his best in spite of being not only quite blind, but fairly deaf as well. Like George Johnson, the only other male Eyak speaker after the 1950s, Sewak was born in Bering River village, maybe a dozen years earlier than Johnson. That village gave way to the development of Katalla, and was already thoroughly bilingual Eyak-Tlingit, if not dominantly Tlingit-speaking by 1900. After the disintegration of Katalla in 1912, there would certainly have been little occasion for Sewak (or Johnson) to speak Eyak. Sewak seemed able to speak words or phrases, but what Eyak he could speak had two traits that made his Eyak more different, closer to being a different dialect, than that of any other speaker, including George Johnson. His full vowel /e/ was more like Tlingit (or European) *e* than everyone else's (which was more like the English *a* in *bad*), no doubt due to Tlingit infl uence. Sewak's Eyak was far rustier than Johnson's. Most important is that Sewak had two separate sounds, a *g* and a *gw* that were consistently distinguished in his speech, whereas in the speech of all other modern Eyak speakers, those two originally different sounds are no longer distinguished. It is not clear whether Sewak still distinguished them exactly as they had been in the old language, whether a given word had *g* or *gw*, but, since Tlingit still clearly distinguishes them, under that infl uence Sewak kept or somehow reinstated that distinction in what he remembered of Eyak. In 1963, 1964, and 1965, Krauss visited Sewak, and managed to elicit perhaps 500 words from him, especially, of course, those with the consonant distinction in question. One of the last visits is hard to forget: Sewak answered some question with "*sila't' yitl'a'ts*," i.e., 'my tongue is _____,' which Krauss had to take to Lena to understand: "Oh yes, that's an old word I haven't heard in years. It means 'stiff'." In other words, in the very act of complaining to Krauss that he felt tongue-tied, Sewak salvaged another Eyak word (to boot, probably a good cognate with one in Athabaskan meaning 'hard').

Chronology and Results
of Krauss's Eyak Work

The first phase – intensive – of Krauss's Eyak work began in 1963, when he determined to make that commitment himself, and ended in 1970. During that entire period, Krauss had full-time teaching and administrative responsibilities at the University of Alaska, now called the University of Alaska Fairbanks, for the full academic year, with only the summer for lengthy absences. His Eyak research, as had been his more general projects of 1961-1962, was funded entirely by the National Science Foundation throughout. The period then can be subdivided into 1963-1965, during which he combined (phenomenally!) productive fieldwork during the summers, with work-up and preparation for the next field season during his "spare time" in the winters. A fairly clear record of that can be found in Krauss's field notebooks, annual reports, and proposals to NSF. Reviewing the reports and proposals not only reassures Krauss that a decent record of that history remains, which it is not necessary to detail here, but it also reminds Krauss how lucky he was in those days to work as productively in the field with these Eyak speakers as he did, being reminded that his repeated claims of success were, in fact, true. He is profoundly grateful to them.

The first summer, June 27-July 9, and July 28-August 19, 1963, was spent in Cordova and Yakutat, with Lena, Marie, Sewak, Anna, and George Johnson; the second, June 6-August 14, 1964, was spent in Cordova, with Lena, Marie, and Sewak; and the third was spent in Cordova and Yakutat, with Lena, Marie, Sewak, and Anna; for a grand total of barely half a year in direct contact with Eyak. The days averaged between five and nine hours of actual fieldwork time. This was only possible because of the good will of the speakers, on the one hand – most especially Lena's patience, and because Krauss had spent all the available time during the intervening months of the academic year preparing the materials. This included putting every single word onto a secondary file of ledger sheets organized by stems, showing all the inflectional and derivational details of the verbs, classification of nouns, etc., constituting an actual concordance of the entire corpus, including all occurrences of each word in the texts, by text number and sentence number, as well as in the notebooks. By the end of the third summer there were 12 notebooks containing about 1,600 pages, about 500 of those being texts, and 1,100 pages containing up to 25,000 elicitations. In addition [210] to the texts, mostly from Anna and reviewed with Lena, that last summer consisted mostly of long days with Lena going over very systematically the prepared enquiries in order to fill out the noun classes and derivational potential of the verbs for the lexicon. By that time over 1,100 stems and basic elements of the language had been identified and clearly described, a score similar to that of the average well-documented Athabaskan language, in spite of the limited resources of Eyak. The sum total of connected text was decent but not abundant, about the total length of the Book of Genesis. Nevertheless, by the end of eliciting that text corpus, an average of a dozen pages would go by without new or unexplainable forms showing up, suggesting that getting more new text was not going to be a very productive way of getting better coverage of the language itself – though coverage of possible Eyak oral literature was, of course, another matter.

In view of all this, in summer 1966 Krauss decided to draw the line, not to return to fieldwork, but, having ledgered the third summer's results (now a file of 4,000 sheets), to begin composing the Eyak dictionary from that. In 1964-65 he had published a sketch (Krauss 1965), 20 printed pages, of the grammar, which remains almost entirely correct as far as it goes. That remains to this day the only published grammar for Eyak, but Krauss then felt and still does strongly feel that the dictionary and texts, as prepared in that second part of the intensive period from 1966 to 1970 along with the ledgers, do readily provide the information necessary for someone, with a start from the 1965 sketch, to construct a rather full detailed grammar of Eyak, whether Krauss lives to do that himself or not.

In 1966 the priority was therefore to prepare a typescript of a dictionary and full corpus of Eyak texts for publication. In order to include completely all the forms in the texts in the dictionary, Krauss first typed all those texts, numbering 80 (including duplicate versions), on a typewriter with specially designed characters for the relatively technical alphabet he was then using. These include the one brief text in Reynolds's hand from 1933, the eight from Liin 1952, the three from Austerlitz in 1961, and the rest dictated to Krauss by Lena (27), Marie (14), and Anna (1); and the largest part by far coming from Anna on tape (24 texts, itself about 6 1/2 hours of speech). The total percentage of that text corpus from Anna is over 70%. The sequence is arranged by and divided into the categories of Raven Cycle (pp. 66-222), Animal Tales (pp. 223-441), Land Otters (pp. 442-476), Mythical Beings (pp. 477-543), Cautionary Tales (pp. 544-579), Legends of People (pp. 580-674), Wars (pp. 675-700), Witches and Shamans (pp. 701-726), and Miscellaneous Ethnographical (pp. 727-912). The format is double spaced, each sentence numbered; first the Eyak text, then the English, translated phrase by phrase as marked by comma or period, then fairly detailed footnotes for each text. The main editorial devices are parentheses, enclosing segments present on the tape that should be eliminated in the fully edited text, and square brackets enclosing segments not on the tape that need to be supplied in a fully edited text. Thus reading in the parentheses and leaving out the brackets, one gets very exactly what is on the tape, while reading in the brackets and leaving out the parentheses, one gets the fully edited text. This work was done May 20-December 10, 1966.

The dictionary was organized and first handwritten from the ledgers and typed – perhaps the first third – by Krauss, the rest by Irene Reed, during 1967-1969. The writing-out and typing was only 90-some percent complete with mainly the verbs ('singular goes,' 'plural go,') classificatory plural object verb stems and various other items listed in the foreword to the typescript. It fully includes all the then-known earlier Russian work, i.e., Rezanov, Wrangell, Furuhjelm, and also the 1933 material, but not explicitly Harrington, Li, or Austerlitz, although all of those had, of course, been checked.

The work was typed double-spaced on approximately 3,300 pages (with perhaps 200 pages to go), Eyak-to-English, technically organized, by stem. It was also provided with an English-to-Eyak index, on about 10,000 file-slips. Krauss figured then and still believes that that dictionary (when finished) will include well over 90% of the lexicon left in living Eyak memory as of the 1960s, perhaps in the high 90's – and of course as time goes by, sadly, it will necessarily become 100%. An estimate of the number of lexemes or entries is perhaps about 7,000 in a fairly strict sense, not a bad score for a language in the relic-like state of Eyak. Coverage of subjects like kin-terms, for example, is quite thorough. For fauna (217 terms) and fl ora (123 terms), for another example, it is still rich, but the speakers were all too aware of incompleteness and uncertainties that would have been far fewer if the work had been done fifty years earlier. We must certainly consider ourselves very lucky that Eyak therewith became one of the better documented languages of North America, for what was left of it in the twentieth century.

Krauss is sometimes tempted to compare that documentation with what we had of Hebrew, basically the Old Testament. For one thing, only the consonants were written in that language and the vowels had to be filled in. There was never any deliberate or systematic enquiry of vocabulary, e.g., biota names, or anatomy while the language was still alive, but only whatever the Old Testament happened to mention (no explanation), thus [211] no dictionary, and no grammar were available – only whatever happened to get mentioned. The Old Testament is an amazing document to have included by chance so much of the language, enough actually to provide the basis – and inspiration! – for the modern revival of Hebrew, now spoken by millions. The point here is that, in a real sense – technical, linguistic – Eyak is documented better than Hebrew was not so many years ago, leaving in principle the technical possibility for reviving Eyak too, insofar as Eyak also might ever have the social resources.

During his sabbatical at MIT 1969-1970, Krauss had both the Eyak texts and dictionary materials Xeroxed, reduced basically four pages to one, double-sided, the texts thus down to 250 pages and the dictionary to 666, with 10,000 shingled slips for the English index to the dictionary ending on page 760 (plus the German and Russian for Rezanov, ending on page 782). That work was thus physically reduced to just over a ream of paper, printed in fifty copies, which could be bound in a single portable volume. Given that Krauss's personal goal was and remains the documentation itself, preservation of the record rather than publication as such, especially where the real need in the academic community is felt by a small number of persons and the number of those interested now remaining in the Native community is also small, Krauss felt that this specialized need was fulfilled, more or less, by the very limited form of publication made in 1970. More complete publication had not only the roughly 200 dictionary pages missing i.e., those still not typed up as of 1970, but subsequently soon also the additional Eyak material collected during the second "intermittent" phase of Eyak fieldwork. Even more decisive though was the rise of other priorities in Alaska Native language work for Krauss, that resulted in the postponement of a final edition of the dictionary.

By the late 1960s the political scene was changing for Alaska Native languages. In 1967-1968 the Federal bilingual education bills had been passed and implemented. By this time at

Fairbanks the subterranean movement to get Yupik into Alaskan schools had surfaced in the form of the course added to the University Yupik curriculum called "Yupik Language Workshop," where "advanced composition" Yupik students were writing, in a newly designed practical orthography, drafts of schoolbooks to be used in schools attended by their younger siblings. There were still setbacks, but by 1970, while strident Krauss was 4,000 miles away at MIT (becoming in those days still more militant), Irene Reed's diplomacy succeeded in persuading Alaskan authorities to experiment with Yupik in Yupik public schools. By 1972 the result was Alaskan legislation mandating Native language use in schools and the establishment of the Alaska Native Language Center with Krauss as Director in Fairbanks. Priorities of the new opportunities and obligations severely limited Krauss's time for Eyak for the 29 years he headed the Center. Nevertheless, during what we may define as the second phase, there were occasional spells of activity in the further documentation of Eyak. Already in 1967, Constance Naish, scholar of Tlingit, had recorded on tape from Anna at Yakutat what Krauss in 1971 transcribed as 14 pages of text. In 1971 Krauss was able to return to Yakutat (June 9-12) for more fieldwork with Anna, which included 50 more pages of text. Krauss was then able to check that with Lena in Cordova on June 13, his last session ever with her. The next year (June 14-18, 1972) Krauss had what turned out to be his last meeting with Anna in Yakutat and recorded 82 more pages of text. For the final editing of that, without Lena, he was now on his own. In 1973, Jeff Leer and Karen MacPherson taped about 40 more minutes of text from Anna in Anchorage, another 13 texts, then transcribed by Krauss. All told, these supplementary texts from Anna add about another 20% to the corpus. Also during the period 1964 to 1981 Krauss wrote about ten academic articles and monographs on Comparative Athabaskan-Eyak, in which Eyak figures prominently, of course. These can be found listed in Krauss's recently published bibliography (Krauss 2006).

By 1980 it had become clear to Krauss that probably the most severe shortcoming of his Eyak work was that he had neglected to define clearly the different classes of verbs in Eyak according to basic criterion of which different conjugations are used with them in the present according to whether they are active, stative, progressive, etc. In summer of 1980, May 27-29 in Anchorage and June 16-19 in Fairbanks, Krauss was able to go systematically through a large proportion of these with Marie, who rendered a major service in filling in this gap. This had been a shortcoming on Krauss's part, and Marie's fundamental grasp of Eyak was exactly what was needed to help with that.

In 1982, on the occasion of Anna's death, Krauss published a volume of her stories in her memory, *In Honor of Eyak: The Art of Anna Nelson Harry* (Krauss 1982). That labor of love featured ten of Anna's most outstanding texts, edited as carefully as possible from the tapes, first shown in double column, her Eyak on the left, phrase by phrase, with English translation of each in the column next to that, line by line, with footnotes and also looser English translation in ordinary paragraph form. Krauss included a historical introduction to the whole, and an introduction to each section, philosophical and literary, as the whole [212] point is that the way Anna told those tales is indeed highly philosophical and high literary art. As she told them in her maturity, these stories no longer have merely their traditional meaning, which would still be interesting enough to anyone who cared about Eyak; and they are not merely suffused with her own personality, which is of course what gives traditional oral literature its artistic quality. In fact – and this is a point not adequately presented by Krauss in 1982, in spite of the fact that he had been pondering Anna's stories for years in efforts to understand them layer by layer – since Eyak society was long gone, and Anna was a survivor who had taken refuge in Yakutat Tlingit society, she had a unique perspective on Yakutat, and on the world. The traditional Eyak forms and stories were now merely her raw material, with which she was – tragically – free to express her own vision. There was no longer any traditional or Eyak society to hear those stories as they were expected to be told. There was only Krauss, who could understand merely the language, and beyond that only the ages for her to speak the meaning to. Anna's art, then, transcends the original tradition altogether. At one level she is speaking to Yakutat and Tlingit, but at another she is speaking to the world, as only Anna can from her Eyak perspective, about such matters as the fate of nations, good, and evil. The book is offered in deep humility to the memory of Anna and to Eyak. Krauss also remembers with great pleasure and cannot resist quoting Freddy's remark to him, "that's a good book."

During the 1970s and 1980s, Krauss was of course preoccupied with the whole Alaska Native language situation, including, increasingly, the fundamental relationship with the same and related languages in the North, now especially Russia – a relationship which had been almost totally cut off by the Cold War. Finally, however, in 1989, Krauss was able to return to Cordova, June 20-24, to work with Marie's sister Sophie, for the one and only time. That too was a pure delight, just getting to know Sophie and to hear Eyak from one more person. Moreover, as noted above, the Eyak Sophie remembered proved to include certain very fundamental verb usages which had not been elicited from anyone else, and which cast significant light on the basic system of Eyak verb classes.

In 1990, Krauss made a long visit to Leningrad, in part to visit Soviet archives there, which contain still the bulk of the Russian work done on Alaskan languages. There he had the pleasant surprise to find three "new" Eyak language manuscripts, Anonymous 1810, Baranov 1812, and Khromchenko 1823, described above. These of course provided just that much more inspiration to write the present history. Virtually all the material in them could be fairly readily identified from the rest of our data, but they provide interesting continuity to our history between 1805 and 1839, with Eyak declining at Yakutat, and becoming prominent in the Cordova area instead.

We now come to a kind of Epilogue in the history of Eyak fieldwork. With the death of her sister Sophie in 1992, Marie Smith Jones became the last speaker of Eyak. Krauss has remained in touch with her, has visited her 15 to 20 times during the period between 1992 and 2006, and has often spoken to her on the phone. The relationship has become, of course, increasingly social and personal, but there are Eyak work sessions too, bringing new information and understanding. Krauss recalls, with unending amusement, that one of his early proposals to NSF, ca. 1963, noted, with sincere concern, that there were very few speakers of Eyak left, "and the youngest of them is already quite elderly," referring of course to Marie – who was then 45 years old and seemingly quite ancient to Krauss, then 28. Marie was, moreover, affl icted with a terrible hacking smoker's cough, and did not seem long for this world. Forty-three years later Marie still has the hacking cough, but is more often worrying about Krauss's health than the reverse. Krauss could feel some satisfaction should Eyak outlive him. He is in fact determined that in some important sense the Eyak should indeed outlive both himself and Marie (Fig. 11).

The Eyak Preservation Council, a fractious Eyak Indian splinter group of the Eyak Village Corporation, under the leadership of Dune Lankard of Cordova, grandson of Lena Saska Nacktan, with the help of Carole Hoover and others, has been militating to prevent the destruction of Eyak traditional lands, especially by logging. The Council has also moved to provide support for the preservation of Eyak history, culture, and language. It has particularly engaged the talents of Laura Bliss Spaan of Anchorage, to do videotaping where possible of

Marie speaking Eyak with Krauss on a number of occasions. One such occasion in particular was in 1995, when a memorial potlatch of sorts was held in Cordova to mark the return or repatriation from the Smithsonian of an Eyak skeleton. Freddy was there, 65 years after her fateful visit of 1930. Dune Lankard's message was made clear, and Freddy, Marie, and Krauss were somehow put together in a very touching film by Laura Bliss Spaan, entitled *More than Words* (1995, 60 minutes) and featuring the situation of the Eyak language. Since then, Laura has filmed Marie and Krauss several times, and has also filmed a series of presentations by Krauss on the Eyak sound system, writing system, and how to use the dictionary, as well as basic grammar, both for the record and for practical purposes for anyone wishing to learn Eyak or to use the extant materials.

The Eyak Preservation Council also supported the digital reproduction of the entire paper [213] archive, patiently and devotedly done by Karl Bergman, of the Eyak section of the Alaska Native Center Archive. As this is the ultimate record and result of all the work that has been done on Eyak, it deserves description as the final section of the present history.

The Eyak archive fills an entire five-shelf bookcase, containing about 15 linear feet of written material. All the material previous to Krauss, i.e., Anderson 1778 to Austerlitz 1961, fills the top shelf. The contents of that are, in fact, well accounted for or described in some detail to constitute most of this history. The second shelf from the top includes Krauss's field notebooks, 18 in number, and the original typed text and dictionary up to 1970, filling eight heavy-duty spring binders for the dictionary and three for the texts. The third or middle shelf contains the reduced texts and dictionary, the 1982 *In Honor of Eyak* draft and derivative material, but also about 35 manuscript files, mostly not mentioned so far, studies by Krauss of various aspects of Eyak grammar, phonology, verbal affixes – done mostly between 1963 and 1969, stem lists, studies in format for a final published dictionary, and supplementary texts from Anna. (Those materials, to 1980, are catalogued and described in Krauss and McGary 1980.) Some of that spills over to a fourth shelf, or the second from the bottom, that is occupied mostly by files of historical material. In this respect the Eyak section is exceptional for the Archive, in that Krauss has collected – though not catalogued – not only all linguistic material he could find for a given language, but here also historical, not necessarily containing anything about the language, partly because of his special interest in Eyak but also because such material is relatively limited. That part is in seven substantial files, 1783-1789, 1790-1799, 1800-1867, 1867-1879, 1880-1889, 1890-1899, and 1900-. The bottom shelf is occupied mostly by the dictionary ledger-concordance files. There are also slip-file boxes, microfilm reels (especially Harrington, Austerlitz, as well as printouts thereof), tape-recordings, video-recordings, some correspondence, and photos.

Krauss does hope he may last long enough to publish more on Eyak, even edit a final version of the dictionary. More importantly, however, he feels that with the preservation of this archive, a full and worthy record of the Eyak language and intellectual heritage of the Eyak people will be preserved for future generations to study and cultivate. It is an interestingly unanswerable question, how much of this would exist today, were it not for Frederica de Laguna.

Acknowledgments. I would like to thank Molly Lee, Thomas Alton, Susan Kaplan, and Stacy Ericson for their assistance in the production of this paper.

References Cited

Abercrombie, William Ralph 1900 Report of a Supplementary Expedition into the Copper River Valley, 1884. *In* Compilation of Narratives of Exploration in Alaska, 1900. Pp. 381-408. Washington, D.C.: U.S. Government Printing Office.

Adelung and Vater (see Mithridates)

Allen, Henry Tureman 1887 Report of an Expedition to the Copper, Tanana, and Koyukuk Rivers, in the Territory of Alaska, in the Year 1885. Washington, D.C.: U.S. Government Printing Office.

Andreev, Aleksandr Ignat'evich 1948 Russkie otkrytiiv Tikhom okeane iv SevernoiAmerikiv XVIIIveke. Moscow: OGIZ.

Birket-Smith, Kaj 1933 Plan før en arkæologiske ekspedition til Alaska sommeren 1933. Geografisk Tidsskrift 36:62-65. [214]

1934 Die dänisch-amerikanische Alaskaexpedition 1933. Ethnologischer Anzeiger 3 (2): 1.284-286.

1935a Foreløbig beretning on den dansk-amerikanske ekspedition til Alaska 1933. Geografisk Tidsskrift 38: 187-227.

1935b Guld og grønne Skove. Copenhagen: J.L. Schultz Forlag.

1953 The Chugach Eskimo. Nationalmuseets Skrifter, Etnografisk Række 6. Copenhagen: Nationalmuseets publikationsfond.

Figure 11. Marie Smith and Michael Krauss in 2006.
Photograph by Molly Lee, courtesy of Michael Krauss.

Birket-Smith Kaj and Frederica de Laguna 1938 The Eyak Indians of Copper River Delta, Alaska. Copenhagen: Levin and Munksgaard.

Black Lydia T. (trans.) 1989 The Round the World Voyage of Hieromonk Gideon 1803-1809. Translated with an Introduction and notes by Lydia T. Black. Richard A. Pierce, ed. Alaska State Library Historical Monograph, 9. Fairbanks and Kingston: The Limestone Press.

Boas, Franz 1936 Research in American Native Languages, Report of Progress, 1935. American Council of Learned Societies, Bulletin No. 25: 85-88.

1972 The Professional Correspondence of Franz Boas. Wilmington: Scholarly Reprints.

Buschmann, Johann Karl Eduard 1855 Verwandtschaft der Kinai-Idiome des russischen Nordamerikas mit dem grossen athapaskischen Sprachstamme. Königliche Akademie der Wissenschaft zu Berlin. Bericht aus dem Jahre 1854, pp. 231-236.

1856 Der athapaskische Sprachstamm. Königliche Akademie der Wissenschaft zu Berlin, Abhandlungen, aus dem Jahre 1855, pp. 144-319.

1859 Die Spuren der aztekischen Sprache im nördlichen Mexico und höheren amerikanishen Norden ... Königliche Akademie der Wissenschaft zu Berlin, Abhandlungen, aus dem Jahre 1854, pp. 1-819.

1860 Systematische Worttafel des athapaskischen Sprachstamms. Königliche Akademie der Wissenschaft zu Berlin, Abhandlungen aus dem Jahre 1859, pt. 3, pp. 501-586.

1863 Die Verwandtschafts-Verhältnisse der athapaskischen Sprachen ... Zweite Abtheilung des Apache. Königliche Akademie der Wissenschaft zu Berlin, Abhandlungen aus dem Jahre 1862, pp. 195-252.

Colnett, James 2004 A Voyage to the North West Side of America: The Journals of James Colnett, 1786-89. Robert Galois, ed. Vancouver, Toronto: UBC Press.

Cook, James 1784 A Voyage to the Pacific Ocean Undertaken by Command of His Majesty, for Making Discoveries in the Northern Hemisphere, Performed under the Direction of Captains

Cook, Clerke, and Gore, in the years 1776, 1777, 1778, 1779, and 1780. Vols. I and IIwritten by Captain James Cook, Vol. III written by Captain James King. London: Printed for J. Stockdaaled, Scratcherd and Whitaker, J. Fielding, and J. Hardy.

Dall, William Healey 1870 Alaska and its Resources. Boston: Lee and Shepard.

1877 Tribes of the Extreme Northwest (Contributions to North American Ethnology, vol. 1). Washington, D.C.: U.S. Government Printing Office.

Dauenhauer, Nora Marks, and Richard Dauenhauer 1990 *Háa Tuwunáagu Yís*, "For Healing Our Spirit": Tlingit Oratory. Seattle and London: University of Washington Press and Juneau: Sealaska Heritage Foundation.

Davidson, George 1868 Report of Assistant George Davidson Relative to the Coast, Features, and Resources of Alaska Territory ... November 30, 1867. Russian America (40th Congress, 2nd Session, House of Representatives, Executive Document No. 177, pp. 219-363).

Davydov, Gavriil Ivanovich 1812 Two Voyages to Russian America, 1802-1807. [1977] Richard A. Pierce, ed. Colin Bearne, trans. Kingston: Limestone Press.

1812 Dvukratnoe puteshestvie v Ameriku morskikh ofitserov Khvostova iDavydova, pisannoe sim poslednim. 2 pts. St. Petersburg: Morskaia Tipografia.

de Laguna, Frederica 1933 Frederica de Laguna Finds Prince William Sound District Rich in Lore of Many Alaskan Tribes Now Fast Dying Out. *Cordova Daily Times*, September 9, 1933.

1934a Ceremonial Paddles from the Eyak Indians, Alaska. The University Museum Bulletin 5 (1): 57-59.

1934b The Archaeology of Cook Inlet, Alaska. Philadelphia: Published for the University Museum by the University of Pennsylvania Press.

1937 A Preliminary Sketch of the Eyak Indians, Copper River Delta, Alaska. Publications of the Philadelphia Anthropological Society 1: 63-75.

1956 Chugach Prehistory: The Archaeology of Prince William Sound, Alaska. University of Washington Publications in Anthropology, 13. Seattle: University of Washington Press.

1972 Under Mount Saint Elias: The History and Culture of the Yakutat Tlingit. Smithsonian Contri butions [215] to Anthropology, 7. Washington, D.C.: Smithsonian Institution Press.

1990 Eyak. *In* Handbook of North American Indians, vol. 7, Northwest Coast. Wayne Suttles, ed. Pp. 189-196. Washington, D.C.: Smithsonian Institution Press.

1996 Cook Inlet Adventures and Afterthoughts: Alaska 1930. *In* Adventures through Time: Readings in the Anthropology of Cook Inlet, Alaska. Compiled and edited by Nancy Yaw Davis and William E. Davis. Pp. 65-92. Anchorage: Cook Inlet Historical Society.

2000 Becoming an Anthropologist: My Debt to European and Other Scholars Who Influenced Me. *In* Coming to Shore: Northwest Coast Ethnology, Traditions, and Visions. Marie Maduzé, Michael E. Harkin, and Sergei Kan, eds. Pp. 23-52. Lincoln and London: University of Ncbraska Press.

Efimov, AlekseiVladimirovich 1964 Atlas geograficheskikh otkrytiiv Sibiriiiiv severo-zapadnoiAmeriki, XVII-XVIIIvv. Moscow: Nauka.

Gallatin, Albert 1836 A Synopsis of the Indian Tribes within the United States East of the Rocky Mountains, and in the British and Russian Possessions in North America. Archaeologica Americana. Transactions and Collections of the American Antiquarian Society, vol. 2. Cambridge: Printed for the Society at the University Press.

Goetzmann, William H. and Kay Sloan 1982 Looking Far North: The Harriman Expedition to

Alaska, 1899. New York: Viking.

Grinev, AndreiVal'terovich 1987 Zabytaia ekspeditsiia Dmitriia Tarkhanova na Mednuiu Reku. Sovetskaia Etnografiia 1987 (4): 88-100, 174.

1988 Indeitsy eiakiisud'ba russkogo poseleniia v Iakutate. Sovetskaia Etniografiia 1988 (5): 110-120.

1989 The Eyak Indians and the Fate of a Russian Settlement in Yakutat. Native American Studies 3: 2: 1-6 [translation of 1988 article].

1993 Indeitsy eiakiv period russkoiAmeriki. Etnograficheskie Obozreniia 1993 (5): 77-83.

1997 The Forgotten Expedition of Dmitrii Tarkhanov on the Copper River. Alaska History 12 (1): 1-17 [translation of 1987 article].

Grinnell, George Bird   1901   The Natives of the Alaska Coast Region. *In* Harriman Alaska Expedition. Alaska. C. Hart Merriam, ed. Volume 1: 137-183. New York: Doubleday, Page and Co.

Henry, Joseph   1868   Suggestions Relative to Objects of Scientific Investigation for the Expedition under Captain Howard along the Coast of Russian America, from the Smithsonian Institution. Russian America. 40th Congress, 2nd Session, House of Representatives, Executive Document No. 177, pp. 192-195.

Harrington, John Peabody 1945 Phonematic Daylight in Lhiinkit, Navajo of the North. Journal of the Washington Academy of Sciences 35: 1-6.

Hodge, Frederick Webb (ed.)   1910   Handbook of American Indians North of Mexico. Smithsonian Institution. Bureau of American Ethnology Bulletin, 30. Washington, D.C.: Government Printing Office.

Humboldt, Alexander von   1811   Essaipolitique sur le royaume de la Nouvelle- Espagne.... Voyage de Humboldt et Bonpland, 3. Ptie. Paris: F. Schell.

Index to Baptisms 1964-1973 Index to Baptisms, Marriages, and Deaths, in the Archives of the Russian Orthodox Greek Catholic Church in Alaska. Four volumes, 1964-1973. Manuscript Division, Reference Department, Library of Congress, Washington.

Jacobsen, Johan Adrian 1884 Kaptain Jacobsen's Reise an der Norwestküste Amerikas, 1881-1883, zum Zwecke ethnologischer Sammlungen und Erkundigungen, nebst Beschreibung persönlicher Ergebnisse. A. Woldt, ed. Leipzig: M. Spohr.

1877 Kaptein Jacobsens's Reiser til Nordamerikas Nordwestkyst. A. Woldt, ed. John Utheim, trans. A. Cammermeyer, Kristiania.

1997 Alaskan Voyage, 1881-1883: An Expedition to the Northwest Coast of America. A. Woldt, ed. Erna Gunther, trans. Chicago: University of Chicago Press.

Johannsen, Uwe   1963   Versuch einer Analyse dokumentarischen Materials über die Identitätsfrage und die kulturelle Position der Eyak-Indianer Alaskas. Anthropos 58: 868-896.

Krause, Aurel 1885 Die Tlinkit-Indianer: Ergebnisse einer Reise nach der Norwestküste von Amerika und der Beringstrasse. Jena H. Costenoble.

1956 The Tlingit Indians: Results of a Trip to the Northwest Coast of America and the Bering Straits. Erna Gunther, trans. Monographs of the American Ethnological Society, 26. Seattle: Published for the American Ethnological Society by the University of Washington Press.

Krauss, Michael E. 1965 Eyak: A Preliminary Report. Canadian Journal of Linguistics 10: 167-187. [216]

1970a Eyak Texts. Typescript texts and translations, approximately 912 pages. University of

Alaska and Massachusetts Institute of Technology.

1970b Eyak Dictionary. Typescript, approximately 4,000 pages. University of Alaska and Massachusetts Institute of Technology.

1982 In Honor of Eyak: The Art of Anna Nelson Harry. Fairbanks: Alaska Native Language Center.

1986 Edward Sapir and Athabaskan Linguistics. *In* New Perspectives in Language, Culture, and Personality: Proceedings of the Sapir Centenary Conference. William Cowan, Michael K. Foster, and Konrad Koerner, eds. Pp. 147-190. Amsterdam and Philadelphia: J. Benjamins Pub. Co.

2006 Bibliographic Notes and Bibliography of Michael E. Krauss. Études/Inuit/Studies 29 (1-2): 38-46.

Krauss, Michael E. and Jane McGary 1980 Alaska Native Languages, A Bibliographical Catalogue. Part 1: Indian Languages. Alaska Native Language Center Research Paper, 3. Fairbanks: Alaska Native Language Center.

Krusenstern, Adam Johann von (Kruzenshtern, Ivan Fedorovich) 1813 Wörter-Sammlungen aus den Sprachen einiger Völker des östlichen Asiens und der Nordwestküste von Amerika. Druckerey der Admiralität, St. Petersburg.

Li, Fang Kuei 1930 Chipewyan Consonants. Bulletin of the Institute of History and Philology of the Academia Sinica. Suppl. vol. 1: 429-467.

1956 A Type of Noun Formation in Athabaskan and Eyak. International Journal of American Linguistics 22: 45-48.

Malaspina, Alejandro 1885 Viaje Político-Científico alrededor del Mundo por las corbetas Descubierta y Altrevida al mando de los capitanes de navio D. Alejandro Malaspina y Don José de Bustamante y Guerra desde 1789 á 1794. Imprenta de la Viuda é Hijos de Adienzo, Madrid.

Mills, Elaine L. (ed.) 1981 The Papers of John Peabody Harrington in the Smithsonian Institution 1907-1957, vol. 1, A Guide to the Field Notes: Native American History, Language, and Culture of Alaska / Northwest Coast. An official inventory for the microfilm edition of Harrington's papers in the Smithsonian Institution, 1907-1957. Prepared in the National Anthropological Archives, Department of Anthropology, National Museum of Natural History, Washington, D.C.: Smithsonian Institution. Millwood: Kraus International Publications.

Mithridates 1806 *Mithridates*, oder allgemeine Sprachenkunde. [1970] 1806-17 (by Adelung, Johann Christoph, et al.) Vossische Buchhandlung, Berlin. [Reprinted 1970. Hildesheim and New York: G. Olms.]

Olson, Wallace M. 2002 Through Spanish Eyes: The Spanish Voyages to Alaska, 1774-1792. Auke Bay: The Heritage Press.

Ortiz, Lorenzo Sanfeliu 1943 62 Meses a Bordo: La expedicion Malaspina según el diario del Teniente de Navio Don Antonio de Tova Arredondo, 2 commandante de la "Atrevida" 1789-1794. Biblioteca de Camarote de la Revista General de Marina 13-14, Madrid. [Reprinted 1988. Madrid: Editorial Naval.]

Petroff, Ivan 1884 Report on the Population, Industries, and Resources of Alaska. U.S. Census Office, 10th Census, 1880. Washington, D.C.: Government Printing Office.

Postnikov, AlekseiVladimirovich 2000 Russkaia Amerika: v geograficheskikh Opisaniiakh na kartakh 1741-1867 g. DmitriiBulanin, St. Petersburg.

Radloff, Leopold 1857 Über die Sprache der Ugalachmut. Bulletin historico-philosophique de l'Académie Impériale des Sciences de St. Pétersbourg 15: 468-524 (Mélanges Russes III). Radloff, Leopold and Anton Schiefner 1874 Wörterbuch der Kinai-sprache. Mémoires de l'académie impériale des sciences de St. Pétersbourg.nVIIe série, t. 21, no. 8. St. Pétersbourg: Académie Impériale des Sciences.

Shelikhov, GregoriiIvanovich and Richard A. Pierce 1981 A Voyage to America 1783-1786. Kingston: The Limestone Press.

Simpson, Sir George 1847 An Overland Journey round the World, during the Years 1841 and 1842. Philadelphia: Lea and Blanchard.

Smithsonian Institution 1942 Smithsonian Annual Report for 1941. Washington, D.C: U.S. Government Printing Office.

Spaan, Laura Bliss (director and producer) 1995 More than Words. Alaska Moving Images Preservation Association, Anchorage, and Cinema Guild, New York.

Strange, James 1928 James Strange's Journal and Narrative of the Commercial Expedition from Bombay to the North-West Coast of America, together with a chart showing the tract of the expedition. Madras: Government Press. [217]

1929 James Strange's Journal and Narrative of the Commercial Expedition from Bombay to the North-West Coast of America, together with a chart showing the tract of the expedition. Madras: Government Press.

Tikhmenev, Petr Aleksandrovich 1863 Istoricheskoe obozrienie obrazovaniia Rossiiskoamerikanskoikompaniiidieistviieia do nastoiashchago vremeni. E. Veimar, St. Petersburg, 1861-1863.

1979 A History of the Russian American Company, vol. 2, Documents. Richard A. Pierce and Alton S. Donnelly, eds. Dmitri Krenov, trans. Kingston: The Limestone Press.

Veniaminov, Ioann (Innokentii) 1840a Zapiskiob ostrovakh Unalashkinskago otdiela [Notes on the islands of the Unalaska District]. 3 volumes. Tip. St. Petersburg: RossisskoiImperatorskoi akademii.

1840b Sostoianie pravoslavnoitserkviv russkoi Ameriki [The state of the Orthodox Church in Russian America]. St. Petersburg: Tip. Imperatorskoi Akademii Nauk.

1846 Zamechaniia o koloshenskom i kad'iakskom iazykakh iotchastiprochikh rossiiskoamerikanskikh s prisovokupleniem rossiiskokoloshenskago slovaria, soderzhashchago bolee 1000 slov, iz koikh na niekotoryia sdielany poiasneniia

[Remarks on the Tlingit and Kodiak and other language of Russian America, with attached Russian-Tlingit dictionary, containing more than 1000 words, some with explanation]. St. Petersburg: Tip. Imperatorskoi Akademii Nauk.

Walker, Alexander 1982 An Account of a Voyage to the North West Coast of America in 1785 and 1786. Robin Fisher and J.M. Bumstead, eds. Vancouver/Toronto: Douglas and McIntyre and Seattle: University of Washington Press.

Wrangell, Ferdinand Petrovich von 1839 Statistische und ethnographische Nachrichten über die russischen Besitzungen an der Nordwestküste von Amerika ... Edited by Karl Ernst von Baer. St. Petersburg: Buchdr. der Kaiserlichen Akademie der Wissenschaften.

Michael E. Krauss, Alaska Native Language Center University of Alaska Fairbanks, Fairbanks, Alaska 99775. A History of Eyak Language Documentation and Study: Fredericæ de Laguna in Memoriam Michael E. Krauss, Arctic Anthropology,, Vol. 43, No. 2, pp. 172-218, 2006 ISSN 0066-6939; E-ISSN 1933-8139 © 2006 by the Board of Regents of the University of Wisconsin System

Anna Nelson Harry
6 January 1906 – 1982
Lament for Eyak

Anna's heroic efforts save what we know of Eyak language and culture, despite enormous hardships. Both Eyak and the Athapaskan family shared a common ancestor some three thousand years ago, with Tlingit also distantly related. After they came from a sheltered homeland in the interior, a few hundred Eyak settled on the coast between Yakutat Bay and Prince William Sound at the mouth of Copper River as they shifted north into Chugach Alutiiq territory. During the 1700s, a Tlingit leader and shaman named x̲atga•wé•t married, traded, and organized among Eyaks, helping to Tlingitizing communities like Yakutat. Like Tlingits and others, Eyak had three classes of chiefs, commons, and slaves, along with matrimoieties of Crow and Eagle, though the latter's name derives from Alutiiq ~ Chugach, as does Eyak itself referring to the "throat" outlet of Lake Eyak. Moieties were based in epically famed houses linked within matriclans now named in Tlingit.

We know this ethnography because of Anna and her kin who survived the trauma and catastrophe when four American canneries set up in the summer of 1889, bringing in 200 men only crews which dynamited salmon runs for a quick profit while spreading disease, disorder, and destruction among Eyaks. After Anna's pregnant mother was murdered, she was barely tolerated by another family, sleeping with their dogs whose tongues cured her wounds. Understandably, she married at 12 in 1918 to Galushia Nelson, who born in fateful 1889 at Alaganik, the other Eyak town, as Anna was born the same year that Cordova was founded as the disastrous terminus of the Copper River Railroad, then TransAlaska pipeline. They had four sons, the last twins, all of whom later died tragically, but provided grandchildren.

Galushia had been "gathered up" like many native children and shipped to religious or federal boarding schools. He went to Chemawa in Oregon at 13 and trained as a mechanic until, ten years later in 1912, his family lured him home with false hopes to a disappointing, frustrating life with few outlets or opportunities. Yet his schooling and English ability served us well when Frederica de Laguna realized the distinctive status of Eyak during her 1930 archaeological survey aided by Gus Nelson, a brother, then returned with the Dane Kaj Birket-Smith and Seattleite Norman Reynolds to record the language and culture in 1933, with Galushia translating for Anna many of the tales formerly told by Old Chief Joe.

When Galushia died in 1939 after a lingering illness, Anna "fled" Cordova for Yakutat, the Tlingitized Eyak village, where she married Sampson Harry and had two more sons, and two grandsons. Anna learned Tlingit, but used Eyak with a few resident speakers who had moved there from Bering River and Kaliakh about 1912.

Fearing the loss of this crucial language, sporadic efforts were made by scholars to work on Eyak: by John P Harrington with George Johnson at Yakutat for six weeks in 1940; by Fang-Kuei Li, a Chinese student of Sapir send to look for tones in 1952, working with George and Anna at Yakutat and Scar and Minnie Stevens at Cordova; by Robert Austerliz of Columbia in summer 1961; and by the sustained effort of Michael Krauss at the University of Alaska from 1960 on, helped by Johnson's daughters Marie and Sophie and Galushia's niece Lina Saska Nacktan (- 1971).

After her sister Sophie Borodkin died February 1992, Marie Smith Jones (14 May 1918 – 21 January 2008) of Cordova was Eyak's last native speaker, and the last full-blood. Four marriages, seven troubled children, alcohol, smoking, and a hard life finally took their toll.

The linguist of record, Michael E. Krauss, works extensively on the Na-Dené language family, especially on proto-Athabaskan, pre-proto-Athabaskan, the Eyak language (- 2008), and other Athabaskan and EskAleut languages. With his 1991 address to the Linguistic Society of America, Krauss was among the first to create an awareness of the global problem of endangered languages. He has fulfilled the linguistic dictate of producing texts, dictionary, and grammar of Eyak.

Remarkably, in France, Guillaume Leduey, beginning at age 12, taught himself Eyak, utilizing print and audio materials obtained from the Krauss's Alaska Native Language Center, without ever visiting Alaska or conversing with Marie Smith Jones. When he finally arrived, Michael Krauss aided Leduey with speaking proper Eyak sounds and assigned further instruction in grammar and morphology, including morphemic analyses of traditional Eyak stories.

In June 2011, Leduey returned to Alaska to facilitate Eyak language workshops in Anchorage and Cordova. He is now regarded as a fluent speaker, translator, and instructor of Eyak. Despite his fluency, Eyak remains classified as "dormant" as there are no native speakers. On the Expanded Graded Intergenerational Disruption Scale (EGIDS) Eyak is graded a 9 (dormant); the language serves as a reminder of heritage identity for an ethnic community, but no one has more than symbolic proficiency. Currently, Leduey provides instruction and curriculum assistance to the Language Project from France.

The Eyak Preservation Council received an Alaska Humanities Forum Grant that enabled them to start a website devoted to the Eyak Language. Other funding supports the annual Eyak Culture Camp every August in Cordova, with countless language resources as well as immersion workshops, an online dictionary with audio samples, and a set of eLearning lessons. In June 2014, the Eyak Language Revitalization Project announced an online program called "dAXunhyuuga'", which means "the words of the people."

Cites

https://en.wikipedia.org/wiki/Eyak_language

1982 In Honor of Eyak ~ The Art of Anna Nelson Harry. Michael Krauss, ed. Alaska Native Language Center.

19   Eyak Legends of the Copper River Delta, Alaska. John Johnson, ed. Chugach Heritage Foundation.

1990 Eyak Frederica de Laguna. Handbook of North American Indians, Northwest Coast 9: 189-196.

Language of the Land
by Marilee Enge

Alaska's last Eyak speaker wages a battle from her Anchorage home to save ancestral lands
HEROIC AGE: The 75-year-old Marie Smith Jones grew up roaming the wild bays and forests of Prince William Sound.

The home that Marie Smith Jones has chosen for herself in downtown Anchorage offers no window into the remarkable life she has led. The modest and rather shabby apartment in one of the city's poorer neighborhoods is a far cry from the wild shores of Prince William Sound, where she was born and reared three-quarters of a century ago.

Yet this Eyak Indian, among the last of her people, is waging a battle from her city home to save her ancestral lands. She is an unlikely activist who found her voice only recently and has used it to argue for a halt to clear-cutting in the coastal rain forest and for placing timberland in a preservation trust.

A frail 75-year-old, Jones is the last native speaker of Eyak, a distinct language related to the Athabascan Indian tongue of central Alaska. Linguists say that upon her death, Eyak will be the first Native Alaskan language to become extinct. She achieved her lonely place in linguistic history when her older sister, Sophie Borodkin, died in February 1992. The media spotlight fell on Jones, suddenly chief of the tribe's elders council and of the tiny Eyak nation. With that role, she also became leader of a fledgling movement to create a wilderness homeland for the Eyaks.

Her message is a simple one that might sound naive within the lexicon of seasoned environmentalists. "Give the birds and animals back their home," she pleaded at a public ceremony in July. "Ask the loggers to put down their saws."

In July, when Cordova fisherman and activists formed a flotilla to protest clear-cutting by the local Native corporation, Jones stood on the deck of the lead vessel. Later, some loggers suggested that she was being manipulated by white activists who needed a symbol for their public relations campaign. "Nobody is guiding me," she responds.

"She is her own person," says David Grimes, a Cordova environmentalist who grew close to Jones during the protests. "What she keeps saying is, I want the grandchildren to be able to see the beauty of this place as it was when I was young." Simply having lived in such a rich and unspoiled place makes Jones' message valid. Grimes argues, "Prince William Sound is the finest marine ecosystem in North America. The Copper River Delta is the largest contiguous breeding wetland [for shorebirds] on the continent. Marie grew up between those two." [24]

In her youth, Jones followed her father into the woods, picked berries on the river flats, and helped her parents catch and smoke 500 silver salmon each fall. "I wish I was back there again, in that time." she says. The journey that brought her to where she is now was a difficult one, and her story is emblematic of the cultural dislocation experienced by Native Alaskans. Jones was born in 1918 in Old Town Cordova, the last settlement of the Eyak people. Historically, the Eyaks probably never numbered more than 1,000, and by the turn of the century their population had shrunk to about 60. Cordova was a rowdy frontier town — a busy salmon canning center and the terminus of the Copper River Railroad, built to transport coal. In that climate, the Eyaks were wracked by alcoholism, disease, and racism.

Jones remembers an idyllic childhood spent with her parents, Minnie and Scar Stevens, around the bays and forests of Prince William Sound. She also recalls being punished for speaking her native tongue at the government school she was required to attend. Nevertheless, she and Sophie hung on to their parents' language. They were the last Eyak children to do so.

Her adult life was far from idyllic. Jones drank heavily and married four times. Her seven children by her third husband were placed in foster homes in Anchorage. She stayed in Cordova and drank even harder.

But it was in those years, the 1960s, that she made perhaps her greatest contribution to the preservation of Eyak culture. A young linguist named Michael Krauss traveled to Cordova in 1961 to record what he recognized as a dying language, and Jones became one of his chief informants. There were other, older women whose knowledge of the language and of Eyak ways was stronger, but Jones gave Krauss his introduction to Eyak because she had the best grasp of English, "The language is documented as well as I can do it in its last days," says Krauss, now director of the Alaska Native Language Center in Fairbanks.

Jones quit drinking in 1970 and several years later moved to Anchorage to be closer to her children. She lived quietly in the city until her sister's death two years ago. It was about that time that she was reunited with her third cousin, Dune Lankard, a young man whose radical ideas were putting him at odds with the village-owned Eyak Corp.

Eyak, a for-profit organization, was formed in 1971 under the Native Alaska Claims Settlement Act, which gave Alaska's Native tribes $1 billion and 44 million acres of land in exchange for their agreement not to press aboriginal sovereignty claims. The act established 13 regional corporations and numerous village corporations. Eyak Corp represents all the Native people in the Cordova area, not just Eyak Indians. (Chugach Aleuts occupied Prince William Sound long before the Eyaks migrated west, and they remain the largest Native group in the area.) Lankard, a former board member, began arguing three years ago that the Aleut-dominated corporation was clear-cutting on traditional Eyak lands.

Although the Eyaks were once spread along the Gulf of Alaska coast from Cordova west to Yakutat, in recent times they lived on the shores of Prince William Sound, roaming the Copper River flats and the deep coastal rain forest there. Their last major village was at Alaganik Slough, a tributary of the Copper River and home to plentiful red and silver salmon runs. Jones regards this land surrounding Cordova and the delta as ancestral Eyak territory, which must be protected from logging.

In the fall of 1992, she and Lankard went to court to stop Eyak Corp from logging at a place called Mile 6, a former village site where her parents where born and lived their youth, and where her ancestors died. They argued that the logging violated a state law that protects historic areas and infringed on the Eyaks' right to practice their religion. This lawsuit was unsuccessful.

Last summer, they joined a broad-based coalition of Cordova environmentalists and fishermen in trying to halt cutting by the Eyak Corp in Orca Narrows, the waterway that leads from Cordova into Prince William Sound. The Exxon Valdez Oil Spill Trustees Council (EVOSTC), which oversees settlement money from the 1989 spill, was considering buying that land to set it aside as untouched wilderness. When Eyak Corp resumed logging in the middle of the negotiations, protesters cook to the sea. Tense talks between EVOSTC and Eyak Corp followed, but ultimately collapsed. So far, the EVOSTC has not purchased any timberland in Prince William Sound, the area most directly affected by the oil spill.

In September, Eyak Corp's logging contractor unexpectedly shut down its operation on Eyak land, saying markets for the wood had slumped. Officials have not said if or when cutting will resume. Negotiations with EVOSTC reopened in November before failing a third rime, and there was talk that Eyak Corp was trying to sell the timber to another logging operator.

Jones and Lankard say they will continue pushing to set aside ancestral wilderness land for the Eyaks — forever protected from logging, mining, and other intrusive development. Lankard estimates that as many as 100 people with Eyak blood remain — only Jones and two others are full-blooded — and he argues that they arc entitled to their own land. He dreams of a place where Eyaks could establish summer camps, gather traditional foods, and cash in on the popularity of ccotourism by leading wilderness expeditions. But a true Eyak homeland would require an act of Congress to amend the '71 lands settlement, and he acknowledges that that will be a long, hard-fought battle. Jones urges him on, saying whatever he does is with her blessing.

In the Eyaks' struggle for recognition, the land and the language are inextricably linked. "When Marie dies, what dies along with the language is the Eyak culture — its heritage, religion, and way of life," Lankard says. But as long as she is alive, he argues, there is still a culture that needs protecting. "They can't say she doesn't exist."

The Eyak elders council is working with the Alaska Rainforest Campaign, a new coalition of eight environmental organizations formed to protect the coastal rainforests of Southeast Alaska, Kodiak, and Prince William Sound. "This area of Alaska is one of the few places on earth that has such a rich, pristine, and beautiful temperate rainforest. It's much more endangered than the tropical rainforest," says Pamela Brodie of the Sierra Club in Alaska. "Marie Smith Jones is the last person with her language and therefore with her culture. It would be tragic if she sees the forest fall around her."

Last spring, Jones paid a visit to Mile 6, the old village site on the Eyak River where her parents lived long ago. She had not been there since Eyak Corp's logging contractor clear-cut a 50-acre swath up to the river's banks. Says Jones, "When I saw that, I stood and cried." A.

ecoheroes

23-24 PACIFIC NORTHWEST FEBRUARY 1994

LETTER FROM ALASKA

LAST WORDS
A language dies
By Elizabeth Kolbert

The last full-blooded member of the Eyak nation, Chief Marie Smith Jones, lives in Anchorage, Alaska, in a two-story, tan-colored building posted with a notice that warns "No dogs" and "No water beds." On a gray Saturday last spring, I arranged to go visit her. When I arrived at her apartment, no one answered the door. I thought perhaps she had forgotten our appointment and had gone off, but when I called up from the street it turned out that she had decided she did not feel like talking to me that afternoon, or, she implied, ever. I probably never would havc got to meet her except that a friend of hers had advised me to bring along, as a gesture of respect, some halibut, a fish prized by the Eyak. Smith Jones asked me if the halibut could fit inside the mailbox. I said I didn't think so.

The Eyak are a mysterious people. By the eighteenth century, they were living near Prince William Sound, in close proximity to other, more formidable nations. (The Chugach called them Ungalarmiut, meaning "the people living to your left as you face the ocean," or, in this case, "Easterners," and the Ahtnas called them [b] Danggane, meaning"uplanders.")Yetfor millennia they somehow managed to maintain not only their own culture but also their own language: Eyak is as closely related to Navajo as it is to any tongue spoken by native Alaskans today. In addition to being the last full-blooded Eyak, Smith Jones is also the last remaining native Eyak speaker. When I asked her how she felt about this, she said, "How would you feel if your baby died? If someone asked you, 'What was it like to see it lying in the cradle?' So think about that before you ask that kind of a question."

Smith Jones is eighty-seven and legally blind, with white, wispy hair, a face covered in fine wrinkles, and wrists no wider than a child's. Our meeting that afternoon ended up lasting for several hours and consisted in large measure of exchanges like this. At one point, Smith Jones told me that, like most white people, I had an "iron face"; at another, she announced, "I'm sorry to say, but I hate reporters." In response to a question about an appearance she had made a few years ago at a United Nations conference on indigenous peoples, she brought up the [c] Dalai Lama: 0987 "Beautiful words come out of his mouth, but his actions tell differently." In between such pronouncements, Smith Jones periodically softened. She talked about being sent off to work at a cannery at the age of twelve, about her struggles with alcoholism, about the stories her mother used to tell her, and about the difference in taste between a fish that has been caught in a net and a fish that has been harpooned, so that the blood slowly drains from its body. Smith Jones is a heavy smoker, and whenever there was a lull in the conversation she would light up another Winston and start to cough — a deep, hacking, raspy cough. Arrayed around her in her living room were at least a dozen prescription-drug bottles and an unopened Sierra Club calendar from 1992. As I was getting ready to leave, she pulled a small card out of her wallet. On it was written her name in Eyak — *Udach' Kuqaxa'a'ch'* — which, she said, translated as "a sound that calls people from afar." I asked her again about being the last Eyak speaker, and this time she responded differently.

"I got that strong feeling right here that it's going to come back," she told me, putting a hand over her heart. "God will send down Eyak to start all over again."

Language is often described as mans essential accomplishment, yet nothing threatens the world's languages so much as human progress. A great wave of language extinctions, it is believed, took place eight or nine thousand years ago, [47] following the so-called Neolithic revolution. As people gave up foraging in favor of farming, they started to live in larger and less isolated communities; certain groups prospered and became dominant, while others – and their languages – were absorbed. A second great wave of extinctions began with Europe's colonization of the Americas and Oceania. It is estimated, for example, that before the arrival of the first white settlers in Australia, in 1788, some two hundred and sixty aboriginal languages were in use. Traces of only a hundred remain. By the end of this century, it is likely that more than half of the six thousand languages still spoken around the globe will have vanished.

Besides Marie Smith Jones, the only other person who understands Eyak is a linguist named Michael Krauss. Krauss, who is seventy, lives in Fairbanks, but when I phoned him last winter he had recently been given a diagnosis of cancer, and was preparing to go to New York to consult with doctors about a course of treatment. "What's happened is very ironic," he told me. "I made a proposal to the National Science Foundation to study Eyak in 1963. In it, I remarked there were only a few speakers left and the youngest" – Smith Jones – "was already, I think I said, 'elderly.' Now this 'elderly' lady calls me in alarm over my health."

I finally met up with Krauss in Seattle, a few months after we first spoke. He was staying with his daughter, and convalescing after surgery. Krauss has an open face, wavy white hair, and a manner at once passionate and professorial. Until his illness, he had had a broad, even stout, figure; now he was painfully thin. His daughter kept urging him to eat something. He kept saying that he would, and then leaving the food that she brought him untouched.

Krauss traces his interest in linguistics back to his childhood. Growing up in Cleveland, he was sent off to Hebrew school, where he studied a language that had nearly died and then been resurrected. After Hebrew faded as a spoken language, around two thousand years ago, it was preserved ceremonially and transmitted through texts. Then, in the late nineteenth century, the language was revived by early Zionists. So successful was this revival that today it is the preferred tongue of at least three million people. "It's a very remarkable history of survival against odds," Krauss told me. "It [48] inculcated in me a real sense of what language means to nationhood and the survival of identity." Later, Krauss did graduate work at Harvard, and learned, among other languages, Gaelic, Icelandic, and Faeroese, the last of which is spoken only by the fifty thousand or so inhabitants of the Faeroe Islands, northwest of Scotland. He became fascinated by the way that some languages, like Faeroese, continued to thrive even as many other, much more broadly based languages were vanishing. In 1960, Krauss moved across the country to start the linguistics department at the University of Alaska Fairbanks.

As soon as Krauss got to Fairbanks, he set about assessing the condition of the state's native languages. For nearly three-quarters of a century, children in Alaska had been prohibited from studying, or even speaking, their own languages at school, under a policy established by the territory's earliest commissioner of education, Sheldon Jackson. "Pupils are required to speak and write English exclusively," Jackson, who was also a Presbyterian missionary, wrote in 1888. "Instruction In their vernacular is not only of no use to them but is detrimental to their speedy education and civilization." As a result of this policy, which endured until 1972, virtually all the native languages in Alaska fell into decline. Most imperiled of all was Eyak. Krauss was immediately drawn to it, both because of its fragility and because of its tenacity.

"We must not forget that all the languages we find today, even moribund relics like Eyak, are themselves the relatively few victors in the constant struggle for linguistic survival," he later wrote, for they have lasted "long enough to be at least documented, as compared with the many more languages which have disappeared forever without a recognizable trace."

Eyak is neither a linguistic isolate, like Basque, nor a part of any modem language community. Rather, it might be described as the spinster aunt of the Athabascan language group, whose members include Navajo and Apache. All Athabascan languages descend from a common ancestor — now extinct — that linguists call proto-Athabascan, which is believed to have originated in the interior of Alaska or the Yukon Territory around the time of Christ. Eyak is thought to have broken off from the even more ancient linguistic branch that led to proto-Athabascan sometime around 1000 B.C. (A technique known as "glottochronology" — the phonetic analog of carbon dating — can be used to determine the point at which related languages diverged.) For Eyak to have maintained its distinctive character for so long, its speakers must have spent the better part of the past three thousand years living essentially in isolation. One of the many unanswered questions about them is where.

Various clues within the language itself suggest that the Eyak were, at one point, an inland people. Their word for "downriver," for instance, *li'*, also means "into the closed end of something," hinting that the Eyaks route to the sea was blocked, perhaps by glaciers. By the time the first whites arrived in Alaska, though, the Eyak were living along the southern coast, from the Prince William Sound down to what is now the town of Yakutat. The Russians, who were trying to establish a network of trading posts in the area, encountered them in the seventeen-nineties. Relations between the two peoples were occasionally tense; in 1799 a group of Eyak massacred a Russian hunting party, in retaliation for which the Russians tortured and killed an Eyak man. Nevertheless, some Eyak were converted to the Russian Orthodox Church.

Although few reliable records from the nineteenth century survive — if they ever existed — Eyak territory seems to have shrunk dramatically during that period. Several villages disappeared, probably wiped out by smallpox or measles. Others were assimilated by the Tlingit, a friendly but more powerful tribe that was expanding from the southeast. (If the English-speaking Americans hadn't appeared, Eyak might eventually have been done in by Tlingit.) By the eighteen-seventies, there were only about two hundred Eyak left, mostly in settlements near what is now the town of Cordova, on the Copper River delta. Around 1890, several salmon canneries were built in the neighborhood of Cordova, a development that, in addition to bringing new contagions, disrupted the Eyaks food supply. (A favored fishing technique of the canneries was to use dynamite.)

In 1933, when two anthropologists arrived in Cordova to study the Eyak, the community consisted of just thirty-eight members. The anthropologists, Frederica de Laguna and Kaj Birket-Smith, attempted to chronicle what remained of the Eyaks traditions. Their study, "The Eyak Indians of the Copper River Delta, Alaska," is at once exhaustive and highly sketchy. "Methods of working stone have been forgotten by the Eyak," the authors note. When they try to ascertain the rituals associated with the onset of menstruation, one Eyak tells them that girls are secluded in a special hut for a month, another says for twelve months, and a third says for six months — and not in a hut but in a "special room." Among the many customs that de Laguna and Birket-Smith attribute to the Eyak are building small wooden houses over the graves of their loved ones, observing a taboo against sewing the skins of land and sea animals into the same garment, and burning children's toys in order to secure good weather. Last spring, I phoned de Laguna, who was ninety-seven and living outside Philadelphia. (She spent almost forty years teaching at Bryn Mawr.) I had heard that she had a large collection of photographs from the 1933 expedition, and I asked if she would let me come see them. She said no, she didn't have much time left, and whatever she did have she needed for her own work. "I assure you that growing old is not for sissies," she told me. Six months later, she died.

When Michael Krauss began his study of Eyak, in 1963, only six people who knew the language were left. Four of them, including Marie Smith Jones and her sister Sophie Borodkin, lived in Cordova. The remaining two lived in Yakutat, two hundred and fifty miles to the southeast. The six spoke with varying degrees of proficiency, but none used Eyak in daily life. As it happens, the last person who had preferred Eyak to either English or Tlingit had been Smith Jones's mother, Minnie Stevens. When she died, in the spring of 1961, Eyak ceased, practically speaking, to be a living language.

Krauss decided that the best way to preserve what was left of Eyak was to assemble a dictionary. This meant first creating an Eyak orthography. As is the case with many Native American languages, Eyak uses sounds – [49] for example, glottalized consonants and nasalized vowels — that simply are not represented by the Latin alphabet. For most of these sounds, Krauss used either standard linguistic symbols or symbols borrowed from other languages. (A glottalized "t," for instance, is written t'.)

Krauss next spent several summers shuttling between Cordova and Yakutat, collecting words. He would point to the parts of his face and ask an Eyak speaker to pronounce the terms for "nose," or *siniik'* (which is really "my nose," since in Eyak you wouldn't say "nose" without indicating to whom, or to what, the nose belonged); "mouth," or *sisa't;* and "eyes," or *silaax.* Then he would ask the same speaker to name the features of his or her face unprompted. In this way, he learned, for instance, that the Eyak have a word — *siniik'adach'uuch'* — for the groove between the upper lip and the septum, for which English speakers have only the clinical term "philtrum." (The Eyak word translates roughly as "nose crumple.") Occasionally, his informants had rather vivid imaginations and, failing to recall a word, would make one up. When I suggested that the process seemed treacherous, Krauss dismissed this, saying, "Any linguist worth his salt should be able to do the philological workup."

By 1970, Krauss had compiled more than six thousand terms and come, in his words, "reasonably close to plumbing the depths of living memory in Eyak." The original version of his dictionary ran to thirty-three hundred hand-typed pages. To a non-linguist, it is nearly incomprehensible:

Deme<u>x</u>ch' (variant of qeme<u>x</u>ch'; L certain of authenticity) deme<u>x</u>ch'ł (noun, d-class, with -ł-instrumental suffix) "soft rotten spot or hole in ice over body of water': deme<u>x</u>ch'łda'luw 'large treacherous spot in ice' L., deme<u>x</u>ch'łda'e' q'aGiiyaaq 'don't fall in treacherous spot in ice!' (certain she has heard this) L.

Linguists typically classify languages according to word order. English is an S.V.O. (subject-verb-object) language: the subject of a sentence usually comes first, followed by the verb and then the object, as in "The woman drove a car." Eyak, by contrast, is an S.O.V., or subject-object-verb, language, so that a direct translation of the sentence *"Lixah da<u>x</u>unh sashehł"* would be "The grizzly bear the man killed." As in many Native American languages, both prefixes and suffixes can be added to verbs, resulting in forms that make distinctions not just in tense — did an action happen in the past or in the present? – but also in the degree to which an action has been completed, whether it occurs regularly, what part of the body is affected, and whether it is being done sincerely. Thus, in Eyak, the question "Are you going to keep tickling me in the face in the same spot repeatedly?" is rendered as one word, *xuqu'liił<u>x</u>aa<u>x</u>:ch'kk'sh*.

It is the differences between English and Eyak that are, in Krauss's view, the reason for preserving it. He asked me if I'd ever taken French." *Tout a l'heure il sera la,"* he said. *"Tout á l'heure il était* lá. Well, what the hell does *"tout a l'heure'* mean? We have no English word for that. How would you define it — 'now plus or minus a short while'? The minute you learn French, you have to learn *'tout a l'heure,'* and it makes you think differently from the way you ever thought before."

He went on, "Each language is a unique repository of facts and knowledge about the world that we can ill afford to lose, or, at the least, facts and knowledge about some history and people that have their place in the understanding of mankind. Every language is a treasury of human experience. Eyak doesn't give a damn about tenses. But it sure does give a damn about other things, much more than I do. Therefore it broadens your thinking, enriches your ability to understand the world — to deal with reality and experience." I pointed out that it has always been the dream of a certain brand of idealist that mankind would acquire — or perhaps recover — a universal language. Krauss said he had no objection to that, provided that people continued to speak their native languages as well.

"Having the presumption to think we can do with just one language is a mistake," he told me. "Not until we reach the age of enlightenment do we really know what we're doing. And I'd like to see someone claim we've reached the age of enlightenment." I asked Krauss whether he thought that Eyak, like Hebrew, could ever be revived. He said that he rather doubted it. Then what had he hoped to accomplish?

"I've never defined that for myself," he said. "I'm doing it because I'm me, and Eyak is Eyak."

The town of Cordova, the last home of the Eyak, sits on the eastern shore of Prince William Sound, on a narrow bay called Orca Inlet. To the north are the snow-covered peaks of the Chugach Mountains and to the east the marshy plains of the Copper River delta. Just beyond the delta lies the Bering Glacier, which is the largest glacier in Alaska. Cordova is still a fishing village, and the tempo of life is determined mostly by the comings and goings of various species of salmon. When I went to visit, last August, the silver salmon were running, and the streams were full of enormous, spent-looking fish, [59] lazing around in circles, preparing to die.

The few traces of Eyak culture that remain in Cordova could easily fit inside a suburban garage. A couple of them – a dugout canoe and a spear – are on display at the Cordova Historical Museum. (Also on exhibit are artifacts from Alaska's first oil field, in nearby Katalla, and memorabilia from the town's annual Ice Worm Festival, a Mardi Gras-like affair held the first weekend in February.) Whatever else has survived of Eyak culture is scattered in the woods. One afternoon, I took a hike out to the remnants of an Eyak longhouse. It had been reduced to four logs, arranged in a rectangle. Blueberry bushes were growing out of what had once, apparently, been the floor. Nearby were some graves, marked with Russian Orthodox crosses that were falling into the ground.

The area around Cordova is resource-rich; in addition to the salmon, the oil, and the forests, there is also a huge, as yet unmined coal deposit about fifty miles east of town. In recent years, the pressure to exploit these resources has been growing – as has local resistance, much of it led by a group called the Eyak Preservation Council. In an unusual twist, the development battles in Cordova have often pitted one native group against another. The Alaska Native Claims Settlement Act of 1971 granted billions of dollars' worth of surface and subsurface rights to a complicated network of native-run boards, and the founder and director of the Eyak Preservation Council, Dune Lankard, who is himself a quarter Eyak, has more than once sued a native corporation of which he is a member. A few years ago, *Time* named Lankard a "hero for the planet," in recognition of his work to protect the region. Marie Smith Jones, meanwhile, gave him the Eyak nameJa-machakih, which translates as "little bird that screams really loud." Although he does not speak any Eyak, Lankard says that he would like one day to be able to file lawsuits in the language.

"We are going to save the language whether anybody likes it or not," he told me. "And we are going to save the land whether anybody likes it or not." He added, "I really think that the Eyak have a lot to offer this screwed-up world, and we are not talking rocket science."

As it happened, my visit to Cordova coincided with the conclusion of a seven-year effort known as the Eyak Language Project. The project was largely the work of a former TV reporter from Anchorage named Laura Bliss Spaan. She first heard about the Eyak in 1992, when she was sent to Cordova to cover the Ice Worm Festival. "When Eyak gets ahold of you, it's really hard to escape," she explained to me. Bliss Spaan arranged for Michael Krauss to give a series of lessons on Eyak grammar, which she videotaped. She then gathered up all the records of the language which she could find — Krauss's hand-typed dictionary, transcriptions he had made of Eyak legends, audio recordings of an Eyak speaker from the nineteen-seventies, video of Marie Smith Jones – and computerized them. Altogether, the archive fit on five DVDs. When I arrived in Cordova, Bliss Spaan was there to deliver the archive to the local cultural council. She offered me an extra set of disks that she had brought along. As I took them from her, I had the odd sensation of holding in my hand all that there was – or ever would be – of Eyak.

The only way out of Cordova is by boat or plane. Flying back to Anchorage and then to New York, I loaded the disks that Bliss Spaan had given me onto my laptop. I listened to Krauss lecture on Eyak vowels, heard Smith Jones talk about how to say hello, and read some Eyak legends about fantastic creatures. In "Blind Man and Loon," a man's sight is restored by a magical bird. In "Woman and Octopus," a woman falls in love with a spirited cephalopod. There was also a "Lament for Eyak," which Krauss had recorded in 1972. In it, the narrator describes what it is like to be a member of a vanishing people:

> K'aadih ulah uuch' q'e' iiłi'ee.
> SitinhGayuudik si<u>x</u>a' iinsdi'ahł.
> SitinhGayuu si<u>x</u>a' lisłi'ahłch'aht q'al
>   ahnuu si'ahrGayuu q'uh yaan' q'e'
>   disłiqahqł,
> al iisinh.
> Aan,
> deelehtdal diaGaxuu,
> ts'it diaGaxuu atxsiilahl?
> AtGaxłałaał.
>
> Useless to go back there.
> My uncles too have all died out on me.
> After my uncles all died out my aunts
>   next fell,
> to die.
> Yes,
> why is it I alone,
> just I alone have managed to survive?
> I survive. •

The culture and language of the Eyak endured for nearly three thousand years.
The only surviving speaker is eighty-seven.

THE NEW YORKER, JUNE 6, 2005

Eyak Stories

Raven and Echo
Old Man Dude

Crow first eats mussels.   It was low tide.   He was opening them.   He was eating them — *hwup* (inhale).   Hear someone making same noise behind him.   He throws the shells back over his shoulder.

When he was through he took a walk.   Walk to someone's smokehouse.   It was big.   No one there.   There was a fire there, lots of meat getting smoked.   He sit down looking around.   No one there.   Soon pot came to the fire.   Water in it. Smoked meat dropped in it.   He cut, he go in the pot.   It was cut, it fell into the pot.   It got cooked.   When it was cooked.   Crow put it in the plate.   Crow eat it.   There was seal fat hanging up in the corner.   Crow saw it when he came in.   Crow go outside.   He takes that fat and chewed it.   Two men started to pull his hair from both sides.   Crow said, "Wait a minute.   I give him to you.   Eat, too!"   Crow hung up the fat and went outside.

Raven and the Grass *Blanket*
Old Man Dude

Crow went for several days.   He had a blanket.   He found a blanket on the ground.   He threw away his old blanket.   He had a grass blanket now, but it rotted, so he had no more blanket. He went to the beach.   He was calling the westerly wind.   "Hey Westerly Wind, give me back my blanket!"   He got his own blanket back again.   He used his own blanket. [2]

Raven Steals the Fisherman's Bait
Old Man Dude

He see a fisherman.   He said, "What bait you got?"   "Seal fat, I got for bait," the fisherman hollered.   Crow he picked up the water on a stick and walked under it.   He began to eat the man's bait.   He chew yet.   The man feel it.   He hooked Crow on the nose.   Too much cheat people, that Crow.   Man in the canoe want to haul him up.   No.   Crow held to the bottom of the canoe so he couldn't get hauled up.   Pretty soon he broke the Crow's nose.

Crow fixed his nose with gum before he went to the fisherman's house.   He went inside the house.   "Nobody found something around here?"   he asked, "Fisherman, he found something," they said.   "He hook him."   "Let me see."   He look at him.   "What nose is this? I don't see this kind of a live nose." Before they could stop him, Crow put him on his nose.   He fly.

He hooked crow on the nose.

Raven and the King Salmon
Old Man Dude

He walk again. He see a king salmon close to shallow water. He tell that salmon, "Come ashore, that man talking bad." The salmon came to shore. Crow says, "Wait a minute." He wanted a small stick to club the salmon he couldn't find it. Salmon went in water again. Next time he killed the salmon when he came ashore. [3]

Raven Robs His Partners
Old Man Dude

Crow had two partners, a bluejay and some other kind of bird. He made a fire in the beach and made a hole. He put the salmon in the hole and put fire on top to bake it. Crow told his partner, "Go look for dry wood. It don't look cooked yet." Crow dug it up when his partner went away. He ate the whole thing. Crow put the fire back on the hole. Partner came back and found him and sat down alongside the fire. They asked, "Fish baked yet?" "No!" Crow, he walked again.

Raven and the Owners of the Tides
Old Man Dude

Crow walked a long ways. He saw a sea-egg (sea urchin) in the water. He jump in the water. Can't get it. He got it finally. At that time it was high ride all the time. Old girl kept the ride up. He came to her house. He said, "Jesus Christ, I'm cold! I get too many sea-eggs." The old lady said, "Where you get it?" "Where I get it? Nothing doing!" He put the sea-eggs on her bottom and rubbed it. Old lady, she cried like hell. "Leave me alone! Leave me alone! Tide's going out," she said. He go outside. Look at tide. It was going out already. He leave her there. Don't touch her no more. [4]

Raven and Magpie
Old Man Dude

He walk out and find everything, seal, halibut, codfish, all stranded. He kicked an old stick on the bottom. "Hey, get up! Help me!" Stick get up. He help.
Crow made a house over there. He got a partner yet. (The transformed stick or Magpie?). He smoked all the stuff he found, in the house. He slept many days beside the fire. Soon, "hu hu" he dream. Soon he get up. Said to partner, "Look out, war coming. You go to war," he tell his partner.

Partner went outside. He fought him (the war). Crow stayed inside. Partner come inside and look at the Crow. Crow had already cleaned up all the food in the house. Crow cheated his partner again.

His partner put Crow in a box and tied it up. He don't say nothing. He packed it up the mountain. Crow told his partner, "Fine day, but half the mountain got fog yet. You'll get lonesome. You going to cry."

The partner throw the box with Crow inside it down the mountain. Going to kill the

Crow. Crow, he die. Partner stay in the house, how many days. He got lonesome. Crow was dead and his meat was already spoiled. Partner still waiting for him. Partner found him and poked the Crow right on the ear. Soon Crow scratched his head. Crow said. "What's the matter? I am sleeping now."

"... war coming. You go to war. "

Raven and Echo
Johnny Stevens

Raven ran into a storm and had no place to go. He walked along the beach and every time he came to a headland he would fly around it. As he walked, he picked up mussel shells and ate them, and threw the shells into the wood. Every time he threw a shell he would say something and someone would mock him. It was the Echo. Raven grew angry and said, "If you are a man, then let me see your house." The Echo only repeated. Raven thought it could be no man for it was unable to answer. [5]

Raven Steals the Sun
Johnny Stevens

In early days everything was dark, there were no stars, no moon, and no sun. Raven saw that a rich family had the sun, moon, and the stars hanging in a box from the ceiling.

A girl and a man went after water. Raven made himself into a feather, and dropped into the water. The girl drank the water, and Raven turned into a baby inside her. The child was born a short time later after, and no one knew how it happened. The child kept looking at the box. He was able to fly five or six days after birth. He kept crying for the box, and at last his grandmother gave it to him. Then he flew with the sun, moon, and stars through the smokehole.

People were fishing in a dark place, getting lots offish. Raven had come to them before and had wanted fish, but could not see. He stopped at the fishing place and opened the box. Sun, moon, and stars flew into the sky. Then people could not sleep, it was light all the time. Then Raven turned into a man with leaves (feathers) for clothes, but he still had the Raven's beak.

Then he went to the first house. The people all went to sleep but they had left a watchman on duty. He saw a faint light appearing in the east but he didn't know what it was. It grew lighter and lighter. He called the people and they all came out and looked with wonder. No one knew what had happened except the grandfather who had let the sun go. The people went in to eat and the Raven kept looking at his mother, so everyone suspected he was the strange baby who had been born to her, but they were not quite sure. [6]

Raven made himself into a feather,

Raven and the Owners of the Tides
Johnny Stevens

Raven asked about the seawater, "Why didn't it go down?" No one could answer. He went away, walking and flying along the beach until he came to a house from which smoke was rising. He entered in the shape of a man. He spoke. The woman who lived there turned around but Raven was invisible. She groped around for the speaker.

She said, "Oh, why are my eyes so sore?" Raven said, "Help me, and I'll help you. You make the tide go down so I can get some clams to eat. I'll make your eyes well." The woman who kept the tides said she would do her best to get the water low enough and finally she succeeded. Raven said that would be *why are my eyes so sore?* low water and that it would come every day. The old lady's eyes grew better and she got younger. [7]

Raven Teaches the People
Johnny Stevens

Raven kept going around a point until he saw smoke coming up between the trees. He went over and there was a family who had plenty to eat. "Where do you come from"" they asked. "I come from all over," he replied. They gave him raw meat but Raven didn't like it. "Where I come from," he said, "we cook our meat."

They had never heard of that, so Raven showed them how to boil mean with hot rocks and how to roast it on spits from [7] the fire. The people were grateful and gave Raven a place to sleep in their house. Quantities of fat were hanging from the rafters. After everyone was asleep, Raven turned into a bird, seized the fat, and flew with it out the smokehole. He returned before morning and after changing back into a man, went to sleep again. The people were angry when they saw that all their fat was gone, and they knew that Raven must have taken it, but there were no marks through the doorway to show where he had gone out. They ordered Raven out. He said that he was innocent but left.

He traveled until he came to another house. He took some sea eggs in with him and said, "Have you ever seen anything like this?" (The people never had.) He also showed them game and fish, and they had never seen them either, for they had no weapons and knew nothing of hunting. Raven showed the man how to make bows and arrows with bone points. Then they went and shot a duck. Since that time men have hunted.

Next he took man up a mountain after bear. By and by a large bear began to chase them. Raven threw his spear and cawed. The bear dropped dead. Since that time men have hunted. They packed the carcass back to the house and Raven showed them how to skin it and cut it up with a stone knife. "What can we use the hide for?" they asked. "You can either dry the meat side and make baskets or you can make moccasins." Before that time people had slept on grass, they had no blankets.

"How can we sew the skin?" they wondered. Raven pulled sinews from the bear's back, dried them, and showed the women how to roll them for thread. He also showed them how to cut up and smoke the meat.

The Raven went up on the mountain and killed a goat. He dragged it home. He showed the people what to do with the fat. He took bark and made a pall. The bark is taken from the trees in spring. There is one piece for the side and another for the bottom. It is sewed together with young peeled spruce roots. Holes are drilled for the lashing. Raven put the goat fat in the pail and made grease of it. It got hard, harder than butter. He did that much.

Then he went up the creek and got some fish. The people did not know how to roast meat by the fire, they knew only how to cook on hot stones. Raven then showed how to make a spit of three sticks and roast the fish. [8]

Raven and the King Salmon
Johnny Stevens

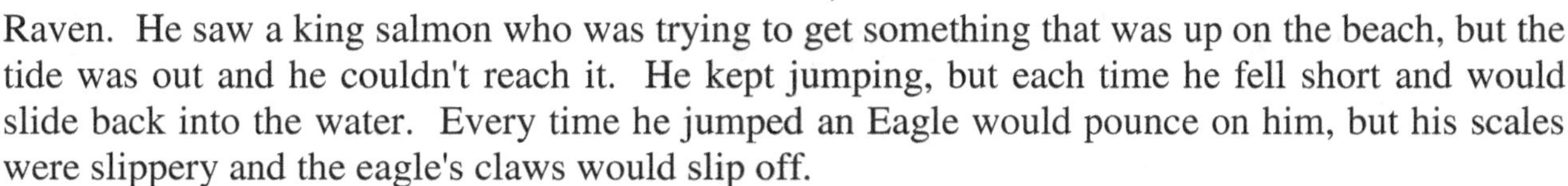

Raven went along the beach to a place where there was lots of fish. He was a smart fellow, that Raven. He saw a king salmon who was trying to get something that was up on the beach, but the tide was out and he couldn't reach it. He kept jumping, but each time he fell short and would slide back into the water. Every time he jumped an Eagle would pounce on him, but his scales were slippery and the eagle's claws would slip off.

Raven turned into a bird and went over to watch him. He cawed to attract the Eagle's attention and then said, "I'll make a big swell so that you can catch the salmon, if you give me that."

The Eagle agreed. The first wave threw the salmon up on the beach but he managed to slide back. Then Raven caused a mightly wave that threw the salmon way up the timber line. Eagle picked it up and the two birds cooked it. Two hungry men came along and asked for food but the greedy birds refused them. They went away. Before the birds could start to eat, a big landslide swept down and buried the fish, so they got none of it. [9]

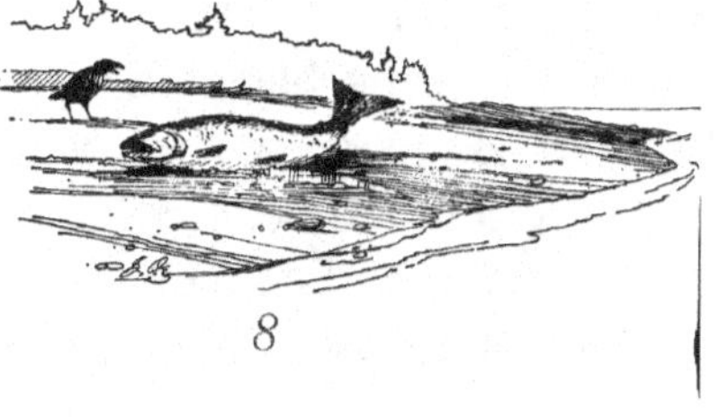

He cawed to attract the Eagle's attention

How Raven Became Black
Johnny Stevens

They separated. Eagle going west, while Raven came east. Ravens were white then, but I don't know how they became black. They made the same noise as now.

Raven Marries
Johnny Stevens

Raven went away again. When he got a little distance from the people, he turned into a bird again. When he was with them he was like a man, all but for his beak, he could not disguise that. Then his clothes were made of different kinds of leaves (feathers).

Raven went away. He came to where there was a family living alone. They had a daughter. Raven wanted to marry her, so he done everything. He stayed with them a long time working for the parents. He married the daughter. The people liked him because he was so industrious and did not sleep late in the morning. Raven went into the woods and collected many small birds and animals. These were the people under him, he told the girl's parents. He would have lots of help in time of war.

After he married the daughter, the parents did not seem to like him. So he left the parents, taking his wife with him. He had prepared a house with lots of food ready for her. His father and mother-in-law came to visit him. He told them that he would live in that place, but that when they got old they could come to him and he would make them young again. He had a comb that would color their white hair again and make them young. That was what happened. [10]

Ravens were white then

Raven and the People with the Magic Canoe
Johnny Stevens

After a while Raven left these people and went to another camp. He found a place where there were many people. He came among them. They wanted to know where he had come from. This was a different tribe from the one he had left, and they spoke a different language. They wanted Raven to guide them to the people that he had just left. Raven told them that they lived far away.

One of the rich men had a skin canoe. The people got into it and Raven showed them the way. All they had to do was to put a pile of fish on each side of the canoe in the bow, and it would go of itself without anyone paddling. When they came to the other people, they wanted to be friends and live together. They had to find out if there was enough for them all to eat. They decided to live together.

Raven and the Killerwhales
Johnny Stevens

Another part of the story tells how Raven came among the killerwhales. They did not like him. They live in the water in rock houses and live on meat and fish. Inside their house they look like people. Raven had to get away from them. [11]

Raven Turns War Parties into Rocks
Johnny Stevens

Finally his helper came and said, "There is war and trouble coming because we are too rich." He saw something coming and turned it into a rock. Soon something, another attacking war party, came again. Raven's helpers warned him and he turned them into rocks. Raven made several islands out of war parties. He lived there many years. He is said to be still living there.

The white people tried to catch him with drink. They got a drug in tea to try to make him fall asleep. Raven, however, made their boat stop and so escaped.

Raven never sits still. The only time he is in the house is at night. He has no children. His parents-in-law came to visit him and he makes them young.

Where Old Raven Made the Earth
Galushia Nelson

ch'iilehshiyah qi' ahh xaah' sałił
Raven-old where earth he made

The Raven was sent down from above. He came down to the ocean. He kept flying around in a circle. Top of the tree stick out from the water and he sat down on it. All the things drifted around close by. He stick it to the tree and said, "Turn into the earth!" for each stick of drift wood. The earth gets bigger and bigger each day.

After it got big, the Raven hop around the earth. "I wish a mountain would come up, too!" After his wish come, he was wishing for more mountains. "I wish there would be a beach, [12] too!" Raven wished for mussels on the beach and all the things in the water.

After he got his wish, he flew around the whole earth. When he came down. Raven said, "Am I going to live on this earth alone?" A seagull came around. "You come to eat up everything, eh?" Then after the seagull came, all the other birds came. When each bird came, he turned them into different kinds of birds. They were all like seagulls at first. He pointed at them, "You turn into this!" He told the ducks and geese, "If there are going to be human beings, they are going to eat you."

After he made the different birds, he walked back and forth along the beach and started to cry. "I am alone in this big world. Am I going to live here alone?" Later, he was still crying for a human being, he saw a human being coming. He told the man, "You live with me here. Where you come from?" The man wouldn't answer. They made a place where they lived. After they lived there for a while, old Raven fly to some other place and the man left for some place, too. [13]

Top of the tree stick out from the water

Raven Makes the Rivers and Other Geographical Features
Galushia Nelson

Two islands near Katalla were made by the Raven dropping rocks. The Raven was flying around and spitting. Where he spat, that made a lake. He drew his finger through the spit to form the rivers. Where he rested and stayed overnight, the spit turned into the ocean.

On the other side of Katalla is a big cave, called Raven's House, (*ch'iilehshiyah ya'yat*) Raven was going to move away from that place. Raven threw his wooden bucket overboard because he didn't have room for it. It is a rock with a deep hole in it. The Natives get sea-eggs there at low tide. The rock is called "Where Raven Threw His Box".

ch'iilehshiyah qi'ch' tsaa'ł uxa' satsaxi

Raven-old where box his threw

Right close by is another rock where Raven dragged his fish rack. There are deep scratches in the rock. This is called, "Where Raven Dragged Along His Rack"

ch'iilehshiyah qi'dax weesh uxa' tsa' salxahti
Raven old along rack his dragged

Besides stealing daylight, and the sun, moon, and stars, Raven also stole water, and put the islands in the ocean. [14]

the Raven dropping rocks

Ugly Baby Crow
(Theft of Daylight)
Galushia Nelson

ch' iileh saqeets' ashiyah
Raven baby-ugly

Once Raven was walking at night. There was no daylight then. He came to people who were fishing for eulachon. He tried to bum them for some but the fisherman wouldn't give him any. "I'm going to make it daylight on you, if you won't give me any fish." The fisherman said, "How could you make it Daylight?"

He left the fisherman and went on his way. He found a chief living in one place who had everything, Stars, Moons, and Daylight. He had two slaves, one for himself, and one for his daughter. The slave of his daughter was to pack water for her.

Raven came and after he saw the Moon, Daylight and Stars, he turn himself into a spruce needle and dropped himself into where they got water. When the slave came to get water he dipped water up with the spruce needle. When the chiefs daughter drank water, she drank water with the spruce needle. The chief's daughter became pregnant.

When the boy was born he grew up awful fast. In a few days he crawled all around. He wanted this and he wanted that. His grandfather think a great deal of him. When his grandfather pick him up he use to say to him, "Looks like a Raven. He got an eye like a Raven."

When the boy wants anything, he points to it and cries. He wants the Stars first. When he got it he went outside, held it [15] up and blew it away, and it went into the sky. Next he got the Moon, after he got through playing with the Stars. Then he did the same thing with the sun. The last was the daylight. It was like phosphorescence. He had an awful time getting Daylight. When he got it he cried "qa" and flew out of the smokehole.

14

his grandfather pick him up
he use to say to him, "Looks like a Raven."

He went back to look for the fishermen. He tried to bum some fish again, and he told them the same thing again if they don't give him some fish he was going to make it Daylight. "How could you?" At first he made it Daylight a little bit. Then when the men saw the light they said they would give him all the fish if he would make it Daylight. So he got all the fish. (Galushia explained that the Eyaks used to fish for eulachon at night with a torch and dipnet.)

Old Raven Was Walking in Back of the Waves
  ## *(Raven & King Salmon)*
Galushia Nelson

ch'iilehshiyah qi" tanhdiiina<u>x</u> g(ał)aal
Raven old where waves behind walking
(where the Raven went beach-combing)

Once a Raven was living as a beachcomber. He goes out on beach for anything that comes on beach to eat. At one time he could not find anything, so next he start with a song which he sing while he was going along the beach. "I am going by the waves. I am going by the waves." [16]

when the King Salmon got mad, rush in so fast it got dry land.

tanhdiiinax gaxtaat
waves behind I-am-going

And the big king salmon got curiosity and came to beach but won't come close enough for Raven to kill it, so he start tease it and calling names, such as, "You big fat fish, you are so fat you could not come closer." But the fish won't come in closer until Raven call it "Fat head and fat jaw." When the king salmon got mad, it rush in so fast it got dry land, where Raven kill it and had a feast.

Old Raven and Magpie
  ## *(Raven and the Owners of the Tides)*
Galushia Nelson

ch'iileh daa<u>x</u> geets'guxaq'
Raven-old and Magpie

Once Raven and an old lady were living by the beach. Raven said, "I wish we had someone to give us good luck." Old lady said, "What is it then?" Raven said, "I don't know what to do to make the tide low." Old Lady said, "You wait till tomorrow morning. There will be low tide." Raven said, "How will that be?" Old Lady said, "You will see." Raven said, "If you made this ocean, that will happen all right." Raven didn't really believe her.

Raven had another companion in another place. That was Magpie. He went back to Magpie and told him to get up *early in* the morning. Next morning Magpie got up early and went outside without waking the Raven. Everything was dry, the tide was so low. Magpie went beach-combing. Magpie found all kinds offish and clams high and dry. He packed them all up on dry land. He found even seals.

Raven happened to wake up and he missed the Magpie. The Magpie had packed up all kind of things above the high tide line. Tide was coming in already. Raven went clam digging too. He didn't know there was so many things high and dry. So Raven started to dig butter clams, but he got only two butter clams. When he got these, he happened to look up, saw Magpie dragging a seal up above the tide line. So he went to Magpie and he helped Magpie to drag the seal up above the water line. [17]

"You wait till tomorrow morning. There will be low tide."

Magpie told Raven, "I think we got enough seals now. We get some more halibut and fish." They only made one trip after the fish. But when they went for the second trip, the tide was coming in so fast they didn't have time to get another load. So Raven didn't have anything but two butter clams for himself. At high ride the Magpie started to clean his game. Raven got some driftwood, although he had never done that before. Magpie always had to do the work. When Magpie finished, he started to make grease out of the seal. Raven left and let Magpie do all the work.

When Raven left he went to the other birds, like Robin and other small birds and told them to make war on this Magpie. Raven told the other birds to attack on a certain day. Then he came back to Magpie. Magpie was all through with his work.

Magpie asked Raven, "Where were you when we had so much work to do?" Raven said, "I was looking for dry wood." Magpie got mad and said, "You are not going to get any of these things that I have pulled up." But Raven didn't mind what Magpie said. He said, "Nephew, if you're tired, lay down and rest." The Raven never called him that before. So Magpie lay down. When Magpie slept. Raven started to cook some of the fish. Raven was taking down some of the fish that was hanging up and he knocked the whole thing down on Magpie. Magpie woke up. "What are you doing?" Raven said, "Bluejays stealing your dried fish! I'm chasing them away." So Magpie told Raven, "Let's bring all the rest of the things in." Raven said, "Let's hurry then."

When they were about through, Raven said, "Hurry up! Someone is making war on us." Raven told Magpie, "When [18] they attack us, you go outside and I stay inside."

So Magpie *was* defending from outside, and Raven stayed inside. Raven was helping himself to all the food inside. He was eating it up. When Magpie was getting the worst of it, he went Inside to get Raven to help him. Raven was halfway in the big square box, drinking seal oil. Magpie pushed Raven in and pushed the top on it and tied the top down. The other birds left as soon as Magpie went in.

When they were gone. Magpie told the Raven he was going to pack him up on the mountain. "I'm going to pack you up on the mountain and throw you down." So Magpie started to pack him. It was heavy. Raven began to sing. "You'll feel sorry when you see the fog halfway down the mountain. You'll think of me."

idagaleh iyaa qa'l'k'a't iti'aana'q' gadaq'ayiiny
you'll feel you sorry mountain on fog
innaa'x li yax igada'ahdaax
on-the-side hanging-halfway-down

But Magpie threw him down anyway. Magpie went home. Some time afterwards the clouds happened to be halfway down the mountain when Magpie got up, so he thought of what Raven said. He started to look for Raven and began to cry. When he found the box, the Raven was lying there, Just the bones left. Raven lifted his head up. "Didn't I tell you, you were going to be sorry?"

Where Raven Went into a Whale
Galushia Nelson

Once Raven was out in the ocean, hunting fish. He saw a whale which he went after. Every time whale came up. Raven would be over it, waiting for a chance to go in through the blow hole of the whale, which he finally did. When he got inside the

whale, he made a fire and start to roast all fat inside whale. After he roast all the fat, he cut off the heart and roast it too, so the whale died and float to beach where some of the beachcombers were and found it. [19]

When they came to the dead whale, they heard someone singing inside, which was, "I wish someone would cut it open right over me!" And one of them happen to cut it open over him and old Raven flew out and said, "qa qa" and away he went.

Where Old Raven Pitched the Seals Eyes Together
Galushia Nelson

Once a Crow or Raven had an army of warriors of light animals and birds. When they were on their way to war, they stopped on a seal bar where there was lots of seals. As they landed, these animals and birds jump out and act as if they were light as a feather and the seals want to know how they could be so light and they want to be as light as Crow's or Raven's warriors.

So Raven told the seals he took all the birds' and animals' intestines out as they want to be light. The Raven asked the seals if they want him to remove their intestines, but the seals want to know how it was done and Raven told the seals that he had to stick their eyes together with pitch.

So seals want their stomachs and intestines removed. And old Raven was glad and started to pitch the seals eyes together, but he did not have enough pitch for the last seal. But the Raven started to remove their stomachs Just the same, until he came to the last one without pitch in its eyes. It Jumped up and ran away. The Raven and his warriors, which was animals and small birds, had a feast on the rest of the seals. [20]

I Am Light
(Raven Kills His Partner)
Galushia Nelson

Raven and his partner (some fat animal), went for a walk. They came to a deep ravine. Raven put a piece of dry wild celery across the ravine and covered it with moss so it looked like a big log. He hopped out on it sideways. He sang, "I am light. I wish the others were as light as I am." He called to his partner, "Come on. See? It's all right!" His partner was scared but he finally came out when the Raven kept calling to him. When he got halfway out, the celery broke and he fell to the bottom and was killed. Raven went down and cooked and ate him. He had another big feast. When he got back, the people asked, "Where's your partner?" "Oh, he fell in the river."

Raven Pretends to Use His Body as Bait
Galushia Nelson

Raven was living with the other birds. They went out fishing with lines for halibut. Raven used a red sweet-tasting clam for bait and caught lots of fish. He had his bait under his seat and wouldn't let the others see it. The others couldn't get a single bite.

They asked Raven, "What are you fishing with?" "I cut a piece of muscle from my leg where the blood veins run and make it red." The other tried it and bled to death. Raven ate them up. When he got home, the people asked, "Where is your partner?" "Oh, he's still fishing."

The next day someone else went with him and the same thing happened. Whenever he lost his bait and put new bait on his hook, he would hold a clam down by his leg and pretend to cut his leg, hollering with pain. [21]

Raven and Porcupine
Galushia Nelson

Raven fooled around the Porcupine and Porcupine hit him with his tail. Raven got quills. To get even with Porcupine he took some of his feathers and tied it into a tree (to simulate a tree). Porcupine was going to an island on the feather log. When he got on the island. Raven took his feathers away, and the Porcupine couldn't get off. The Porcupine was singing because he couldn't get away. Finally it got cold, the water started to freeze, and at last the ice was thick enough for Porcupine to cross to mainland. (Galushia explains, if you laugh at Porcupine it will bring cold weather and the north wind will blow.)

Finally it got cold

Raven Raises an Army in the Sky
Galushia Nelson

Raven went to the sky. He raised an army there and lowered them on a rope. They thought the trees below were men with spears pointing up and were afraid to come down. [22]

Raven Journeys to the End of the Earth
Galushia Nelson

Raven once went to the edge of the world. There is a hole there where the tide rushes in and out. Raven got too close and fell in.

Porcupine and Beaver in Partnership
Galushia Nelson

Porcupine and Beaver were partners (*si'la'xan na*). Porcupine was like a Beaver and lived in the water but he had quills even then. Once when he was traveling on the ice. Porcupine fell through the ice and couldn't get out. Beaver chewed a hole through the ice and came up under Porcupine and packed him back on the ice. They went ashore and built a fire. Porcupine started to dry himself. Beaver sat down beside Porcupine, who didn't hear him come and he touched Porcupine and kind of scratched him. Porcupine hit him with his tail and got him full of quills. Beaver got mad and beat him up. Porcupine got mad then and left and went on dry land to live by himself. Beaver went back to his place. They lived apart for a while.
Later they met again and were good friends. They were getting water supplies, cutting brush, when Porcupine hit Beaver again with his tail. Beaver got mad and threw all their cutting tools away. Porcupine got mad and said, "Now all you can use for tools is your teeth." Beaver answered, "Well, you're going to be so you use only your teeth, too. You'll live any place, under rocks and under roots. You won't make a house like I will." Porcupine said, "I won't have a hard time like you in the water, though. The only time you ever get out in open water is when it's warm." Beaver said, "They (the hunters) will find you quicker than they will me. Go away! Beat it!" Porcupine went on his way. [23]

porcupine has to climb tree

Porcupine and Beaver
Galushia Nelson

Porcupine is a bad friend of Beaver. Beaver takes trees away from Porcupine. Beaver can chop tree down, but Porcupine 1 to climb tree to get his food. Beaver can build a house, but Porcupine has to look around for a crack in the rocks or a place under a stump. Beaver can work for himself, can trim limbs trees for winter. Porky can't. That's why they are bad friends (This is a Copper River story.)

Wolverine and Fox Were Cousins
Galushia Nelson

Once Wolverine chose Fox for his cousin. He got him to live and hunt around with him. Fox was very willing because Wolverine would kill anything, he was a good hunter.

They went hunting and found a cache and Wolverine got up and threw down a goat stomach. Fox said, "Throw them all down and I'll pack them home." But Wolverine said, "There's nothing up here, only that goat stomach." He stayed up there for quite a while. Fox said, "What arc you doing up there all this time? If there's anything up there, throw it down and we'll pack it home. Somebody will catch us." Wolverine answered, "There's nothing here but the blood from that stomach. I'm scratching it up." Then Fox replied, "I didn't hear anything but those wild canaries in the trees." [24]

Fox said, "I told you to hurry

Fox saw the people coming and told Wolverine, "Here they come!" He grabbed the goat stomach and ran away. Wolverine yelled, "Wait for me!" Fox said, "I told you to hurry and now I won't wait." Woverine jumped down from the platform. He had eaten so much that he burst open.

Wolverine Man
Galushia Nelson

Wolverine Man was a good hunter, hunting goats all the time. Although he killed lots of game and brought it home, he only ate after he killed something. When he chased goats and got tired he said to himself, "Hurry up. What's making you tired?" He picked up rocks and put them under his shirt. When he ran on the side of a hill he moved the rocks under his shirt around to the side towards the hill.

Another time when he chased some goats, he ran so fast that he got so far he couldn't get back, couldn't get no place from there. While he was stuck there, hanging by one hand from high place, it got dark. The biggest goat came down backwards to him. He got a hold of the goat by the tail. The goat started to pull him up and then he asked, "Are you going to kill us like you used to?" "No," said Wolverine Man, Goat kept asking, "Are you going to kill us and leave us [25] without using us? What do you use us for?" "No". Then the goat pulled him out.

But Wolverine Man did the same thing when he got out. He happened to kill the one who saved him. While he was packing the goat home he fell over a cliff and the goat and Wolverine Man smashed to pieces.

Taken by the Fish People
Galushia Nelson

It was winter and the people were eating dried fish. *he was stuck there, hanging by one hand* Somebody gave a boy a moldy one. He wouldn't eat it but threw it outside, kicked it and threw it in the river. He did that all winter, throwing away moldy fish.

In summer, when the fish were running, he went to spear some fish and he got lost and never came back. They looked for him around the fish creek but couldn't find him. They thought he had drowned. They couldn't find him for over a year.

Next year they were fishing with a dipnet. They got one that made a funny noise. An old man said, "Don't touch it but put him in some feathers and put him on the drying platform above the fire." When the fish started to get warm, he sang, "I turned into a fish' I turned into a fish!"

te'ya' (...) siłe'ł
fish I-turned-into

When [26] he finished, the old man said, "Take him down." The boy had a mother and father there. When they took him down he turned into a human being again. He told his parents and the other people, "When you people get fish and clean them don't leave the blood laying there. Throw the blood and guts in the lake or river."

All the people did what he told them. In the fall the boy told his father to make him shavings and a fish rack and spear. He told him, "Bring these things down to the beach for me. Give me a small box of oil. We're ready to go out again." When they got to the beach, the boy put them in the water. He told his father, "We're going now. If nothing happens to me, you'll see me next year when the fish start to run again." He went in the water and left.

While he was away with the fish people, something happened that he didn't like. He got mad and wouldn't say anything. The Fish Chief told his people, "Go take him to the Creek-Where-We-Feel-Better (*k'udagalehdzuu aa*h)." When they got near the creek, the boy started to laugh again. After that, when the fish started to run next year again, the boy got up the wrong river and a woman cut off his head.

He turned into a groundhog

Turned into a Groundhog
Galushia Nelson

There was once a man out trapping with deadfalls. He was having bad luck. He got nothing at all. He couldn't catch anything. He trapped for a long time. Finally an old woman came to him. The old woman told him, "You know why you are having bad luck?" "No." "You lay in bed while these young ladies get up before you. You eat, too, while your women are combing their hair. You are in the house when the sick women come back in from outside. You go take a bath in devilclubs. Rub the devilclubs on yourself."

He did that. The old lady had a cane. She laid her cane on his back. He threw up nothing but women's hair. She told him, "Tomorrow all your deadfalls will have something in them." He went out next day. All his deadfalls held some kind of animal. He brought them home and skinned them. He had the same kind of luck every day. The woman told him, "Later [27] on you are going to catch a pretty white animal in your last deadfall on your trap line. Don't take it home. Take it out and let it go."

The man caught a lot of animals and then in his last deadfall he caught a white animal, a pretty animal. He took it anyway and started home. He had a big load. He put it on top of his pack. On the way home, the animal kept falling off every little while. Finally, it started to run away. He put his pack on the ground and chased this animal. When he was chasing it, just when the animal was going in its hole, he grabbed it by the end of its tail and pulled off the end of the tail.

He sat down and felt sorry. Towards evening a woman came out of the hole. He still had a piece of tail. The woman said, "Give me my sister's hair band." The man said, "No. You send your sister out." "No, she's not going to come out." The man still wanted to see the woman. Finally she came out. She was a pretty woman. She wanted that hair band back again. The man wouldn't give it back, he wanted to go inside with her. She said, "No." The man said, "I'll give you your hair band back if you'll let me go inside with you." "No," she said, and started inside. The man followed her in anyway. He turned into a groundhog.

Living with the Black Bear
Galushia Nelson

ts' iyuhqa'l waxiit' inhinh
black bear-among living

There was woman out picking berries. She had on a ground squirrel skin shirt. This young woman was married. They were out berry-picking. She stepped on bear dung. Bear been eating berries. She got mad and called the bear all sorts of names. "Big nose, big feet, big face!" They kept picking berries after that. Towards evening all started home. On the way home the handle of her basket was breaking every little ways and spill her berries. It happened quite a few times. When the last one passed her, she told the women, "Send my husband to meet me right away." [28]

While she was on her way her husband met her. It was a bear who pretended to be her husband. This man started off with her. It was dark already. Finally she caught on that they were going the wrong way and she started to pull the squirrel tails from her shirt, one at a time and left them tied to the bushes every little way. When she used them all up, she started to break off the tops of the bushes as she passed. They got above the bushes into the grass. She could leave no more signs for her brothers to follow. Finally they came to the bear's den.

28

bear pretends as husband

110

When they missed the woman, her real husband looked for her. The found the squirrel tails and followed them, but they couldn't find her. They lost the trail amongst the grass. She was gone till next spring. She lived there with the bear, just like man and wife. She got away while the bear was out eating. When she got home she used to point where the bears' dens were to her people. She could see the smoke from their holes. Brown bears and grizzly bears make a different kind of smoke from the black bears. Some say it's a true story. [29]

Brown Bear People
Galushia Nelson

lixahwalahyuu
brown bear people

There was a bear who was married. He had an old father-in-law. They were hunting around creeks after fish. When they caught fish the young bear gave his father-in-law the worst fish and kept the best fish. There were two human brothers who watched it from far off. They watched several times.

Once when the bears were going home with fish, the old bear was taking a rest. The young men came up to the old bear. Young men asked him, "Is that the way he treat you all the time?" "Yes, that's the way he treats me all the time."
The young bear had two faces (two heads). The bears went fishing again, and the young men watched them. When the old bear was resting, the young men asked him the same question.   "Is that the way he treat you all the time?" "Yes, that's the way he treats me all the time." The young men asked, "Where is the young bear's heart?" "Between his eyes," the old man said.
While he rested, the two brothers got good fish and gave them to the older bear. The two young men asked him what time they came to get fish. "Just evening?" Old Bear said,
[30] "Early in the morning and in the evening."

the two brothers got good fish for the older bear

When the bears came back, the two brothers killed the young bear and skinned it and put the skin over themselves. Got a load of fish and took it home. Old bear didn't take anything home because the brothers took it all home for him. The bear's wife got suspicious that it wasn't her husband that came home with her father. She got mad. She talked loud. Her father said, "Leave him alone. He done good for me".

The she-bear went in her room. She stayed in her room until her father called her out again. Then they were living there as her husbands. After they were living with the bears over a year, in spring when the bears were coming out, the younger brother went out and was killed by two other bears. The female bear told her other husband, "Your brother is killed by two other bears by the creek." The man and father-in-law went to look for her brother. When they found his body they took him home. They made eight rings out of devilclubs and another plant (*tcvkck*) and cover him with them, and brought him back to life.

This plant is rare. It is like skunk cabbage, the wrinkled leaves grow in radiating groups at intervals along the stalk. It has green flowers which turn black when it goes to seed. The natives use the roots for medicine.

Porpoise People
(Blackfish People)
Galushia Nelson

qe 'xuuti 'walahyuu
porpoise people

Once a woman bring a porpoise head in her room and make believe it was human. She had this head in a box. When she goes into her room in evening to go to bed, she talks to this head as if she was talking to a human being, and others asked her who she was talking to. She always say, "To nobody." She goes out to pick berries for her and this head and put the berries in the box the head was in. And it becomes a human being in evening.

At one time while she was out picking berries again, some of the people take a look and saw a head of a big porpoise. [31] They find the highest place by the ocean to throw this in the ocean. When she come home from berry picking, she saw that the berries was still on the box and she came out of her room. The other people asked her why she had the head of a porpoise in her room. She did not answer but asked what they did with it.

They said they throw it in the ocean. "What is it good for?" She wants to know where, but they won't tell her. But she went and look for it, and she find the place to where she could go under the ocean to look for the head. She find the Mussel People and asked them if they saw anybody. They said to her, "Just before you came there was a Chief's son pass."

So she went and came to Clam People and asked them if they saw anybody. They also answered that the Chiefs son passed a little before she came. So she went on again and asked same question to the Butter Clam People, then the Razor Clam People, who told chiefs son was next to them, not very far off. So she went there and find him, sitting head of the house. As soon as Chiefs son saw the woman, he stood up to her and told his father not to say anything to her as he had lived with her for a long time. Then he said to her, "I don't believe you would follow me here." And the woman answered, "How couldn't I follow you as I brought you to my room myself." They lived there forever. [32]

she talks to this head as if she was talking to a human being,

Blackfish People
Galushia Nelson

qe' xuuti' walahyuu
blackfish people

They had landed, had a fire

Once there were some people going out hunting. While they were on their way, coming around a point, the first canoe in the hunting party saw a lot of people. They had landed, had a fire, there were lots of boats. The first canoe, before others see him, back-paddled, turned back and told the others, "There's lot of men over there at the point."

The men who back-paddled thought they were coming to make war on them. They land where they start from. They chose one man to go through the woods and come up behind the party they saw to find out whether they were acting warlike. The man came back from spying on the people. He told his people, "I don't think they come to make war on us. They have a lot of seals roasting around the fire. They are happy. They don't act like they were going to make war." So they all went over there with their canoes.

The Blackfish People, they thought this hunting party were coming to make war on them. So they grabbed their seals, some half cooked, and some cooked, and threw them in their canoes and went off. Instead of boat going as it should go, their boats went under water. They come up some distance off shore. So the hunting party talked to them. "We were afraid of you, too, when we saw you when you came around this point."

So they came back to land when they heard that. They landed where they had a fire and the hunting party helped them roast the seals. After they got through eating, they had a shooting match with bow and arrow. The Blackfish People didn't have bow and arrow but they used the hunting party's. They bet each other whatever they got. The Whale People had the hunting party beat. [33]

He Came Back to Shore Together with the Seal People
Galushia Nelson

geettaakwalahyuu uti' qi'yaq'sdiqehtinh
seal people together towards returned-he with shore (by water)

There was once a man who killed more seals than anybody else. Wherever he went he always killed a seal. One time he went out hunting, he ripped over all of a sudden for no reason. One seal came and got him when he went underwater and brought him to where the seals came from. So he lived among the seals under the water.

At one time, the Seal People's chiefs son got speared between the shoulder blades. He got away with the spear point. The Seal People asked the man if he knew anything about it. The oldest Seal Man pushed the man from behind. "Do you know anything about it?" The man said, "Maybe. Wait a while."

The old Seal went out with the man and told him, "Don't help him until they promise to bring you back to your old [34] home, if you know anything about it." So when he came back inside they asked him again, "Do you know anything about it?" The man said, "I know. If you people take me home, I'll help him."

A devilfish is chasing" us

The Seal People thought the wound was a boil. They said, "If you help him, we'll take you home." So he went over to the chiefs son and looked. There was a big spear sticking on his shoulder blade. He hid it and didn't show it.

The chief said to his people, "The fastest underwater swimmer, take this man home."

Before he started to swim with the man, he told him, "Put your head against me as close as you can. If I go fast with you, you'll smother if you don't do as I say." The Seal told him, "I'm going to come up three times. Remember that."

When they started to swim, in one place, he went the fastest he ever went. The Seal Man told him, "They are almost up to us." The man asked, "What is it?" "A devilfish is chasing us." The man told the Seal, "Slow down. Let him catch up with us." So he slowed down and the devilfish caught up to him. The devilfish put all his tentacles around the seal's head. The man used the spear point and broke the devilfish's bag of blueish stuff and the devilfish died. The Seal told the man, "We like this devilfish, but this devilfish kill us. We don't get saved from this devilfish."

Before they started again, the Seal ate up the devilfish. Then they started on again. The Seal said, "I am going to come up now. I hear somebody rowing. The last time I come up, if he should spear me, make a noise."

When he came up the last time, somebody speared the seal, and the man made a noise as he was told. The man who speared the seal asked the seal when he heard the noise, "Are you a man?" He said, "Yes. Let's hurry to shore." The man towed the man and the seal ashore. When they came ashore they dragged up the seal, and the man told the others, "This seal was sent with me to take me home. Don't touch it. Don't do anything to it." [35]

Boy Turning into a Loon
Galushia Nelson

Once there was people living in Sheep Bay. They used to spear fish in a lake near by. Sometimes when they speared a fish it would get away and they would never find the fish or the spear again. They wondered why because the lake had no outlet.

The boy was born in one family. They started to train him to hold his breath a long time, fed him seals and big loons, animals that dive a lot. They got a big loon and skinned and dried it. When the baby was born they put him in the skin and feed him meat of animals that stay long under water.

When he got grown up and when the fish ran, he went to the lake with a fishing party. He went in the water and they never saw him again. In the evening when they started home they landed near Anderson Island in Sheep Bay. They heard something hollering out in the water. He hollered every rime he came up. He went back towards the lake and kept hollering. They heard him again in the lake and went back to look for him.

They found the loon. They went back home with the boy-loon. He told them there was an underground channel to the lake. Then he turned back into a loon and went back. That's why people never bother the loon. [36]   *he turned back into a loon*

Where a Man Killed Lots of Land Otters
Galushia Nelson

daxunh qi' gatatsitt' iinsal'ahtinh
man where land-otter killed-lots-he

Once a man went hunting. His canoe tipped over with him. He saved only himself and one stone axe. He landed on the shore. He had no way of making a fire and it was cold. In the evening some of his relatives came and landed. When they came they said, "enya" (an expression of sympathy). The man jumped up and got mad at them. He knew they weren't his own people. They were Land Otters disguised as people. He said, "You people here already? You're not going to fool me." He grabbed his axe and chased them away.

Next morning at daylight he found some dry punk and made a fire-drill and started a fire. He started to build a house. His axe wasn't good enough to build a canoe and he was a long way from home. He was making a canoe at the same time. Every once in a while the Land-Otter People came disguised as his relatives.

After he built his house they came again. He had some pitch hanging up above the fire, drying. When everything was finished, some of these people came again. He called them in the house. He pretended that he was fooled, that he believed them. He was going to kill them. When he called the Land-Otter People up, he stayed behind on the beach and bite the edge of their canoe. It quivers. So he knew that wood wouldn't quiver.

He had dug out a urine tub before. He was saving his urine. He put it in front of them. "Wash your hands," he told them. The animals just dipped the rips of their fingers in and turn their heads away. Then he knew they weren't real human beings, got their paddles and put them above the fire inside the house. Then he put pitch on the fire. It made black smoke. The paddles got limber and turned into dead minks, (Land-Otters use live minks for paddles. Their canoes are live skates.)

Then the man killed the Land-Otter People, and they turned back into Land-Otters. He skinned them, and he cut their canoe up and dried it. He kept doing that till he built his [37] canoe. Finally his own people came. He had been gone a long time. He still didn't believe they were his own people even when they washed their hands. He put their paddles over the fire and put pitch in it. They cracked and popped in (he heat and started to burn. Their canoe didn't quiver, either, when he bit it. His house was full of land-otters and mink skins. They took him home and all his furs. He was so rich he got to be chief of the tribe.

He put their paddles over the fire

This story is supposed to be true. That's how they found out that the Land-Otters get people when they drown.

The Big Mouse [38]
Galushia Nelson

ƚuundiyahsluw
big mouse

Big mouse living under a cliff. He come out every time someone pass in a canoe. Kill them and eat them. He killed several people like that. There was one old man taking three women to pick berries. Old man knew the mouse's song. If you knew it, he wouldn't bother you. Sing it when passing. Old man was singing. The youngest women said, "I wish we see this mouse." Old man said, "Don't! What you say that for?"

Just a few minutes later, the water turned red under the cliff and spread out to the canoe. The old man was still singing the mouse's song. Mouse come out backwards halfway out. He put his tail out of water and dropped it on the canoe. The old man, when he dropped his tail, jumped on the mouse's tail. He hang onto the tail. The women were all killed.

Mouse went back under the cliff with the old man. He was saved. The mouse came into a big room under the cliff. The man went to the other side of the cave from the mouse. The man sang the mouse's song so the mouse didn't bother him. He got some feed for the man. The mouse only went hunting at time of no moon, when it's dark. When the mouse goes hunting, there was a root of a tree sticking down from the roof of the cave, he (the man) tried the strength of the root. Later he climbed to the roof. The mouse had a hole clear to the top of the ground where he stuck his tail out. Man climbed clear out but came down before mouse came back from hunting and sat down where he was before. When mouse comes back sometimes he brings back seal or halibut. He puts it under himself to cook them. When it gets cooked, he brings it out and give it to man. The man eats it.

At one time the mouse went out towards morning. The mouse was supposed to be home before the raven started to make noise. When the mouse left, the man climbed the roof and got out. Before he got very far, the mouse came back. The mouse was making all kinds of noise in the cave because he missed the man. He stuck his tail out of the hole and swung it around. The man got home.

At full moon the mouse sleeps sound. When old man got home he told the young man to try to snare a crow. If they snare a crow in full moon time they're going back to mouse's den. "Sharpen all that you use for your old knives, and sharpen all that you use for your old axe," the old man said. [39]

The old man sneaked up on him .

When they caught the raven they have all knives and axes sharp. They go to where mouse sticks out his tail. Mouse had his tail sticking out the hole when he's sleeping. (Tail was like a watchman.) The old man sneaked up on him with an axe. He chopped the mouse's tail twice before he cut it off. The mouse pulled the rest of his tail down.

The young man said, "Throw the crow down that hole!" So the crow started to make all kinds of noise down there. The mouse started to go under the cliff. He got halfway out before he died. After the mouse died, the old man went down on

116

the root and looked at the mouse. When he found the mouse was dead, he came back up and told the other man. This young man would like to see it, so they went down and looked at it. When they came out, the mouse turned into a rock. The crow came back out of the hole, too.

The hunter must rise before the crow makes a noise in the morning, or he will not get any game. All the animals are up before the crow. If the crow gets up before an animal does, the animal will die. [40]

Giant Animals
Galushia Nelson

A devilfish was supposed to live in the deep hole outside of North Island in Cordova Bay. It would grab canoes if they came too close at night. When it came up, water would get so slimy that the canoe could not paddle away. The water was so deep there that a fish line could not reach the bottom. The tentacles of the devilfish were always sticking out of the water. The Natives were afraid to go on the outer side of the island, even as recently as Galushia's boyhood. Some times people might escape from the devilfish by making a noise like a crow. The devilfish was finally driven away when the boiler from a stern-wheel fishing boat was thrown in the water.

A giant bear used to live in a lake near Martin River. There is a little slough running out of the lake that was made by the bear when he left. The name of the slough indicates that it was made in this way.

A giant beaver used to live near a glacier near Mile forty-nine, on the Copper River Railway. He had a big dam. You could see the water coming over it. He left.

There was a giant bear that lived in a lake near Gravina Bay. He was supposed to be growing bigger all the time. People were afraid to go there. They might make the bear mad. He would shake and make the earth quake.

These monsters were called *et'stll'yatl*. They always lived in the ground or under water. They were all bad and ate people.

Alder People and Sun People
Galushia Nelson

Once there was a war between the Alder People and some other people. The Alder People killed off all but a woman and her daughter. Afterwards the woman and her daughter stayed outside and cried all the time. "I wish someone would come around and marry my daughter!"

She cried there for a long time until a Frog came and asked, "What about me?" The woman asked him, "How you going to get revenge for my brothers who were killed?" The Frog said, "Every time when I jump from under a man's feet, I [41] think I done something great." But the woman thought that wasn't enough.

"What about me?" The next was a little bird. The woman asked, "What could you do?" "When I scratch up the ground I think I done something great." But the woman didn't think much of that either.

Then came a Snipe. "What about me?" "What could you do?" "When I jump around the edge of the fiver I think I done something great." But that wasn't enough.

The Blue Jay came next. "What could you do?" "When I pick up all the salmon eggs around the beaches I think I done something great." But that was not enough.

Then Magpie came. "What about me?" The woman asked him, "What could you do?" "When I find something that is hidden away, I think I done something great." But she did not think that was enough.

Then Robin came. "What about me?" "What could you do?" "When I pick those red (elder?) berries, I think I done something great." But that wasn't enough.

The Kingfisher said, "What about me?" "What could you do?" "When I catch those little fish I think I done something great." But the women didn't think much of that.

Then came the Goose. "What about me?" The women asked him, "What could you do?" "When I fly over seven bays without rest I think I did something great." But that was not enough.

The Fox came next. "What about me?" "What could you do?" The Fox said, "When I traveled around the world in the night I think I done something great."

The Brown Bear came. "What about me?" "What could you do?" "When I start to get mad and start to run after something and tear up all the earth and break everything, then I think I done something great." The woman thought a long time before she refused the Brown Bear.

Then came the Black Bear. "What could you do?" "When I slap anything and make it fly away from me I think I done something great." But the woman refused him, too.

The Wolverine asked, "What about me?" "What could you do?" "When I find a cache and rob it, I think I done something great." But that wasn't enough.

The Goat came. "What about me?" "What could you do?" "When I climb the steepest hill, I think I done something great." But he was refused. At last came the Sun Man. He had a cane. The woman asked, "What could you do?" "When I start to make these rivers boil and heat it all the way down the mountain. I think I done something great." [42] The old lady said, "Show us how you make this water boil and heat up the mountains."

The Sun Man gave the woman his cane and said, "In case I start a fire and the fire comes towards you, put this cane over the top and the fire will stop."

He left them and crossed the river and the rivers boiled. It started a fire. When the fire started to reach the woman, she raised the cane over it and put the fire out. The woman thought it was great and gave her daughter to him.

The Sun Man went home with the girl up in the sky. The woman told the Sun Man before he left that her people were all killed by the Alder People and that she wanted revenge. The Sun didn't say anything, but went home. The Sun Man had eight boys by this girl. The eight boys didn't have no sister. Their mother said, "When are they going to be old enough to take revenge on the Alders?"

The Sun packed half a basket of water. He dipped the boys in it and threw them above the door. When they fell on the floor they were full grown. Then the mother said, "Are they going to be without a sister all the time?"

The man took out his bow and cut off the end, where the string is tied. He dipped it in the water and threw it above the door. When it came down it was a girl. They called her *Djtmite'ki'*, "talkative." The youngest son was .....?..... He was the boss of his brothers.

The Sun's wife made a basket around her husband's thumb. When it was finished they took it off and blew in it, and it became big. They tied a rope made of roots to it. He put the oldest boy in the basket and sent him down to earth. When he got too far he saw the trees sticking up. The father had told the boy to shake the rope when he wanted to come up. He did so. The father asked, "What's the matter?" "Someone sticking spear up under me." That was the trees.

The father said, "Maybe not a spear." So he sent the next oldest down. All the others was sent down, one at a time, but they all had the same story about spears. Then the girl was sent down last, and she found out it wasn't spears (because she was made of wood). When she came back, they sent all the boys and the girl down at once in the basket. The father gave them all his tools, spears, bows and war clubs. He gave the oldest a branch, like a blueberry branch. If one got killed he was to hit him with the branch and he would come alive again.

When they landed it got foggy. Their father made it foggy. They started to build a fort. The other people couldn't see them but they heard them building a fort. But they couldn't see them. The chief of the Alders heard them and said, [43] "What's that making a noise? I don't like it. I'm suspicious." The Alder People said, "That's only some birds making a noise." The chief kept repeating his question. But the Alders said, "Maybe it's just the ghosts of the other people we killed off."

When they got the fort finished, the clouds drifted away and were gone. The Alder People were surprised when they saw the fort and prepared to attack it. The Alders attacked the Sun People. Seven of the Sun People went outside the fort to meet them. Just the youngest and the girl were inside. When they were fighting, the Sun People killed about half the Alder People, but none of the Sun People were killed yet. The youngest wanted to holler for the father, but the others wouldn't let him. His sister begged him not to call his father. The sister went outside and talk so much that the Alders' war canoe tipped over. The youngest boy started to rush down to meet the Alders, He ran halfway down and then ran back to his brothers. He made a bluff of attacking the enemy alone. When the woman and the youngest boy started to talk, and the youngest went inside again finally, they found that about half the Sun People got killed. The youngest wanted to call for help to his father again. The sister was scared and let her brother call for help. They did not give the oldest a chance to use his branch. The brothers didn't know he hollered. The oldest used his branch afterwards and made the others come to life.

The father heard the call for help and started to make the river (ocean) boil and that killed all the warriors in the canoes and those on land were killed by the heat. Alder were all killed off, the Sun People stayed there and hunted together.

In the evening, when the sun hit a cloud and it was pretty, the youngest said, "I wish we could kill that color animal." The oldest always tried to stop him from saying that kind of remarks. When the youngest said that next time, he found an animal colored like a cloud. He chased it and kept chasing it, and finally chased it into the sky. All the brothers went back to the sky. (The "blisters" on the alder bark are supposed to be wounds made by the Sun People.) [44]

Calm Weather's Daughter (diiyeextsii)
Galushia Nelson

There was a man and his wife. She was always getting mad at her husband. Every time she gets mad, she says, "Get out of here. Get out of the house!" She tells him, "Go marry the daughter of the Calm Weather." Finally the man got tired and left her.

He kept going until she saw smoke from another house. When he came to the house, he hang around outside for a while. There were two women living there. When they heard him outside, they said, "If you arc a human being, come inside." He stayed overnight.

Same evening they asked him, "What are you doing here?" The Man told them that his wife chased him out and told him to marry the Calm Weather's daughter. Next morning before daylight they woke him up and told him to take a bath in devilclub water. He stayed around all day. The second day they told him to get up early and go. They put up a lunch for him. They told him to look for a pretty bird that will fly ahead of him, to follow bird wherever he flies. So he did.

He came to a slave who was chopping wood. He watched him from a distance. Slave broke the edge off his axe. He talked to himself about it. He was sorry. "I guess I will get a good licking for this." The man took pity on the slave. He went up to him and asked the slave if he knew where Calm Weather's daughter lives. Slave said, "What you want to know for?" The man told him, "If you tell me, I'll fix this axe for you again."

The slave told him he was the slave of the Calm Weather. So the man knew where they lived. The man fixed his axe. The old slave was glad and told him, "There are two sisters living close by their father's house." The man told the slave, "Don't tell that you saw anybody."

The slave went home with a load of wood. Although he never drop any wood before, he dropped a piece of the wood from under the bark. The slave didn't know that he had lost k. The man followed him and found the wood and took it along with him. Late in the evening, everyone was in bed, when he was ready to come in, he put the wood in front of him and slipped in behind it into the house. He happened to go into the youngest girl's room. The girl didn't say anything though she knew someone had come in her room. The oldest girl heard [45] the man and girl playing in the room but she didn't say anything either.

Next morning the man and girl stayed in her room. So the oldest girl went to her father's house. She didn't say anything, so her father asked, "Where is your sister?" She said, "I don't know. I heard her playing all night." Girl's father sent his slave over to find out who she was playing with. The slave came back and told his master, "She's laying down with a man."

The oldest girl ran back without saying anything. They tried to take the man away from the girl but she wouldn't let him go. The oldest girl had a dentalium shells on the hem of her skin. She bought the man from her sister with it. So they lived together. When the youngest lost some of the dentalium shells, she wanted the man back. But she couldn't get him.

The woman told her husband, "Lets row somewhere. I got a boat on the beach a little ways." The man went to look for the canoe but he could find only a razor-backed clam shell turned upside down on the beach. The man told his wife he couldn't find any boat but saw only a razor-back shell turned over,

She said, "That's the one. That's our boat. Turn it over and kick it on the smaller end." So he did and the shell turned into a big canoe. Then they were ready to go. The slave was taking things to the boat. The slave brought eight bundles of dried fish and four wooden boxes of seal oil. So they got in the boat and started to go.

This man told her he had a wife before. The new wife told him, "Don't say anything to your wife if it's true you had a hard time to come to our place." They got to the man's first home. They lived there. The second wife used to send her husband out for water. When the man came back with water, the second wife would dip a leaf in the water. The first wife used to follow the man and get water, too. The woman always spoke to him but the man never answered. Finally the man took pity on the new wife. "How will she know if I answer my first wife?"

The second wife was making a big basket. She never went outside. She kept on working at the basket. When the man came back after speaking to the first wife, the second wife dipped a leaf in the water and when she pulled it out, the leaf was shiny.

The second wife told her husband, "You better live with your first wife. I'm going home." The woman got all her things together and started home. The man followed her down to the beach. The woman never stopped. He walked right on top the water after her. "Turn back," she said. "I'm going to look back at you if you don't turn back." The man kept [46] following her until they got close to the woman's home. Then she looked back at him. The man sunk then.

When the woman got home, her father asked her, "Where is your husband?" The woman said, "Around the point. I looked back at him and he sunk." The father said, "Why did you do that?" "I told him not to speak to his wife and he spoke to his first wife and he spoke to her. That's why."

The chief told his slave, "Hurry and look for this man!" The slave went to look for the man. He walked right under the ocean. The first the slave found was a big Bullhead under the water. "Let's see," (looking into the fish's mouth), "maybe you swallow this man." (He didn't see anything inside the fish.)

He saw a Shark, and asked him the same question, "Let's see, maybe you swallow this man." Then he found a Devilfish and asked him the same question. "Let's see. Maybe you swallow this man."

Then he found a Dog Fish and asked him the same question. He just looked in their mouths. The young shark or Dogfish happened to be the one that swallowed him. So the slave cut up the Dog Fish. He just find the man's bones in there. He picked up all the bones but couldn't find one of the knee caps. He went to take them home.

When the slave got home, the father put the bones together and tried to make them stand up, but the bones always fall down again. The chief tried to make them stand up several rimes, and then he found out that one of the kneecaps was missing, and sent the slave to look for it. The slave went but couldn't find it.

When the slave come home, he cut out the slave's kneecap to put on the man. He made the bones stand up and turn into a human being again. He told the oldest daughter not to stay with the man again, so the youngest one stayed with him. So the father gave slave to man. Before he gave the slave, he put a shell, called the "cockle's baby" in as a kneecap for the slave. They lived there then. [47]

Around-The-Lake-People (maaqudati 'a 'ah daxunhyuu)
Galushia Nelson

Dwarves as big as a thumb used to hunt and fish around the country. They were found around Strawberry Point (on Hinchinbrook Island, near Boswell Bay) at the small lake there. The little women row, the little men hunt and fish. A human captured a little man who had become tangled in some roots. The dwarf gave the man all his hunting outfit, spears and bow and arrows, to let him go. One spear with an agate point he hated to part with.

When he was turned loose he returned home, but his people had gone outside the breakers. He hollered for them to come back and get him. One of his relatives came through the breakers for him. They all started home in canoes and on the way they saw a mouse, which was a brown bear to them. They all landed to try to kill him.

The little man without hunting implements was killed by the bear for he had no way to defend himself. The other people killed the bear. The bear was cut up in small pieces and left there because he had killed one of their people.

They put the body of the dead in a canoe without examining it at all. His relatives took the body home. The wife ran down to meet her husband, she didn't know he was dead. The skin of his head had been pulled off. The wife and [48] children ran down to meet him. They were happy that their man was coming home.

The wife, when she saw her husband's head, tore a piece from the bottom of her skin and bandaged his head. They took the body and placed it in front of the left front house post. They left the body outside for eight days. On the eighth day they took the body inside.

Towards noon, the body began to move. Only the wife was there. Right at noon he moved more and more until he lifted his head. He sat up and scratched his head. He asked his wife what had happened and she told him that a bear had killed him. He asked what they had done with the bear. She said they had killed it, cut it in bits and left it there. He asked who had brought his body home.

He told his wife not to worry about him and left, taking two men with him. They went to Yakutatik. They were gone about a year. They came back at the time when the birds start to lay eggs. When the people saw them coming they were excited. Each man was coming in a separate canoe and all three were full of brown bear skins. When they landed the people lifted them up and carried them to the house. The man was made chief of the tribe. When he finished eating, he said to his wife: "I guess I got even with those bears."

He gave his eldest daughter to a man. She knew everything — all about making baskets and keeping house, she had already promised to marry another man, but had to obey her father and left the first man. The first man asked her husband to dig clams with him. They were digging as the tide was coming in. He made the husband stay on a sand spit. He drown there and they found the body. He turned into shrimp (sand-hopper).

The other man went home and told several different stories about what had happened. The drowned man's wife had a dream that the man had caused her husband to be drowned by the tide and in the dream her husband told her he had become a sand-hopper. People asked the man if that was true. He said yes. But they did nothing to him. That's all. (*daqaidaqaeu*)

These dwarfs had many different tribes around the lake, like the different tribes of Indians.) [49]

human captured a little man

Wolf People
Galushia Nelson

The Wolf People had been taking people from a village. They took quite a few away. Once a young girl was playing outside. Some old people smelled something. "Oh, there's something smell like a muskrat," chey said, "It's queer this muskrat smells in the fall."

They were suspicious. It was fall and muskrats smell only in the spring. While the girl was playing outside they called her but she would not come in,

A Wolf Man was back of the house in the brush. He was showing the girl different kinds of pretty birds. The girl went up to him, and he tied her up and put her among some feathers and packed her off. While he was packing her the little girl started to throw the feathers out one by one through a little hole in the bag. They went a long way. They came to a big lake. He hollered to his people. They got him with a canoe and brought him home.

... the girl was playing outside they called her but she would not come in.

The Wolf Man was a slave of the chief of the Wolf people. He put the bag with the girl in front of the chief. The chief looked in and only found a little girl in the bag. He said, [50] "How did you do this? What did you do this for? Didn't you take pity on this little girl?"

When he took the girl out, instead of killing her, he killed the slave who brought her home. Another slave cut up his body and they ate him. When they cooked the slave meat, they gave some to the little girl. She pushed it away and started to cry. After she didn't eat the meat the chief sent his sister after some goat meat. All she ate was goat meat and bear meat. She lived with them there.

She started to grow. She got old enough to pack water and to get up in the morning. The Wolf People thought the girl was just like themselves because she was growing up with them. Every morning before the others got up she packed water for the whole village. She tried to get on the good side of them so they wouldn't kill her. The chiefs sister told her to do things for everybody so they wouldn't kill her. She gave the girl a knife and told her while she was packing water early in the morning to put holes in all the Wolf People's canoes, except one small one the girl could handle alone. "These people go hunting early in the evening and come back in the morning," she told her.

One morning while she was packing water, the girl cut up all the boats. It was easy because the Wolf People had birchbark canoes. Then she started away in the small canoe she saved for herself. Before she got to the other side the Wolf People found out she had got away. They put their canoes in the water and Jumped in. Before they got far the boats sank. One boat with some men bailing and others paddling got clear across. It nearly caught her.

The girl landed and ran behind a little waterfall and hid there. A Wolf Man landed and tracked her to the falls and lost the track. He walked around and cried and sang a sad Wolf song. (Galushia and Annie Nelson had heard the words of this song but did not remember them.) The Wolf People gave up searching after a half a day. The girl followed the feathers home to her own people. [51]

Tree People
Galushia Nelson

There were people living together. In one family there were nine boys and one girl. They were hunters, always talking turns hunting. At one time the oldest went out hunting and he never returned from his hunting trip. He was caught in the Tree People's snare. The Tree People eat people. The snare opens and shuts all by itself all the time. Only time it don't move is when it got something. Next to oldest one looked for him and got into the same snare. It caught eight of the boys. Finally the youngest and the sister went out to look for their brothers.

When they were on their way, the boy was leading, the boy's head was almost in the snare. The girl saw it, grabbed her brother, pulled him back. "Didn't you see the snare?"

When they saw that snare they turned back. On their way back they picked up a rotten piece of wood. They made it in shape of a human being, put some of the boy's clothes on it. And they went back and threw it in the snare. They climbed a tree where the snare was set.

When the Tree Man saw he caught another man in the 5nare, he laughed. "Hehehehehe! You got one again?" He asked the snare. He built a fire before he started to eat the dummy. He started to cut it and found it was only rotten wood. After he found that out, he cut off a piece of muscle from his own lower leg and cooked that. After he got through eating it, he went home.

The boy and his sister trailed him home. They liked the man before he got home. Then they saw smoke and wanted to sneak up to the house. The house was made of the boughs of the tree. They looked in without the woman seeing them. They saw a foot sticking out of the woman's pot. They came into her bough house and sat across from this woman. She tried to feed them with their own brother's flesh. The boy and his sister shoved it aside. The woman tried them with another dish. She offered them hair.

"Try this seaweed." They shoved it aside. Woman got mad and threw her *wakck* (woman's knife) at the boy. He jumped and it went under the boy. He grabbed the knife and threw it back and cut the woman's head off. [52]

One-Eyed Frog
Galushia Nelson

Once there was an Invisible being that they sent for everything. If people wanted anything they would ask him to get it, wood or anything. He was called,

dik' gada'anhginh yax daku'txinh
not-seen-one-sent-for-something

Another village heard about this being. There was a shaman there who claimed he could find anything. If nobody else could find a thing, he could. They asked him if he could find this unseen messenger.

He said, "Maybe I can, I'll try. I'll try early tomorrow morning." He started out early next morning. He kept going and traveling until he came to a one-eyed Frog. When the Frog saw him, he asked, "What are you doing here so early in the morning?" "I am sent to find this unseen messenger. Do you know where he is?" The frog told him, "I do not know exactly where. There's another people live next place, Geese People, two Geese Women." "Is it very far?" The Frog said, "It's not so far, but you can't make it tonight."

He stayed overnight and started next morning. He found the Geese Women. They asked the man, "What you doing here?" "I'm sent to find this unseen messenger. Do you know where he lives?" They said, "He lives around the next point. You go over right away. You come to a house and go in it and call "Malshaa!" When you find Malshaa you come by here again."

He went over there. When he got in the house, he called "Malshaa". Someone answered without being seen. He said, "I'm sent for you. Could you go with me?" Malshaa asked, "Is it very far to where you are sent for me?" "No it's not very far. It took me three days to get here." Malshaa said, "I'll fix up my things. You wait for me at those two women's. I'll get my things ready before these people get home. You better go. If they find you, they'll eat you."

He went to the Geese Women. They said, "Did you find Malshaa?" "Yes." "Is he going with you all right?" "Yes." "If you aren't going right away you better eat with us," they told him.

While he was eating, Malshaa came over. He came just like any human being, he could be seen then. He told the shaman, "Let's stay overnight. It's too late to go now." They stayed overnight and started next morning. When they were on their way, they went around the first point and found a canoe. [53]

Malshaa said, "Let's take this boat. We'll get there quicker with this boat. The Shaman said, "No, they'll see us going." Malshaa said, "No they aren't going to see us" /*

They went in the canoe. The boat belonged to some people there. A boy was playing outside. He came in to his parents. "There's an old canoe over there. There is nobody in it, but the paddles are moving!"

They ran out. They didn't believe him but they ran out and saw nobody was in the boat and it was in motion. They got scared because the boat was in motion with nobody in it. The boat never acted that way before. They followed the boat along the shore and tried to find out what made it go. When they couldn't find out what made it go, they turned back.

The shaman got home with Malshaa. When he got there, the people came to meet him on the beach. "Did you find |lum?" they asked. "Yes, he's right here." They told him, *"Tell him* to get out of the boat and we'll bring the canoe up."

The shaman told Malshaa, "Malshaa, get out of the boat now. This is where they sent me for you." He got out and they went into the house. They went to the shaman's house. The shaman's wife had everything ready, things to eat. The shaman could see Malshaa but the others couldn't see him at all.

While they were eating, the shaman told Malshaa, "You will live here with us all the time." So he lived with them there in the village. When people brought fish to dry, all the fish started to get cleaned without anybody touching them. All the wood started to pile up around the house without anybody seeing anybody pile it. The fish hung themselves up. The fires were built. Malshaa was doing all the work. Malshaa died. After he died, everybody saw his body. He was nothing but i a little bit of a man. [54]

The Man and the Salmon Tail
Galushia Nelson

A man was walking along the river bank near Eyak. He heard someone call, "Save me!" (xuul la'!) He looked everywhere, but at first he saw no one. At last he saw a salmon tail on the

ground, full of maggots. He washed the
maggots off and put the tall back in the
water.

They had a hard time that winter.
One day he went to the river to get water.
He saw two fish tails sticking up out of
the ice. He pulled up the two fish by the
tails. This was a reward for being kind.
That is why people always put salmon tails back in the water.

He saw two fish tails sticking up

The Man Who Fed A Starving Animal
Galushia Nelson

A family were halibut fishing during the winter. They
were having no luck. An animal (like a gorilla, large, hairy,
without a tail, that travels in the woods) came out and cried
behind the camp. The man went out to ask what was the matter.

He said, "Come to my camp." The animal came and asked for
food. The man had only a little, but he gave what he could [55] spare.
The animal went away without thanking him. Next morning the people
found a pile of halibut in the camp. This happened for several days,
until they were able to catch fish again for themselves.

An animal (like a gorilla,

The Girl and the Dog
Galushia Nelson

There was a man and his wife. They had a daughter
who was always playing around with the dog. Her mother told
her, "Don't play around with that bitch. Leave her alone."

They were going to move to another place. When they
were ready to move, she was playing with the dog. So they left
her playing with it. Before they left they tied the girl's head and
the bitch's head together and left them like that.

They had a female slave, too. The slave said, "Wait a
while, I forgotten my *wakck* (woman's knife)." It was Just an
excuse to go back and cut the girl and dog apart. She told the
girl, "Don't show yourself. I'm going to get a licking if they
find I cut you loose."

Before they left they tied the girl's
head and bitch's head together

The slave went back to the boat and they left. The girl
was still crying. They went home to where they were before. After a year, the girl's mother told
the slave, "Go to our camp, and throw their bones out. Shovel them out."

So the slave went over there. The slave find the girl and the dog. They were still alive.
The house was almost full of things to eat. The dog was a good hunter. When the slave went
over there, they fed her and gave her all she want

to eat. She sneaked a piece of fat under her shirt for her son. The slave says, "I'm going home now. I'm staying too long. They're going to get me for it." The girl said, "If they come back with you, when they land, you run in first. We're not going to let my father and mother in."

The slave got home. The mother asked her, "Did you shovel the bones out?" The slave said, "Yes." That evening [56] when they went to bed, the slave went to bed with her son and gave the fat to her son. After the son ate up the fat, he started to cry for some more, and called for fat: "*k'uq'axdee!*"

The woman asked the slave, "What's wrong with your son? He never cried like that before." "I tried to feed him with the breast, but it slipped out of his mouth. That's why he cried."

The boy still kept crying. The woman asked the same question. The slave got mad, and said, "That daughter of yours that you tied to your dog got a house full of meat and gave me all I could eat. I hid a piece of fat for my son. After he ate it up he wants more."

"You want to get up early in the morning. We got to go there early in the morning. Try to stop your son from crying." So next morning they started before . When they land where the girl and dog were living, the slave grab her son, Jump out and run. The girl asked the slave, "Is that my mother and father?" The slave said, "Yes." The girl's mother started to run up, too. She and her father said, "My poor daughter! My poor daughter!" The girl pulled down a piece of fat that was hanging and threw it towards her father and mother, and said, "You didn't think I was your daughter when you tied me to a dog." She said to the fat, "Turn into a glacier!"

It did, between her and her mother and father. The glacier got long, and the father and mother made a bird noise, "Dak Dak." It sounded farther and farther away. [57]

A Tlingit War Story
Galushia Nelson

(This is a Tlingit war story, referring to Tlingit villages. Mrs. Scar Stevens, who is supposed to be of Tlinget descent, confirms this opinion.)

There were some people going to visit another village in canoes to have a good time. They had had a war with those other people long before. They had killed most of the people in the other village but thought they had forgotten about it by now.

They landed at a place for overnight. A raven started to eat their extra clothes in the evening. The oldest man said, "That's a bad sign. Let's go back." But another man had a brother-in-law in the other village and he wanted to visit him. They had married two sisters.

The old man said, "All right, we will," but he was kind of sore. When they were about halfway there in their canoes, the sky above them cracked and they saw their own shadows in the crack. The old man said, "This is a bad sign. Let's turn back." But the man who had a brother-in-law said, "I want to see my brother-in-law."

When they got there a man came to meet them where they landed. He was the brother-in-law. He had a blanket over his shoulders and a short spear under it. When his brother-in-law stepped from the canoe he just turned away from him without speaking and went back to the house.

The people went to another house. They started to dance next night. The man who had snubbed his brother-in-law wouldn't come. They sent a man after him. The messenger came back and said, "He's having a row with his wife," Instead of having a row with his wife he was sharpening all his war spears.

Finally he came as far as the door. He heard a song referring to his sons and daughters. He stopped then and almost changed his mind about killing those people. Then he thought to himself, "Maybe they'll think that I got scared."

When he came in there were two fellows dancing. He pulled out his spear and pushed them aside with his spear. He didn't mean to kill them but he pushed them apart so hard that they hit the two opposite walls and broke their heads and died.

He said, "Do you people think I forgot you killed my uncles?" His name was Qaduwina. He started to kill them off. Some fell down and pretended to be dead. They had done that [58] same trick before. Qaduwina said, "Do you think you can play that trick on me again?"

Even while they were down he ran his spear through them. One of them was under some others and he didn't get him. After Qaduwina left, he sneaked off. The blood was *Raven started to eat their extra clothes* halfway to a man's knees in the room.

The man that wasn't killed got a bundle of dried eulachon that was soaked in blood. On the way home he washed them off and ate them. He had nothing else.

Qaduwina had saved one woman for himself but his slave killed her without Qaduwina's knowledge. Before he killed her, the slave said, "Come on out. What's the use of hiding? What's the use of trying to save your life?" She had a daughter. She cut her daughter's head off and jumped out of the room.

Qaduwina' brother-in-law had a wife at home. When the man that wasn't killed got home, she asked him if her husband was killed, too. "Yes." She didn't believe him. "How is it gets daylight again then?" She finally believed it. "It's all right, too," she said. "My people were killed off by these people and we aren't even with them, yet." She was from Qaduwina's village.

They started to prepare for war again. It was the next generation. When they were on their way they met another people, another tribe. They mistook them for Qaduwina's tribe. After they killed about half of them they found their mistake. [59]

The Man Who Killed His Children
Galushia Nelson

Once there was a man and his wife living away from the others. This man won't let his children grow up. He kills them off as soon as they were born. Finally the woman got to think of a way to raise her children by digging in the ground and hiding her children there. When her husband returns from fishing she hide her children until they were old enough. Sometimes they would come out to play when their father was out fishing, and sometimes their father would hear them make a noise as there were twelve boys by now. When their father come in, they go in the ground again. When their father heard them make noise, he would come in and the boys would hide,

Their father would say: "Who's making that noise?" The mother said: "I throw some clam shells out. I guess that's what your heard." The next day father heard them and asked:

"Who's making the noise?" The mother answered: "Oh there were a lot of crows on the beach making a noise. Maybe that's what you heard."

there were a lot of crows on the beach

When they were old enough, the mother told that their father had killed all of their older brothers and sisters. So they killed their father.

The Man Who Left His Wife
Galushia Nelson

A man who wanted to leave his wife pretended to die. He told his wife to put him on the beach with his canoe and all his belongings on top of him. In a few days he disappeared. He went away to live with another women in a different village. His wife heard about it. She went to that village and killed them both.

(This is the bare skeleton of a story told also by the Prince William Sound Eskimo. The Chugach version serves to explain the formation of Middleton and why the brown bears on Montague Island are so fierce.) [60]

The Illegitimate Child
Galushia Nelson

A chief's daughter gave birth to a child, although she was unmarried. She killed the child and hid the baby behind the sloping board used for a pillow. Her younger sister discovered the dead baby and told the parents. The girl admitted what she had done and named the father of the baby.

Her brother told the man to get wood. They built a pyre for the baby. The girl asked her mother to fix her hair, so that she would not be mistaken for a slave. When they were burning the child, the girl jumped on the fire. Her lover pulled her off, and climbed on the pyre himself. She got on top of him, and they *They built a pyre*
 both burned with the baby.

There was a famine. There was very deep snow, so deep that they had to climb out of the house through the smoke hole. After the girl burned herself, the snow stopped. (This is supposed to be a true story.)

Good For Nothing
Galushia Nelson

Once there was one man who was good-for-nothing among rest of men who were preparing for war with other tribes. While young men and old men were in water to be strong, this good-for-nothing man would be in bed which he made by fireplace with few skins of animals. When someone have a fire going, his bedding would start to steam. The others were in water from daylight until they see smoke coming out of house. They start [61] come out of water one by one and try to pull a part

of limb on old partly rotting tree to see who was strongest, and when they come back to house, each would move this good-for-nothing with their feet and making some remarks about him.
one by one and try to pull a part of limb
They thought this man was too lazy to go out doors to urinate.

This man who was good-for-nothing heard about others trying to pull a limb off tree, so he started to go in water early in morning before the other men and be in bed again before the others were out of their bed. That is reason when someone start fire going, his bedding would start to steam. But others thought otherwise. At one of the early morning's try at limb, he pulled it out but put it back in so others won't know about it, and was in bed again. When the others try it, the strongest man pull it out, and was given strong man's spear for the war.

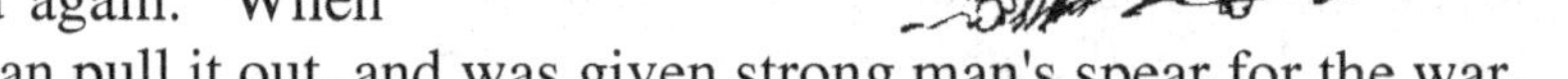

The war was not very far off. All men was making spear points and arrow points and war clubs, but still this man who was good-for-nothing was still making believe he was good-for-nothing. And then when rest was ready to go, he want to go with rest of the men, but was told that they haven't any room for useless, but begged so much they did let him go as a bailer of one of the canoes. When they got where the fight was to take place, he stayed behind rest and when they start to fight he also stayed behind, too.

But when his side was losing he take the strongest man's spear and told him to stand back and watch. The first man he killed, he did not spear him, he got a hold of him with the spear and throw him so far when he came down he was killed by the fall. And then he started on rest.

When he start he said to them, "What do you think you are doing, killing my-people?" He only spear them once to kill them. So he won the war for his people. [62]

The Little Girl Who Played With Dolls
Galushia Nelson

Once there was a village where there were lots of children. They is not allowed to play with toys or dolls. But the children were always playing with her dolls by the fireplace and she was told many times that something would come up out of the ground to get her. But she would keep on playing night after night. One night her mother told her to go to bed and not play any more but she did not do as her mother told her to do, so she let her alone. While she was playing something *she was told many times* did come out of the ground and pulled her down into the ground and was *something would come* never seen again.

(This is a story told to children so they won't play with toys in evening. They are taught to go to bed early.)

Taking Away by Owl
Galushia Nelson

Once there was a very bad boy at one of the villages who was crying for this and that. No matter what you gave him he would want something else and would cry until he gets it.

and one night a Owl did come

One of the wise men use to tell his mother that Owl will get him [63] if he does not stop crying for everything. But he was hard to please, and one night a Owl did come down through the smoke hole on top of the house and take him away and was never seen again.

Taking Away by Checkers People
Galushia Nelson

Once there was a boy who likes to play checkers and who is a good checker player. As there is a season for checkers, the checkers was played for about a month. But this boy who likes to play checkers would keep on playing as long as he could get someone to play with him. There was old man who use to tell him that the Checkers People would come and get him if he didn't stop playing checkers, but would keep on playing. Finally one night while he in bed and sleeping, someone told him to get up and go with them. This men and women was all small people and he had to go with them and was never seen again. [64]

Salmon Boy
Galushia Nelson

Kid went to spear fish

One boy had a home. They were hungry. Wanted dry salmon. Kid said, "No, me go." Kid went to spear fish, but silver fish took him away, spear and all. He went to the fish home outside, and stayed all winter. The fish were like people there. Next year, when the fish came, the kid came, too. The Natives used to scoop the fish in a net. Someone caught the kid in the net with the fish. He heard the little fish make a noise.

The kid's father said, "What's the matter with that fish? Take him in the house!" He told them to wrap him up and put him in a warm place. So the boy told the people how the [65] fish went outside to their home. When the fish went home, the kid went outside, too. The fish outside used to eat meat spits. The kid made a boat and went to another place.

Every year the kid came back as a fish. Every year they used to catch him when the fish came. All the Natives were scared of that fish that was moving. One bad woman cut the fish's head off and found beads around his neck. He was wearing his sister's necklace. How many yards the head came back to the body and it came alive again. When they cut his organs, the white stuff started to run out from his liver. This time he died. That's all.

The Woman Who Married a Bear
Old Man Dude

Old ladies go after berries in the summer. Had bark baskets for berries. Packed them all home. Then packed them berries in a barrel. One women slipped on bear dung, going home. Lost all her berries. She got the basket and picked up all the berries again. Again she slipped. Three times she sent a girl to the home to get her husband to help her. The rest went home, but she waited for her husband. Husband came and was packing her berries.

"What's the matter with that bear around here, making dung? He's got big hands, big feet, big nose, big ears, big mouth, big head, big buttocks!" she said. Husband said, "Look at my hands! Where's my big hands? Look at my eyes. Where's my big eyes? Look at my nose. Where's my big nose? Look at my ears? Where's my big ears? Look at my mouth, Where's my big mouth? Look at my head. Where is my big head? Look at my buttocks. Where's my big buttocks?" He was a big brown bear! He said, "Come on! Lets get inside the mountain." He got halfway up the mountain. "You sit down here," he said. "I'm going fishing."

He stayed with her all summer and bring her fish. Then he said, "Let's go now into the winter-time house." That girl had seven brothers. They didn't sleep with their wives because they wanted to find out where their sister was. They looked all fall. In Christmas month last, one didn't look yet. He stayed in the house. Some day, he go up Simpson Bay alone, early in morning, looking for sister. Bear and girl stay in hole six [66] months. Last brother look all over on snow, don't see nothing. Soon he see snow balls his sister had thrown down the mountain. He saw marks of someone's hand on it. He go back to the house. Oldest brother asked, "You see anything over there?" "I see something."

Next day all seven brothers go over there after their sister. They have a dog that finds bear hole and barked there. The bear already had two kids by the woman. She told the two young bears to go over to their father's den. Now she goes back home. She stay in the house. Blowing snow, nobody walk. Everybody hungry. The girls told her brothers, "Get up early in the morning. I'll tell you where to find bear's den." Early in the morning she told them, "You see that smoke?" And pointed up the mountain. He said, "No, I don't see it." She put something on her brother's eyes so he could see the smoke from the bear's den. That's all.

The Man and the Land Otters
Old Man Dude

One man went hunting all the time in a canoe. He went to the beach, got out of canoe, alone. Soon he got up. He hear something. On the side of the canoe he see two brown bear's hands. He grabbed the tree because he was afraid. When he looked back at the canoe the bear was gone. Bear looked back and saw the man up the tree. The man had a spear. When the bears came to the tree, he killed both.

One bear watched them and went to the hole to call another bear. Thousand bear coming. The man cleaned them all up. The watchman bear called more bears. The man is tired now. The watchman bear got some more bears. The man saw a big waterfall and went under it. The bear was looking for him but couldn't find him.

Two days man stayed there. Then he went to salt water. He see another canoe coming. He had two brothers. The brothers found him. "Come on!" they said. "We've found him." He go to the canoe. He went home. He had a wife and two children. It was dark when he lay down. He got up in the night. He looked at his wife. She was a Land Otter! He thought he was home but it was a Land Otter's hole. He killed all the Land Otters with a piece of stick.

He went out. It was [67] too far to walk home. He went and

67

Bear looked back and saw the man up the tree

when he saw something to eat he ate it. Some time later he saw a canoe, it belonged to the Land Otters. The Land Otters had taken his brother who had drown, long time ago. He had turned into a Land Otter.

The Land Otter asked him, "Do you recognize me?" "No!" It was his brother who had turned into a Land Otter. "How long ago the Land Otters got me! I know what they do. The Land Otters are people." The Land Otter said, "Let's go home. I'll take you home." The man was scared. The Land Otter took his brother on his back and took him into the water. He didn't feel the water. He saw everything under the water. He didn't know how long, but his brother took him home and said, "Now you go ashore." He saw his wife. He killed his wife. He eat her. Then he went back to the Land Otters' home. He was a devil already. [68]

The Porcupine Dance
Old Man Dude

Porky in the hole. A man watching him at night. Heard someone in porky hole. He sing, he dance. Man looked in hole. Porkies was dancing in there. One porky said, "I'm going out to get something to eat." The man killed twenty-five porkies. He quit, he got enough. That man die next day. Taqeiki, that's all. Other people watch porky hole at night, but don't see porky dance.

The Giant Mole
Old Man Dude

In Yakutat was a big mole. Canoe were going away. Fifty man in a canoe. Saw mole in the water. Mole hit canoe with his tail. Tipped canoe over with his tail. Broke canoe. One man from canoe went into mole's hole. Mole was asleep. Mole didn't close its eyes. After a whole month he go outside, as soon as mole shut his eyes.

They were looking for crows in the night time. It wasn't daylight when water was coming into the mole hole. He (the man) looked up and saw the upper entrance to the mole hole, like a hole in the mountain. The mole put his tail out of the hole. The man was in the hole. The mole stuck his tail in the water and pulled it in full of animals. All the different animals were on his tail. The mole put a big seal under his right arm. In two minutes it was already cooked. He gave it to the man. [69] Man stay there three months. When mole was sleeping his eyes were like lamps. Three times when mole was hunting the man was watching him. Three times he cooked the seal under his arm.

Mole hit canoe with his tail

The mole went out. He (the man) climbed the rocks hanging into the hole and went up the mountain. Mole went far away from home. Then he went back to his home. Water was coming in the hole from below. When he slept his eyes were like lamps. The man watched the mole. When he saw his eyes closed, he went out of the hole.

Crow filled his basket full of live people (crows). When he got enough, he went up the mountain. The mole was so big his tail stuck out the hole. The man saw it. One man went on one side, the other man went on the other side. "Look out, don't miss! You chop it." Two men chopped at the same time. Cut the mole in two. Crow helped them to throw it in the hole. Crow was making a big noise inside. Crow was scared. Mole went out the hole and floated up dead in the water.

The Giant Devilfish
Old Man Dude

Devilfish near Natives house. Two brothers went out hunting in a canoe. Two days they go hunting, go back next day. One place they paddled but canoe didn't go. Don't see nothing. Kept paddling but canoe didn't budge. Soon look in water. Looks brown under them. That's big devilfish. Legs thick as a dishpan.

Two fellows tie knives to their wrists. He put his paddle down to test the depth of the water and the devilfish came up. It was four feet deep. They jump off canoe. They cut the devilfish. One fellow was lucky and stuck the heart. Devilfish all die, and floated up. Hundred-fifty yards wide. Another big canoe went after him. Can't make it. Can't paddle across. Water is too heavy. Was too many scales on the water. [70]

Mosquitos and Water Bug
Lena Nacktan

Mosquitos flew back out over the water. They had gotten full and water bug saw this and asked the mosquitos, "Where have you come back from with big bellies?" The mosquitos said thus, "Do you see that yonder that land? It appears black." The water bug said thus "Yes, that's where their big bellies are from," The water bug said that "We too, we shall go there, to get big bellies." Thus the mosquitos saved us humans.
Dictated by Lena Nacktan in Cordova, 1963.

Greedy For Fishers
Lena Nacktan

Once long ago, a child was crying. His mother said thus to him, "No more fisheggs." Nevertheless he continually cried. "Give me fisheggs," His mother said thus to him, "All gone." Pretty soon his grandmother came in and said thus, "I've got fisheggs. Come here, come with me. I'll feed you fisheggs." He went with her. She fed him fisheggs. Then she went back with him. He sat down by the fire. He was getting warm and he vomited. It was all just spiders that he vomited. He died after that. It was an owl, his grandmother.
Dictated by Lena Nacktan in Cordova, 1964. [71]

Raven at Controller Bay
George Johnson

An old time story is told. Raven was with his wife, he lived there. Then a whale surfaced. Then he went out to it. The Raven in a Kayak. The whale surfaced and he speared it. Then his line, his buoy too he flung in the water. It surfaced with it. Nine miles it extended, it extends about that far over the water, his line. His buoy behind him, behind his back it floated to the surface. It became a rock. His line became a sand spit.

Lots of strawberries on it. The whales head, it's there they camped. His kayak is called Kayak Island. This fat which he cut out from its neck, he flung it in the water. That's what became Martin Islands, He kept some grass in his canoe, that too he flung in the water. That is what became Kanak Island, Thus this is told. His wife looked at it. That's why it became an island, the whale. His kayak too became an island. The fat became an island. That's what became Kanak Island. His wife looked at it. That's why, that sea otter surfaced. Then rocks, that's what he threw. Right there, amongst them, when the tide sets low they can be seen. That's what he threw it and that's what's called thus, Raven pelt it; Raven's harpoon-line.

whale surfaced and he speared it

This text was transcribed by Fang Kuei Li from the dictations of George Johnson in Yakutat, in 1952. This story is similar to the story recorded by BS/DL called "Raven Makes Rivers and Other Geographical features." [72]

Man Fixes Crane's Beak
Lena Nacktan

A crane, it's beak was broken. It couldn't do anything. A person was boating along. He saw it. He went over to it. He asked it, "What's a matter?" The crane said thus, that his beak was broken. I can't eat anything. The person went over to it and cut the beak off with a knife. He saved it.

A long time passed and he was boating around, that person. He saw it again and the crane said thus to him, "You'll have good luck." After that the person got rich.
Dictated by Lena Nacktan in Cordova, 1963.

Bear-Man Killed
Lena Nacktan

Long ago there was a man who was a hunter. He was always going around hunting. He would come back home, wherever he had killed something. He went some more again, hunting. That time he didn't come back home.

His companions kept searching around for him. They kept going around looking for him, all the time. Something had abducted him. He became a grizzly-bear. A year passed for him and this shaman-woman, she dreamed about him. He said thus **to** her, "I yearn to come back here. I shall come back here in the form of a grizzly-bear. You should not do anything to me. I won't do anything to you. When I've walked around you four times, then I'll become a person again, when I've walked around you four times. If you kill me, down-feathers will rain down."

It became daylight, a grizzly-bear was coming towards them. They became afraid. They barred the door shut. The grizzly-bear kept trying continually to get in. That one person said, "Sharpen your bear-spears. We'll kill it." A child bawled for water. There was no more water. The father said thus, to a slave, "You go get water for him." He ran out by the grizzly-bear. He fetched the water

He ran out by the grizzly-bear

to the child. The grizzly-bear didn't touch him. He climbed out the smokehole, and, he killed it [73] with a bear-spear. Down-feathers rained down. Then the woman thought of what she dreamed. He was a person that grizzly-bear.

Recorded from Anna Nelson Harry in Yakutat, 1963, and first transcribed with the help of Lena Nacktan in Cordova in the same year.

Bride Eats Only Liver
Lena Nacktan

and a Raven was sitting on the beach

Once a young person, a girl, this man wanted to marry her and the girl said thus, "That's all I like, liver." "I'm a good hunter." She married him. The parents however lived way over there, a promontory jutting out there. They too lived in a different place. The husband said thus to her, "I'll go hunting." He boated off. He boated back to her. He brought her just livers.

Again he boated off and again he brought her some more livers. Pretty soon the girl began to get lonesome, [74] for her parents. She said thus to her husband, "Take me to my parents." He said thus, "Soon."

The woman got very lonesome. He took her there. They were getting there and a Raven was sitting on the beach there. "That's your mother sitting there, cleaning fish." Magpies were walking around there. "Those are your brothers and sisters," the husband said to her. "Where ever is my father?" "Sitting on top of a house there, he's an eagle." He arrived there with her father and her brothers and sisters, he had killed them and it was their livers he had been feeding her.

Dictated by Lena Nacktan in Cordova, 1963. This story may be of Chugach origin and similar to the one recorded by BS/DL called "The Woman Who Liked Livers",

Witch
Lena Nacktan

Once a person was a witch, he was invited to a potlatch. They all were having a good time. His fellow guests were dancing and singing. While they were thus distracted the witch went back out, he sneaked back out. He got back home and lay down. Those who were giving the potlatch, he disappeared on them. They said thus to this one youngster. "Take that potlatch food of his to him." He went there with it. He went in there.

The witch didn't hear him, that he had come in. The witch was lying down and counting on his fingers how many people he had killed. He was having a good time, alone. He was laughing. The child was watching him. The witch was saying, "He's another one I killed." Thus it was that child, he set that potlatch food down right there in the doorway. He went back. He said thus to his father, "That man is having a good time with himself all alone. He's lying down and he's counting on his fingers. Here's another one I killed," he's saying.

He's really laughing. The child's father went there with him. He sneaked in. The witch was laughing. "He's another one I killed," he was saying. He said thus to him, "I'll kill you, I'll kill you too." He killed them. [75]

Jealous Wife Walks On Water
Lena Nacktan

She was running on the surface

A man went back, leaving his wife and married another woman. He would go for water. The wife said thus to him, "Don't speak with your former wife." Her husband said thus to her that he wouldn't speak with her. When he fetched water up, the wife would dip a feather down in the water, to see if he had spoken to his former wife. Nothing would happen to the feather. Again he used to go some more for water. Then his wife, his first wife, she spoke to him. Therefore he too spoke to her.

He fetched the water back up and that other wife dipped the feather down in the water again. The feather turned bad. She found out, her husband had spoken to that former wife of his.

Immediately the wife ran out. The husband ran after her. She was running on the surface of the river. The husband said thus to her, "Watt for me a moment! Don't go back!" "I'll look back at you." She looked back at her husband. He sank. [76]

Shaman
Lena Nacktan

Once a shaman, a great shaman, when he boated off, salmon he would stop from running. At about as far as he could boat down stream, he would reach his hand down under water, leaving his glove, he would pull his hand back up without it. He had stopped the salmon from running, until he boated back there. After he had been away a long time, he'd boat back there. He'd reach his hand back down under at the same place. That glove of his, it was back on his hand. He would boat back home. He would dry the salmon.

A year after that again he'd boat off. When he got back to that same place, he'd put his snuff-can this time down underwater there. He would stop the salmon from running. The salmon would swarm right about there. They wouldn't go past it. Again he was away for another long time. He would boat back home. When he boated back to that same place, he would reach his hand down under to get his snuff-can. He would take it back away from there. He would boat back home. He would dry the salmon again.

Some other shaman heard about him. They wanted to kill him, because he was more of a shaman than they. Some things, [77] in the form of tidal debris, they sneaked along the shore to him. When the shaman was sleeping, they would wake him up. He would always hear their sound. Then he fell deep asleep, that shaman. All of a sudden he woke up. He heard the sound of teapots. Two teapots were coming at him, to kill him. He really woke up and so it was he himself killed them. Thus it was those two shamans died.

Shaman Causes Ice Breakup
George Johnson

A story of old time this is I shall tell. I was not yet born and my grandmother that is, they were giving a potlatch. Those who lived on Kayak (Wingham Island) it was they had invited, to Chilkat. That's it, it was cold, a cold spell, a big one. It was quite cold all that water – Bering River, that is froze up. Those whom they had invited couldn't get back onto the island over there, they wanted to get back. That river was frozen. It had gotten thick, that ice.

So then a shaman, a shaman it was, he was powerful, that shaman. So then his kinfold said thus to him, "What shall we do? It's up to you." That fellow, "the ice is starting to break up. Rain, it's starring to blow. Thus it will be." Thus he said, that shaman. Around the fire he was walking. He was singing. [78] His nephews, that is, they were singing. They were beating the drum too for him. The shaman said thus, "Wind blow hither, tremendously. Rain also, let big one come down. Ice too break up!" Thus it was he said. He was saying just thus whereupon rain started to come down. Wind too started to blow. It was strong. All that river ice, thick it was, started to break up. The day afterwards it was good weather. The sun was shining. All those people were in good frame of mind. They all of them boated straight back home, to the island, to where they lived. This is the story I know.

Aleuts Punished for Beating Eyak Woman
Lena Nacktan

He shot the Aleut

Long ago a woman to get fish, she went for it. All the men folk had boated away after ducks and Aleuts were sneaking around there, looking for someone to kill. One Aleut man saw the woman. He beat her up. He was going to kill her. The woman screamed. One Eyak man boated back there. He had heard her. With a rifle he came ready to fight. He shot the Aleut. He wounded him. The other Aleut picked him up onto his shoulders. He ran away with him.

The man went back home with the woman. The chief said thus, "We'll boat there." (Constantine Harbor). They boated there and that woman also. They disembarked. Russians were there. He said thus to them. "Those Aleuts there have been bothering us. They beat up this woman. They almost killed her." Russians, all the Aleuts went into the building there. The Aleuts sat down. The Russians said thus to the woman, [79] "Do you know him who it is?" "Yes." The Russian said thus. "Look amongst them." The woman immediately knew him. He was wearing a skunk-cabbage leaf hat on his head. The woman said thus, "That's him."

The Russians said thus, "Is it certain that's him?" "Yes, that's him." The Russians said thus, "Come here. I'm going to whip you." He was going to whip him and the Aleut said thus, "Don't whip me. I'll pay her for it." A canoe full of things, quantities of flour and quantities of tea. Thus the Aleut saved himself.

Preacher Tempted by Land-Otter Girls
Lena Nacktan

Once a preacher was walking around, he came upon two women. They went over to him. Those women said thus to him, "Come here, let's take a walk," he didn't think anything the matter with that, for they were nice looking women. He went along with them. They were walking along a long time. That man said thus, "This is already a *The man saw their tails* long time we've been walking." The women said thus, "It's not far we're going." The man said thus, "Go, walk in front of me." Those women went in front of him. The man saw their tails, and he grabbed a club. He said thus, "You aren't people." They vanished. The man looked back. Where there was a light in the distance he turned.

Dictated by Lena Nacktan in Cordova, 1963. [80]

Aleuts Betrayed Eyaks
Lena Nacktan

People landed at an Aleut village. The Aleuts invited them over, that they might eat with them. They went up there. This one woman, an Aleut woman, she know it that they were going to kill them. She said thus to this one man, "I'll hide you." He was a young man. She hid him in the sweatbath. At night the Aleuts were going to kill them. In the night they killed them.

head kept walking back up ashore

One shaman they beheaded. He didn't die. They threw his head in the water. That head kept walking back up ashore, on the hair. Again they kept throwing it back in the water. Again it kept walking back up ashore. It wasn't dead. The Aleuts said thus to a woman, "You kill him!" Only then did that shaman die, for good.

They were searching around for that one man. They couldn't find him. He ran off. That man saw a person boating along. He yelled to him. He boated ashore by him and took him away. He transported him back across. He went back home.

The Aleuts asked him, "How did you get back home?" "By myself I boated back across in a bark vessel." The Aleuts knew it that he was telling a lie. The people transported him to Nuchek. There they asked him, "That one person, it was you who transported him across." That person said no. The Russians said thus, "We'll whip him, till he dies." The Russians said thus to the older brothers, "If you help him, we'll whip you, too." Therefore they didn't help him. They killed him. (The location where this story took place is at a winter village of the Mummy Island people called Tauxcvik, on Hawkins Island in 1805.)

Dictated by Lena Nacktan in Cordova, 1964. This story is very similar to the one that is recorded by BS/DL called: "The Slaughter of the Yakutat at Tauxcvik. " Another version of this story can also be found in Bancroft's book called "History of Alaska" (1886, pages 451-452). [81]

Qadyyina and the War with Aleuts
George Johnson

Aleuts with those Gi-sqed people, was war it was. Long ago Aleuts wanted that, they killed all the people. Land it was, that some of it might be theirs. It didn't turn out that way. He was called Qadyyina. He was a Gi-sqed. It was he that killed all those Aleuts. Whoever saved himself, he it was got away from there, to Nuchek, to the island, all. "That's enough," they said, "that's enough war." Aleuts, no longer avenged themself. Long ago that was, long ago. Nobody knows, how much rime it's been. It was then there was a war. Ever since then it is they haven't killed each other. Nobody avenged himself. Qadayytna it was killed them all, Aleuts. That's as far as I know it.

Transcribed by Fang Kuei Li from the dictations of George Johnson in Yakutat, 1952.

Raven Cycle (III)
Anna Nelson Harry

Raven was out in a boat with wife. They were going along, and it got foggy on them. Then that rock, he came to it. He ran aground on the rock. He got mad at his wife. He got mad at his wife and then her strawberries, his wife's strawberries, she had them in a big basket, he threw it in the water. Everything was lost, everything. Then, the wife wept over it, "What, what will become of us? Sweet tasting things and berries, my strawberries you've thrown into the water," Then, "do we live only on sweets?" he said to her and he get furious with her, his wife.

He was mean with her. He said to her, to his wife, "I'm going to put you out here. I'm going to leave you stranded on this rock here." The wife said to him, "Go ahead and do that to me. Do that to me. Throw me out. You won't get away from here. Your boat will sink with you," she said to him, to her husband.

They had words. They speak badly to each other. The place where they had words, they had the quarrel about strawberries. He threw the strawberries into the water. Then those [82] strawberries turned into sea-urchins. It immediately sank, that big basket. Over there at Kayak Island, over in that direction near Kayak Island, they became sea-urchins. There people going along by boat came upon them. Like strawberries taste, that's how sea-urchins taste. They're Just Raven's wife's strawberries. They turned into sea-urchins.

Some other people were boating along there and, they said to her, "Come here. Come away with us. Your husband is mean to you." Then he said to them, "I'll throw you in the water, all of you, and your skiff too, I'll overturn your boat with you in it," he said to them. Then those other people, the woman, the woman was also aboard. People he didn't know had been going along in their boat behind them, they were her relatives. They had been boating along behind them and came upon it.

She went away with them. With those other people. Alone he went along, he went along, in his boat. He was going along in his boat. Foggy, it was foggy and simply nothing could be seen. Nothing could be seen. They couldn't see anything, there was so much fog over them. That's why people simply say, "Raven is boating along, there's a big fog." Then that fog, when Raven is starting out, that's why they don't like k, people, real people seeing it. That's why he makes it foggy on them, right away.

He came to another land over there and, in the morning k was the fog immediately began to lift, and the sun shone and it was gone, the fog. It was gone. Then he said to her (his wife was back with him), "I'm going to he down there a while. I'm going to sleep. Let someone be on guard for it. If people start coming here let him wake me." Then the wife, she too fell asleep.

So the Raven's eye, his eye it was, he set that down on the rock there, his eye. Then he said to it, "I'm sleepy. You though, watch over there. If people start coming here, you'll holler out." He fell asleep and people boating along came upon him, people came upon him. It was a gull-person. They must have been gull-people.

Then some gulls flew there. They saw it. He (one of the gulls) picked the Raven's eye up in his beak and the gull gulped it down, Raven's eye.

He woke up and said, "Huh! A big gull has already gulped down my eyeball. He has eaten it up." So then a blueberry, a blueberry there, he made it into a eyeball, a blueberry. (Don't you see?) Raven's eye is a blueberry, he has that for his eye. The wife woke up, "Who are you talking to?" "Gull people they are, gull people, gulls. My eye is gone. I have no eyes." "Where is it? What happened?" "I said to it to watch [83] southward over there. My eye didn't watch. It just rolled around, right there. Gulls swallowed them down." "Where indeed are you eyes? What are you eyes?" "These blueberries, I've put these blueberries in my eye-sockets here, and I can see fine." She laughed at him, "Your eyes will look like blueberries. Blueberries they are."

Then he was going to go on his way with her again. Again he was going to travel some more with her, her husband, his wife. "Over there, we'll go across over that way. We'll live right there, over in that direction. Over there is the mainland. This is an island. It's not an island that we could live on. When the wind gets strong it'll be too windy a place, that's why. Over there towards the mountains we'll cross. We'll live there. There are lots of small trees there, small trees, small spruce brush, we'll live amongst them. It's those small trees. We'll settle down. We'll perch on their branches," he said to her. Does old Raven do Just about all sorts of things? He does everything. "We'll settle down nicely here. We'll stay living here. We won't build a house. Just the branches of small trees, where there are lots of these small trees, where there are lots of spruce boughs, here under these trees we'll perch," he said to her. "When it's windy, when it rains, we'll perch cozily in the shelter of these small trees. It's too much effort building a house, that's why. Fine it is.

"Fine, good. We'll stay there. When the sun begins to shine, we'll know right away. When the sun begins to shine, on the ride-beach, when the tide's out, at ebbtide, from the tide-beach, mussels, cockles, all sorts of things we'll eat from there, we'll eat. As the tide comes in, we'll go back up. We'll stay over there upland. There are mussels and cockles, cockles, red-tip clams, the ones whose neck stick out. When the sun [84] shines we'll bite them off. We'll bite their noses off. That's how we'll eat.

"Whoever is storing food when the tide comes in we'll descend on it. We'll just help ourselves. Everything, anything, meats, pieces of seal meat hanging up to dry, and salmon too, they hang up to dry. When someone goes away from it we'll eat it up. That's good.

"Fine. Boating around for food, hunting for food. We don't hunt anything down. We don't hunt anything down. Because of that, we'll eat up the things that these people keep for their own food. Sometimes true human beings, these people have mountain goat fat, pieces of mountain goat fat hanging up. I like that, that mountain goat fat. From where it has been hung up, we'll eat it up from there. When it falls down they throw it away. Then it will all be ours." That was her husband. Her husband it was being that way with her, how it pleased her/him. Her husband said that to her, and that's all the farther it goes, this story.

Ravens and Mother of Pearl Canoe
Anna Nelson Harry

Raven likes to do all kind of things. It had dried up, this river. There he came upon it, this mother of pearl. He said thus, "This must be the mother of pearl I've been looking for." He packed it upstream, he packed it upland. Then he made a canoe with it. He made a canoe and then, already he had made it, the canoe. Then he said thus, he sat down having made a canoe, "Perhaps I'll use it to put on the canoe." Then, he didn't see any person. He was alone there. He would talk to himself, that Raven.

Then someone said to him thus,"If you'll give me some I'll help you with it." He didn't see anyone. But someone was talking to him. Then Raven said thus, "Come here. If you help me I'll give you some of this mother of pearl of mine." Then he went over to him. It was a

Raven just like himself. He came to him and he said thus to him. "Let's gather together some spruce pitch." The spruce pitch, they gathered it. After they had collected it, "Whatever shall we do with it?" Then one [85] said to the other thus, "We'll heat up those stones, flat thin stones. Light a fire." He lit a fire and then he said thus to him, "Put the stones down on the fire. When the stones get hot then we'll put them in back."

They put them in back with tongs. Then the pitch, they put it down. The pitch was getting warm and it got warm and then they placed the mother of pearl down into the pitch piece by piece. Then the pitch, they stuck it to the canoe. The gunwhales of the canoe, they finished decorating them and then, they carried it to the water on their shoulders. Then that which was left over from it, that mother of pearl

they packed into the canoe. They got it all put in it *it got warm and then they placed the mother of pearl* and, they boated off in it. They used some on their paddles too, mother of pearl, they boated off in it. They were boating along then, someone saw it. Then those people, "What could that beautiful thing be?" Those people, they threw their canoe into the water and boated towards there. They got to this shore, a distance from it there and then they could see it clearly.

"This must be Raven's canoe," they said to each other, those people. Then they said thus ro Raven, "Where are you boating to?" The Ravens said, "To where you live yonder." The people said thus, "Boat hither. We're tremendously interested in it, that canoe of yours," Thus they boated along with them. They went with them and then they arrived there, and, they landed and those people got right out of their canoe. They landed and then lifted it up onto their shoulders with the Ravens in it, up the shore over there. They set it down off their shoulders with the Ravens in it. There they set it down off their shoulders and then, skunk-cabbage leaves they put over the mother of pearl. They took them off of it.

Then those people asked Ravens, "Where did you get this from?" Then the Ravens said thus, "We drained the water out from under it." "Won't you sell any of it?" Then Raven said [86] thus to them, "If you want some." Then the people said, "Whatever in exchange for?" Raven said thus, "Three black bears and two grizzly bears, mountain goat fat, the fat of four mountain goats, if you give us, we will give you some, dried seal meat, and black bear meat, grizzly bear meat, mountain goat fat, two Storage boxes of it." That pleased them, because the people wanted some of it right away. They gave those things to them and they overturned their canoe, with the mother of pearl. It fell out of it and then they turned it back up off it. "Gather it up from there," the Ravens said to them. They gathered it all up from there, those people, and they brought it inside. Their food, they left it out there.

Then before long, the Ravens had devoured all their meat. They devoured all their meat and then they next sold their canoe to the people. The people, one of them said thus, "Our food will all be gone." Then another one of them said thus to him, "Is there only one black bear or grizzly bear or mountain goat?" Thus they found out about it, that canoe that Raven had made. Then they gave it to them. "What's this?" the one Raven said, "What will happen to us? We've sold our canoe." Then the other Raven said thus, "This wood drifting ashore is plentiful. Trees, we'll make them into a canoe," The makings of a canoe had drifted ashore there by them, driftwood. The Ravens, they went down to shore to it. They dragged it up, and they made it into a canoe. They were going to boat back there, in the canoe. They hadn't yet gotten there and the driftwood canoe sank with them.

Then one of them said thus, "What ever is going to become of us? Our canoe has sunk down." The other Raven said thus, "The Raven who made it into a canoe he said thus, we'll fly up. You take off first." He was going to take off and "Caw!" He immediately took off. The other one however was walking about right there. The first Raven was already perched on a tree and he said thus to his companion, "How is it you're just walking about there? Say thus. Caw." Then he said thus, "Caw!" He took off. He said thus and alighted there by the Other. That's all the farther the story goes. [87]

War with Aleuts
Anna Nelson Harry

It was the first settlement, at Alaganik, that place Alaganik, too much winter, whre there is too much strong wind. The northwind there is too strong. That's why they moved to Eyak. It was too far to go hunting mountain goats. Man people died. Snow, it slide down on them, as they were hunting mountain goats. Snow slid down on them. They would go mountain goat hunting to Kiiwaalaa, from Alaganik. That's why they moved to Eyak.

Those Aleuts sneaked up on some of the Eyaks, Flag Point, below here, at Hedysarum Place on Alaganik Slough. Mummy Island, there is Mummy Island. People from here, Tlingits, some boated to Cordova. Then Aleuts enticed them ashore. They enticed them and gave them something to eat, cockles, they kept giving them dried cockles. Then the Aleuts sang songs. This one man, he must have pleased an Aleut woman and they were two girls, they said to two men, "Get away from here. They're singing a war song. They're going to kill you all, when you sleep at night." Those two girls would not give up trying to warn them. They just told them to hurry, to get away from there. "Get going now, get going." [88]

They went, from there, straight away, in the direction of Katalla here, Katalla. They came ashore and lay down. They were still asleep. Those people who lived there on Mummy Island, they killed them, as they slept. The Tlingits made war. Those two got back and told about it here, to their relatives, Therefore the Tlingits here all winter long prepared bows and arrows, spearpoints, all these things, sharp things, all winter long, they were going to make war with them. Summer came there. One winter passed and, it became summer again after that and then they boated there. Then they made war with the Aleuts. The Tlingits made war with them. Thus many of them were killed. Some of them though they made war right there over yonder over on the far side.

Those of them towards Canoe Passage, on Hawkins Island went in the direction of the mountains over there and saved themselves, Aleuts, they were the ones. They settled at Chenega. Those allies of theirs though were wiped out, all of them. I have seen it the place where the Aleuts were wiped out. Mummy Island. They were wiped out there and since then they have not lived there anymore, at Mummy Island.

They avenged themselves, on the Aleuts. They were boating along for pleasure. They enticed them ashore, in order to kill them. They killed them. They killed them all, every one. Those two girls though spread stories throughout the battle. Those same girls

the porcupines, his canoe, he dragged ashore

tipped them off again, the Thngits doing battle. Where the Aleuts that had hid themselves were hiding, they directed them there. People found out about the place from them, from the girls. They were annihilated there, they two. All of those Aleuts were killed. Those two however they took to Kiiwaalaa, those two girls. The Eyaks said thus to the Tlingits, "Don't do anything to them, to the girls." Thus they were brought to Eyak. They grew up and Eyak men fell in love with them, and they were married there, at Eyak.

From them again it was that people found out about it, that the Aleuts were sneaking up on the Eyak again. They were sneaking there and those girls told about it. Thus it was the Eyaks, as evening fell, went to this fort. They hid behind the Fort, the Eyaks. Two were waiting for it. They saw them and summoned them. Thus they there at Eyak, they shot them with arrows in the river. They wiped them out and the Eyaks took their

kayaks over into the trees. That's as far as it goes. Chief Joe it was told me this. [89]

Giant Strawberry
Anna Nelson Harry

A land-otter it was, a strawberry, he ate it, a man. A strawberry this size, he ate it. Like this, above, a salmonberry-bush, he hung it up on that. The man was going about hunting. He had already killed something. Three porcupines, he killed them, and he came upon it the berry and he said to himself, "Maybe it's a giant strawberry." He plucked it down from there, and he ate it. He ate it and devoured it all and went on his way again.

Everything changed in his eyes, once he ate the strawberry. He got back to his canoe and he put his porcupines down in the canoe and departed. He boated out. But in his eyes, to him that was the way it was.

A point of land, he boated around, people from here lived, here. He boated across in this direction apparently. The house, he saw it. It's a land-otter habitation. In his eyes it's a house. He landed there. There the porcupines, his canoe, he dragged ashore. He entered the house there. He was carrying along his porcupines also.

He went inside there and his grandmother was sitting way inside there. His grandmother said to him, "My grandson, you [90] wife has gone for berries. She has gone for berries, you wife." She was cooking something there for you, and she told me thus, that you should eat. Then his wife came back. She brought him berries and by him, she sat down by her husband. She said thus to her husband, <<! have picked berries for you. Eat some of them." "Yes," he said to her. Then he ate some. Then his wife, his wife said thus to him, "Now lie down, lie down for a while. I'll prepare the berries nicely." He lay down.

Then for three days, he didn't know, it wasn't his wife. For three days and three nights he didn't know. He went out, from there. Thus, he went out and this way, he felt around on his cheeks. Then it was he felt there. There, his face, his whiskers, they were already long. He found out about himself. Not his kinfolk, but land-otters, his grandmother and his wife were. He realized that. People like himself were searching about for him.

Only his canoe was recovered from there and they towed it. He found out about himself and he went after it, his canoe. It was gone. He realized fully they weren't his kinfolk, but land-otters. He went a long time, he was facing upstream and sitting on a rock. Then his kinfolk came boating around the bend toward him. The man sitting in front said thus, "There he is sitting on a rock. Just paddle gently. I'll get ready for him. Paddle close along the shore."

He was sitting on a rock, the missing man, with his knees drawn up to his chin, he had his forearms on his knees and his head down on his forearms. Then the bow-man crept out and sneaked up to his back, and he grabbed him. They recovered him. They boated back with him. They got back home and because he didn't want to go in they carried him in. Someone took care of him.

Three days he stayed inside and after three days he recovered, became more or less normal. He recovered and he ate. He ate something. Then he said thus, having eaten, "Land-otters made a strawberry for me. I ate it and I went out of my mind. That's why I got lost. I went inside a land-otter house. I saw my grandmother there. My wife too I saw there. I went out of there and the wind blew on my face and my cheeks itched. Therefore I felt there and I found them, my whiskers. That's why I left there. I didn't go back there." Thus he recounted it to his kinfolk. He became his normal self again. That's all. [91]

Old Husband and Young Wife
Anna Nelson Harry

From here it was, Tlingits from Yakutat to Katalla, they arrived there in boats. They landed there. So you see young girls at Katalla. So an already old woman, and old man it was, he liked this girl. The young girl was walking along and the man, the man was already old, the man's name was *Ch'aq'iinq'taa'*, the girl, he grabbed her arm. He embraced her. He was holding her tight, but the girl though got angry with him. She didn't like him. She said thus to him, "Who, who you nasty thing, could love such a nasty thing as you?" The man said thus to her, "Yes, yes, yes soon you'll be in tears."

He was still holding her and he cut off some of her hair. Then he gathered them together outside, her clothes. Here, the hem, he cut a piece off it. He cut a piece off her clothes. Her hair also, the hair and her clothes, a crybaby-leaf, he made that for a spell on the girl. "Who will be wife of such a nasty thing [92] as I?" Then she said thus, "I'll be your wife." She moved in with him. She lived with him, of her own accord. She lay down and he lay over on the wall side behind her. He would lie down onto her. He would say thus to her, "What is becoming of you?" the man would say to the woman. She was a good-looking woman. People said thus to the man, "Poor her. She's out of her senses. That's why she said thus to you." Then he grew kind to her, to the woman. Very nice to her, his wife's mother, he was always helpful to her, kindly. Right there it *was* he himself died. At Bering River village they lived. He died right there. She never came back here.

Wolverine People
Anna Nelson Harry

Yonder amongst the glaciers, over there our way, towards Cordova, that man heard them. He said thus, "Those aren't people, they speak to you different from real people." Then they went to bed, it being already evening. They lay down and then they heard them. They could hear them there. Therefore then, the oldest man said, "I can't sleep well." They didn't pay attention to him. The young men however slept well. They said they weren't concerned about anything.

Then they came to them, the wolverine-people, to the humans. They came to them and then, they went about only by night, not by day. Then they looked about amongst them, the people. The old man was watching the wolverine-people. Then the wolverines there, when they had built a fire, they sat down there. Then they sat by the fire, the wolverine-people. The old man woke him up. He pushed him over gently with his hand. Then he got up. Then the young man jumped out of bed and said to the wolverine-people, "Who are you? Who are you?" Then one wolverine said thus, "Your tribe." He said thus and then all the people got up. They got up, and he asked them, "What are you doing?" "We're going hunting."

They were humans in his eyes

They were humans in his eyes. They didn't look like wolverines. It was dawning and, it dawned and then the wolverine-people said to the humans, "We're going to sleep. We're going to sleep, us now." The wolverine-people were going to sleep. They lay down. The real people however they ate something. Then they went to hunt all of them. They went to hunt and then, beavers it was, the people killed many of them, beavers. They took them there. They were already gone, [93] the wolverine-people. Before they had gotten back home, the wolverine-people had gone away from there. It was getting dark and then, they came back to them. The wolverine-people turned into humans with them. The beavers, they had killed many. The wolverine-people hadn't killed anything.

The wolverine-people said thus to the humans, "Come on yonder along with us." But the old man didn't like that. He said to the young man, "Don't, don't. Tomorrow we'll boat back." He knew, that old man. Those beavers were tied to a cottonwood tree. Because they were going to boat back they lay down. The old man fell asleep. The people were asleep and then the wolverines packed all that beaver meat onto their backs. They woke up and there wasn't anything there. The meat wasn't there. Only their skins were there.

Then the old man said thus to the young men, "Do you know where they are?" The young men said thus to him, "We don't know." Then the old man said thus to them, "They're wolverine-people. They're making themselves human with you. If I weren't with you they'd lead you off. You would not get back home." They boated back, those people. They landed back home and then they told them, the people, they had stolen all the beaver-meat from them.

Therefore now, even nowadays they still steal, for exactly that reason also they move their hands around a person's food (wolverines get into a person's food, or a person takes precautionary measures with food). Anything he gets to eat, right away wolverines find it. [94]

Lake-Dwarves
Anna Nelson Harry

A man was out hunting on foot. He came upon some lake-dwarves. He stood there and watched. Before him, boating, were two little canoes filled with these lake-dwarves. Just then mouse came out. To their eyes it was a brown bear, that mouse. Many dwarves shot at it with their bows and arrows, until at last they killed it. Then, lo, they saw a second mouse, and they were going to kill this one too. The man was watching that. "What? What is that?" he pondered.

After the dwarves had killed the second mouse, they landed their canoes and proceeded to tow the two mice to shore. These wee people began butchering the mice the way brown bears are butchered. They took off the skin. Then they cut up the carcass. It was quite a struggle to load that mousemeat into their boats. It took two dwarves to carry the hindquarter, the mouse-thigh. They worked very hard until all the meat from the two mice was loaded into their boats — the ribs, the spine too. That lesser little mouse, for them, was a black bear.

While they were bustling about over their work, preoccupied with the mice, the man reached down and plucked up one of the wee people. He took him and tucked him under his belt.

The dwarf pleaded with the man. "Please, these things I hunt with, I'll give them to you if you release me. They are yours if you let me go. You will become a great hunter if you free me." The little fellow was begging the man quite pitifully. "I will show you my weapon." He handed it to the man. It was the size of the man's thumb, like a strawberry leaf. Then the dwarf said, "Put this inside your rifle whenever you're going to shoot anything." The man set him free.

The other lake-dwarves were at their boats and ready to leave, waiting for their comrade who was missing, who had disappeared from their midst. The hunter had freed him and he was running back to his people. When he arrived they asked him, "Where are your weapons?" "I gave them away. That's how I managed to get back here. A huge man, big as a tree he was, grabbed me. I got him to release me by giving him all my things." "Maybe it was a tree-man," they said to him. "No, no. He was a person. He was the size of a tree, though. A huge person. He was enormous. He had clothes on and he stuck me under his belt. I offered him everything to pay him off. I finally gave him my lucky hunting leaf and for that he let me go." "Quick! Hurry up! He'll come upon us again." The dwarves put out their boats, paddled across the lake, and got home. [95]

My, how their women came running down to meet them! Their little husbands had killed a brown bear and a black bear and had come boating home to them. The little people brought the meat ashore. Although it was already evening, the women hung the meat in the curing-house, right away, just as it was. The next day they would cut it into strips. Some went to bed, but it was expected that at any time the man would come.

They had boated clear across the lake. There was no way for the man to walk across, because it was such a deep lake. He too went home. After all, he was out hunting for black bear when he came across these lake-dwarves.

Two Sisters
Anna Nelson Harry

There were once two sisters. One of them had no sense, didn't care about anything. The other one was good. A man fell in love with her because she was nice and married her. Her husband's parents built a big house for them. But the bad sister lived alone, unmarried.

The married sister moved with her family to another place, where she established another large household. She had six children with her husband. Then her husband died. She would never remarry, however, because other children. She didn't want any new husband to slap her children or beat them up, as she never beats them herself.

Her children were growing, and as their mother was moving to a new place with them, Aleuts fell upon them. Those Aleuts killed one son and one daughter others. They wrapped the little girl's hair around a canoe paddle and thrust her under the water and held her down until she drowned. As for the boy, they stuffed his mouth with moss and buried him under a tree stump.

For eight days the mother ate nothing, traveling along. She found a place to hide her children. She saw a magpie, which flew away. She paid no attention to it. She cut something off a land-otter and her mind became like a man's. On the tenth day her mind became like a man's. She had cut the land-otter for revenge on the Aleuts. After she killed the Aleuts, she went home. Then she told her younger sister, "You should be married by now. You're so wanton you clutch to the underside of dead logs. You lie with men on housetops, anywhere." [96]

They were going to move. They were setting up a camp for drying fish. Their old mother was still alive, but their father had died. They had all moved to this camp for drying fish. As they were preparing to move back from there, the first sister said, "Let's abandon her right here. She's too senseless." They tied the sister together with a dog. As they were about to abandon her, thus tied together with a dog, there, an old slave they had said, "Heavens, we're about to leave and I forgot my old knife! Let me go back for a moment and get it." She ran back. She lied. She cut the dog and the woman apart. Their heads had been tied together so they would die, but the slave separated them and ran back to the shore. The people left the woman and the dog behind.

The second sister stayed with the dog. The dog came out of its skin, changing into a man. Then that dog said to her, "I'll marry you. I'll take good care of you. I'll go hunting for you." She said, "If you will take good care of me, I'll marry you. We'll live alone here." Then that old dog lived as a man with her. The dog would go hunting goats in the mountains. Fish, all sorts of good things, he would bring back to her. He packed in all kinds of good things for her. She would prepare it nicely and dry it, putting up lots in storage for winter.

The people had passed through most of the winter. Spring was about to come. This is the time of year people have the least to eat. The old slave was told to go back and shovel out the bones. She went back there knowing that nothing had happened to the woman and the dog. In fact, she found them well stocked with all sons of food – mountain goat fat that she had dried. When the slave told the sister that she was about to leave, the sister said, "Don't tell my mother I'm alive. Be sure not to tell her that."

The slave went home and said, "I shoveled out their bones." They went to bed. She had put a piece of mountain-goat fat in her pocket for her child. As they went to bed she gave it to him. Then the child cried for more of that mountain-goat fat. She said, "Quiet, quiet down! Where will I get any more to give you?" Then someone said, "Those two you tied together, their house is practically bursting open, it is so crammed with food. It's fairly bursting open." The old mother said, "Hurry, let's hurry, let's get in our boats and go there."

They landed there and the slave Jumped out. She Jumped out of the canoe and ran up the shore. She grabbed her child and ran to where the fat was hanging. The Others were behind. She cut a piece of the fat down and threw it behind her, in front of the others. That piece of fat turned into a big glacier, expanding right together. She was gone. The people never [97] caught up with them. Her husband climbed up on the glacier after her but fell down in and died. The slave and the woman and the dog and the son all turned into owls and flew away. Owls. Since then nothing more is said about them.

This story is similar to "The Girl and the Dog" as told by Galushia Nelson, pg. 55.

Woman and Octopus
Anna Nelson Harry

Once there was a woman who went out picking blueberries with her child. While she was standing about berrypicking, something interfered with her. Something grabbed her foot. Something interfered with her foot and she said, "What's this clinging to my foot?" She look at it. It was an octopus sitting there. "What are you doing?" she said to it. "Long-fingers," she called it, and it immediately wrapped itself around her and started dragging her down toward the shore. She cried out, but who was there to hear her? There was no one to hear her because she was alone with her child. The child wailed for her mother. She said, "It's taking me into the water!" As it dragged her away into the water, she said to the child, "Go home. Tell what happened to me, that the octopus has wrapped itself around me. Tell my uncles of me. This is already my last breath."

Nothing happened to that woman. The octopus dragged her into the water and it turned into a man with her. He took her into a house, a big house. It was probably a chamber under a rock, but in her eyes it was a house. The octopus married her and she lived with him. He would always go hunting for all kinds of things, fish, anything, which she would eat. When he caught a seal, he would lie down on top of it to cook it. That's how he cooked them, by lying down on top of them, and she ate them. Cockles, all those kinds of things too, he would cook them that way, by lying over them and right away they would start to cook.

Some time after that the woman's brothers were traveling along in their boat. The woman was sitting on a rock, a *skerry.* The octopus had gone hunting and she had climbed up onto a skerry and was sitting on it when her brothers saw her, "There she is, our sister sitting on a skerry there." They landed by her and said, "It's time to come with us. That's enough of living with him. You have been missing a long time already." She said, "Let me stay here a little while yet. Let me stay here a little while yet. Your brother-in-law will hunt for you," she [98] said to them. So they let her stay there. They went back without her. Only she did say this, "You'll come back here sometime, won't you?" she said to her brothers, and they went back without her.

The octopus came back and she said to him, "Your brothers-in-law came here to get me. I said to them, let me stay here a little while yet. Your brother-in-law will hunt for you," that's what I said to them. That's why they let me be here. He must have been a big octopus, her husband. Then he said to his wife, "You had better tell them that they must not kill me, your brothers. Let them not kill me. Killing things is all they have on their minds." "Yes, I'll tell them that, that you'll help them when you see them," said the woman to the octopus.

That woman had gotten to know him. In fact she had gotten quite used to the octopus. She had octopus-babies, two of them. Octopus-young- Then he said to her, "We'll go there. We'll go to my brothers-in-law. Take those babies of yours." He had become a person, he wasn't an octopus. They arrived there and she said, "Where" s that octopus you were saying had taken me away? He's a person. He has become a man." He lived with them.

Then one day he went out to sea. He made a mistake. He fought with this whale. The whale got the better of him. It killed him. The whale killed the octopus. After that she went back to his sisters for a last visit, along with her brothers. She didn't stay long after that. Soon she died.

The young octopuses, however, grew big and went into the water. After their mother died they went into the sea. They said, "We'll get revenge on that whale for our father. We'll kill him." After their mother died they went and fought with the whale, those children. They killed the big fat whale for their mother's brothers. That big whale, they killed for their uncles. After that they went to sea for good. They never came back. Their uncles never knew where they went.

Wolf-Woman
Anna Nelson Harry

A woman was traveling about with her husband. While she was asleep in the canoe and her husband was away from her, the Wolf-People came upon the woman. While she was still asleep -Jicy picked up the canoe onto their shoulders with her in it. [99] When they had already carried it on their shoulders a long way, and were still carrying it along, she woke up. She sat up and looked around. She was being carried along in the canoe on their shoulders. She cut open her pillow and strewed the down feathers out. The Wolf-People weren't aware of it. She was tossing them out until they came to a river, and then they crossed the river, to those Wolf-People's relatives over there. They kept her.

That woman lived a long time with them. As it would start **to** get dark, the menfolk would go out hunting, only at night, not during the day. During the day they would sleep. That's how she began to realize who they were. Their boats were at the shore. She would go to get water. That woman would carry the water up from the shore. While she was gone to get water, she would cut those boats. She cut them except for a small one just the right size for her to handle. She kept on fetching water from there. While they slept, after they lay down, she would fetch water. Unlike them, she would sleep at night.

They were kind to her. They ate everything, just like what people eat. The Wolf-People however, ate in their own fashion. They didn't boil anything. They would circle around food howling, those Wolf-People. That was their way of cooking it. She, however, cooked over a fire. They kept good watch over her.

She had already spent a number of years there when she cut those canoes. She set the small one in the water. She kept looking at them to see if they were asleep. They were sleeping. Then she went to fetch water and set it in the water. She got into it running. She launched herself out with a kick. She gave herself a good shove-off and was paddling across the river. She was just this short distance from the other side when they found out about her. Those Wolf-People immediately ran in all directions. Each time they shoved a canoe into the water it would sink. Those canoes were made of skin and would sink. So a number of them sewed up one canoe. She had already reached shore when that one boat set out after her.

Then, where a waterfall comes down from a mountain, from up above, here a lake forms, a lake where the falling water goes downstream. It was behind this, the water falling out in front, here in the recess behind it, there was no water. It was behind that water she stood. They ran there smelling her tracks. But from where she went into the water, they couldn't any more, Right there they stayed, running back and forth, howling. She could hear the sound of those wolves howling. She stayed right there, as night fell, behind the water. As it was night, she settled down there. She stayed there and slept. After daybreak she stole out forward by there. No one was there. So that was [100] how she got back among humans, following along those same down-feathers along the way they had taken her. As it began to get dark she would look around for water. How many — two-mountains she crossed. As it began to get dark she would look around for waterfalls. When she saw one she would try to go in behind it. Thus, in two, three places, she spent the night behind a waterfall. In three nights and three days she ended up safely back home.

She didn't immediately go in among her people. When k was already well into evening, she came down to shore by skirting above where the people lived. She approached the shore from above, in the evening. She looked around for some person to hail. He had gone to get water, at the lake. A child who had gone to the lake for water she saw. She called him over. "Come here. It's me. I've come, tell them, my relatives, to come here to me." He ran back. He didn't fetch any water up, he ran back so. He ran inside there and said, "Somebody, it's a lady, is sitting over there by the water. She called me over to her. She's calling you to come. Hurry!" They ran there. All the men ran over there. Then they brought her back down to their home.

Her husband was already remarried to another woman. When she didn't greet him he said to her, "Ah, is that really you that came back?" She didn't answer him. She said not one word to him. "Not right now." She wouldn't eat anything that day. "Tomorrow, though, tomorrow morning I'll eat, not now." She stayed right there where she lay by her grandmother. Then she told her grandmother what had happened to her, why she had been gone.

Another day came and went. After she had spent that one day there, wolves, that night, descended on the village. It was the Wolf-People, looking for her. In the people's eyes however, they were ordinary wolves. Quite a number of wolves descended on the village. As it got light the wolves went away again. The next day after nightfall they could be heard, those wolves. Staying right indoors, she wouldn't go out at all. From following her trail they knew that the woman had come back there. Again their call could be heard. A number of men climbed onto the housetops with bows and arrows. After eight of the wolves were killed they left the people alone. They didn't bother or interfere with people any more. They didn't come around people any more.

After that she became well again. Her mind had become almost like a wolfs mind. When her mood was bad she would right away feel like biting humans. When she had been living long enough with people again, her mind became pretty much human again. [101]

Then the people with her moved camp. They were going to smoke meat, to dry salmon. They moved camp there with her and one wolf was prowling around there. The woman knew him. She kept telling him, "Mountain-goat, black bear, I have no way to get any of these things to eat. Kill some for me." The next morning when it got light all those things, mountain-goat, black bear, were lying there outside for her.

Only she never would get remarried, that woman. Because she had come to be among the wolves, she would never remarry. She stayed right with her grandmother. That's how she lived. Her grandmother got very old and died of old age. Then she herself would go about in her canoe, alone.

They would come to her, the (Wolf) People. The wolf told the woman, "Tell your people not to kill us. We are people just like them. Our relatives, Wolves like us, are among you. I am a Wolf like your people. When you have a potlatch, your own kind, we are your own kind. *wolf told the woman, 'Tell*
 Tell them not to kill us any more. Those Wolves like us, we'll help them, *your people not to kill us* with whatever they want. They didn't use to kill us, but now they keep killing us. They trap us with deadfalls, they shoot us with arrows. They stab us with spears; they keep spearing us to death. They keep killing us that way, those relatives of yours. So you should tell them to leave us alone. Then we won't bother you any more either."

So that woman said, "Yes, I'll tell them that." The wolf said, "Don't forget to tell them that." "Yes, I won't forget." They filled some canoes for the woman. They killed mountain-goat, black bear, brown bear for her. The Wolf-People killed things for the woman. She took them home. When her people came running to shore for her, woman like herself. "Where did you get so much stuff from?" "Those people among whom I spent the year met me. They're the ones who hunted the food [102] for me." Those women said to their husbands, "Go help her, bring it up for her, what she brought." They carried it up, the women helping. They cut it into pieces and hung it up to dry.

Then she told them the story; she told them what the Wolf-People told her. "Don't keep on killing them any more. That's what they told me. Their relatives, Wolves like them, are among us. That's who you keep killing. That's why they too have bothered us. They're people Just like us. That's all that was said. We won't bother them any more. We didn't know they were people like ourselves. All these things have spirits, black bears, all living beings. That's what they told me, the Wolf-People. There are also song-bird spirits. When we go around after little land-birds, and their spirits speak to us, we won't bother them any more." That's what the Wolf-People told the woman.

After that they weren't bothered any more. Nothing more at all happened to her. Sometimes there are days when quite an amount of mountain-goat and black bear is accumulated. In winter it is hard to kill black bears and mountain-goats. They used to live only on those fish. In olden times those were the things people used to live on. They kept helping them in those ways, and then that woman died. After that woman died they haven't come around people any more. Those wolves don't come around us any more. That woman died. That's all.

Blind Man and Loon
Anna Nelson Harry

A woman had a blind husband. She said to him, "A moose is going by!" "Give me my bow and arrow," he said to his wife. She gave them to him. "Aim it right at the place under its shoulder," and she held him that way. "Is that right?" "Yes, it's aimed right at that spot," He shot. The animal bolted forward, shot right under the shoulder, and fell. She

said, "It's still going." Then he said, "Hand them to me again." He shot it a second time and killed it. It had fallen but she told him, "You missed." That wife said to him, "You didn't get it, you didn't hit it." She went over to get the arrow. She poked it down into the mud and brought it back to him. He smelled it. "It smells like blood." "No, you hit only the mud," she told him. Then she went off. She would leave her [103] husband. He was blind, but she was not. She would leave him, to go over to the moose, which she soon had no doubt gotten ready to boil.

Then down at the shore of the lake something called to the husband, "Come here." "I can't, I'm blind." "Come just grope your way down, by the shore here, come." It was a loon speaking to him. "Lie down flat on my back. Bury your head in my feathers." He dove under with him and swam around the lake. Twice he swam around the lake with him. When they came up, the loon said, "Now then, look over there." "I can see a little," the man said. "Put your head back down." He put his head back down and dove back under. Twice again it swam around the lake with him. A big lake it was. When he came back up this time he could see perfectly. Then the loon told him, "You should go over there."

That wife of his was cooking something there. He came over to her and she said, "Ah! I was just cooking something for you, my dear," she said. He was furious at her. He jammed her head down into the cooking pot. Her head immediately cooked. Because it cooked just too completely, that the woman died. Then the man went home. He had good fortune from the loon. That is how he got his sight back. That's all. [104]

Eyak History and Language
Anna Nelson Harry

There was no Eyaks at Eyak, nor were there any Eyaks at Alaganik. The Eyaks came from far upriver, in boats made out of something like cottonwood. They came down the Copper River. They were following along the river in their boars. They found eggs. They first saw eggs. They boiled them, tasted, and they were good, so they gathered a lot of them. Continuing along they came to Alaganik. They went up past Alaganik. There they settled down.

Of spruce-boughs, they first built shelters and lived in those. After living a long time like that they built houses of ta'xts', wind fallen trees; *ta'xts'*-houses they built. So after many attempts, they made true houses, of hemlock. They made their houses of hemlock. They built large houses.

They were becoming many, those first people who came down the river in their boats, and they never went back upriver. More people after them came down, in turn. That's how Eyak was established. It was Eyak after that.

Summer came and they would go around by boat. They made their first dugout canoes. They chopped down large cottonwood, and fashioned that into a canoe. They went in that into Eyak Lake. Then they tried spruce instead of cottonwood. That too was good. They carved large boats out of spruce.

They went back up by Eyak into Eyak Lake. They liked it at Eyak, and settled down there. They made more boats there. They went by these to Eyak Lake and saw many fish, ripe salmon. So they no longer wandered, but lived right there.

As they remained living right there, their children became many. The Eyak village kept having children, at Eyak. That's how Eyak became populous. Thus we are Eyaks at Eyak Village. When they felt like it they would go to the mouth of the river, to the breakers, to get seals. Over where they had come down the river there are seals. Nor are there many salmon, that swim up that far. When they came down the river they found about all these things. They saw seals, ripe salmon, cockles, eggs, birds, geese, mallards. So Eyak became a village. They were becoming numerous at Mountain Slough, and Mountain Slough became a village too.

Cordova was not a village. The village was at Eyak. Whites arrived there and Cordova became a town. The Eyak people were no longer very many. They moved there from Eyak. After [105] they moved to Cordova still some of them would go back to Eyak, and live there again, not being in just one place. As there came to be these Whites, we moved to Cordova; the Eyaks lived in town.

Recorded in Yakutat, 1965.

The Legend of a Tlingit Warrior:
Kaa-Tee-Na-Ah
Sue Abraham

Kaa-tee-na-ah was a great Tlingit warrior and leader of his people. He would fight the Aleuts all the time. The Aleuts would fight in small packs and use guerrilla warfare. One day the Aleuts waited for all the men to leave, while the women and children were berry picking. Then they came and sole Kaa-tee-na-ah s mother for revenge and to spite the Tlingit [106] leader. The Aleuts thought that he would come and fight, but the warrior said wait till winter when they are grouped together in their winter village (Hawkins Island). A large fleet of war canoes came and attacked the village and many were killed. They would wipe a whole village out at one time.

Kaa-tee-na-ah's mother was saved. But before that, she was not treated very well, except by an old Aleut woman who had a furskin blanket wrapped around her. She would walk by her and secretly drop scraps of extra food for her. She was a very kind old woman who would help during her captivity.

Then the Tlingits came and brought her home. After the battle, she told her son and people, "Do not to harm or kill this kind old woman, for she was a very honorable person who took pity on me and was kind and helped me while I was a prisoner." And so they took this old Aleut woman home with them and they wanted to honor her in the best Tlingit way for her kindness. She was treated by all with great honors.
Then as the years drifted on, they took her back home to her people. This was when that old woman's daughter married Ka-tee-na-ah or his son. (?) This marriage took place on a small island (Mummy Island) near Cordova before European contact. The marriage brought peace again to these troubled waters and opened up the Copper River trade route once again so that trading could be done in a safe and peaceful manner. (The name of this leader was reported to have come from the village of Angoon? He was from the Raven clan, they were also called the dog-salmon people.)

Recorded in Anchorage, 1984 by John F.C. Johnson and is also similar to the war stories recorded in this publication.

The Tlingits and Aleuts Battle in Controller Bay
Sue Abraham

In the winter time there was a big battle between the Chugach / (Aanaoot) Aleuts and the Tlingits. The Indians came in four large canoes full of men, their goal was to attack the Aleuts. The Aleuts heard of the plan and came out in large numbers of kayaks to do battle. The Aleuts pursued the Tlingits in their kayak to Wingham Island. On the way two war canoes full of Tlingits decided to kill themselves rather than be captured, so [107] they overturned their boats and drowned. The other two canoes made it to Wingham Island where there was a battle and many were killed. There the Aleuts overcame the Tlingits and killed them all, they brought their bodies up to a cave and laid them to rest. The Tlingits wanted the heads back from their dead, bur that never happened. It was the custom to exchange heads after a battle. The Tlingits used to take the heads of the enemy and put them on a pole to show their great deeds of battle.

The Aleuts Trapped at the Guyot Glacier in Icy Bay
Herman Kitka Sr.

The Aleuts took off in their kayaks

A Russian boat and Aleut sea otter hunters were at Yakutat. All the Russians were killed. The Aleuts took off in their kayaks and fled towards Prince William Sound. The Tlingits chased them and found them at the head of Icy Bay. The Aleuts knew they were trapped so they started to climb the Guyot Glacier or the Guyot Hills. The Tlingits knew they had them trapped so they just waited. Later they went to look for them and they found them dead from starvation along a river or hill.(?) Before they died they were eating each other. They just left them there. This area is still called Guyot Hills or Aleut Hills.

Recorded in Anchorage, 1985 by John F.C. Johnson. [108]

Ravens Party House (Ka-Ta-Ton-Hit) in Controller Bay
Herman Kitka Sr.

Raven's House was used as refuge for women and children when the men were out hunting on long trips. They felt that this was a safe place because it was Raven's House and they were protected by him with his powers. At this house the people were not afraid of the Kushtaka, for at this cave no harm would come to them. You had to be magical and good to find this place, the doors would open and shut by themselves.

Raven's House is called "Ka-Ta-Ton-Hit", which means: "Raven's Party House". This large cave was given this name because Raven invited all the animals in the ocean to his house for a party. He had shiny and colorful things there to attract the animals (rock crystals). All the animals would come ashore, then Raven would trick them and eat them. This is the rea5on why we have animals that live on the land now. The shiny rocks were used to lure the King Salmon ashore as well.

Long ago before the Russians came the Athabaskan Indians were migrating from the Interior down the Alsek River near Dry Bay. They captured the Raven clan at Yakutat. They were captured because they were surprised and were in such a hurry that they did not have their weapons ready for battle.

The Yakutat Raven clan built a "NU" (fort) for protection. This fort was a stockade just like the Russians built, and it was built before the Russians came to Alaska. During the battle with the Athabaskans, this fort was captured along with the Raven clan.

Sitka was considered at one time the capital of the entire Tlingit nation. After the battle, the Eagle clan went back to Sitka and regrouped. Then the Sitka Eagle clan put their war canoes to the sea and pushed northward. They went to Yakutat and did battle with the Athabaskins. They freed the Raven clan and drove the Athabaskans out of their country. Later the Eagle clan built a fort next to the other Raven fort so that they could help watch over their land.

After the battle the Yakutat Raven clan and Sitka Eagle clan went to Raven's House for a potlatch to settle the ownership of the Controller Bay area. At this potlatch the land surrounding Mount Saint Ellas was turned over to the Eagle clan for better protection. Now the Eagle clan owns Mount Saint Elias and all the land around the mountain.

Recorded in Anchorage, 1985 by John F.C. Johnson. [109]

Tlingit Migration in and out of Alaska
Herman Kitka Sr.

The Tlingits have legends of living in Alaska before the ice age. They say that the winter lasted all year round, so they were driven south to "Sa-Na" (South Wind Country). They migrated slowly to where there was seasons again and stayed until the winter cold pushed them farther south. When the ice retreated north, so did the animals, so the Tlingits migrated back north.

During one of the migrations back to Alaska, the Tlingit Kogwanton organized nine clans together under the Eagle crest. This was done for protection from hostile tribes also living along the coast. All of these Kogwonton adopted the Killerwhale emblem which was worn on their backs.

The Tlingits call Prince William Sound "Cha-Koot-Tha" (Largest Bay in Alaska). Legends also tell of how Raven created the Aleutian Islands by throwing rocks into the water. Oral history records the making of war canoes in Glacier Bay, now the only trees big enough are petrified sequoias. There is also stories ofpre-ice age fish camps where fossilized fish nets were left on the beach.

Recorded in Anchorage, 1985 by John P.C. Johnson. [110]

The Birth of the Tlingit Bear Clan
Herman Kitka, Sr

There is a place in Canada, along the Inside Passage, near Granville Channel where the Tlingits stopped as they migrated back north to Alaska for the second time.

A woman was out picking wild celery in the spring time and slipped on a pile of bear shit, she then insulted the young bear who left it behind. In the woman's eyes, a young man came to help carry the celery, he was really a bear. She was taken to his den. In her eyes he was really a man.

The medicine man told his people that this woman was living with other beings that were not people like themselves. None of the brothers would come near the bear den.

The younger brother found her. She thought she was living with humans. The sister told her brother not to harm small bears. The brother went back to his people and said that she was living with bears, so he prepared his brothers to bring her back. He did this by fasting and then they left.

The woman said, "Brother-in-law is coming, do not do anything," she told the other bears. A big bear came out and it was killed. They brought the head and hide back. This happened during the migration of the Tlingits along the Pacific coast. Those people and that family were thence called the Bear Clan and thus this was the history of the beginning of the Tlingit Bear clan.

Recorded in Anchorage, 1985 by John F.C. Johnson.

Eyak
Current status and revival

Extinction

Marie Smith Jones (May 14, 1918 – January 21, 2008)[4][5][6] of Cordova was the language's last native speaker,[7] and the last full-blooded Eyak. Because of the dying off of its native speakers, Eyak became a symbol in the fight against language extinction.[8]

The spread of English and suppression of aboriginal languages are not the only reasons for the decline of the Eyak language. The northward migration of the Tlingit people around Yakutat in precontact times encouraged the use of Tlingit rather than Eyak along much of the Pacific Coast of Alaska. Eyak was also under pressure from its neighbors to the west, the Alutiiq people of Prince William Sound, as well as some pressure from the people of the Copper River valley. Eyak and Tlingit culture began to merge along the Gulf Coast, and a number of Eyak-speaking groups were absorbed by the Gulf Coast Tlingit populations. This resulted in the replacement of Eyak by Tlingit among most of the mixed groups after a few generations, as reported in Tlingit oral histories of the area.

Revival

In June 2010, the Anchorage Daily News published an article about Guillaume Leduey, a French college student with an unexpected connection to the Eyak language. Beginning at age 12, he had taught himself Eyak, utilizing print and audio instructional materials he obtained from the Alaska Native Language Center. During that time, he never traveled to Alaska or conversed with Marie Smith Jones, the last native speaker.[9]

The month that the article was published, he traveled to Alaska and met with Dr. Michael Krauss, a noted linguist and Professor Emeritus at the University of Alaska Fairbanks. Dr. Krauss assisted Leduey with proper Eyak phonological pronunciation and assigned further instruction in grammar and morphology — including morphemic analyses of traditional Eyak stories.

In June 2011, Leduey returned to Alaska to facilitate Eyak language workshops in Anchorage and Cordova. He is now regarded as a fluent speaker, translator, and instructor of Eyak.[10] Despite his fluency, Eyak remains classified as "dormant" as there are no native speakers. On the Expanded Graded Intergenerational Disruption Scale (EGIDS) Eyak is graded a 9 (dormant); the language serves as a reminder of heritage identity for an ethnic community, but no one has more than symbolic proficiency.[11] Currently, Leduey provides instruction and curriculum assistance to the Language Project from France.

The Eyak Preservation Council received an Alaska Humanities Forum Grant that enabled them to start a website devoted to the preservation of the Eyak Language. Other funding supports the annual Eyak Culture Camp every August in Cordova. The Project provides countless language resources including immersion workshops, an online dictionary with audio samples, and a set of eLearning lessons, among others.

In June 2014, the Eyak Language Revitalization Project announced an online program called "*dAXunhyuuga'*", which means "the words of the people."[12]

Language family

Main article: Na-Dene languages

    Eyak is a part of the Eyak-Athabaskan language family and Na-Dené larger grouping, which includes Eyak-Athabaskan and Tlingit with a controversial but possible inclusion of Haida. The Athabaskan family covers three distinct geographic areas, forming three subgroups: Northern Athabaskan in Alaska and the Yukon; Pacific Coast Athabaskan in California and Oregon; and Southern Athabaskan, also called Apache, spoken mainly in the American Southwest, which includes Navajo. There has been extensive comparative reconstruction of a Proto-Athabaskan-Eyak (PAE). A recent proposal of a Dené-Yeniseian stock has been widely well received by linguists, linking the Dené languages to the Yeniseian languages of central Siberia. If it proves correct, it will be the first validated genetic link between Old and New World languages. Far less accepted is a possible Dené–Caucasian stock that has been pursued for decades.

Phonology

The following charts are based on the material in Krauss (1965); IPA equivalents are shown in square brackets. The orthography used by Krauss and the Eyak people is the same, substituting only **A**, **L**, and **X** for respective [ə], [ɫ], and [x̣].

Consonants

		Bilabial	Alveolar central	Alveolar lateral	Postalveolar / Palatal	Velar plain	Velar labial	Uvular	Glottal
Stop	unaspirated	(**b** [b])	**d** [t]			**g** [k]	**gw** [kʷ]	**G** [q]	
Stop	aspirated		**t** [tʰ]			**k** [kʰ]		**q** [qʰ]	
Stop	ejective		**t'** [tɧ]			**k'** [kɧ]		**q'** [qɧ]	**'** [ʔ]
Affricate	unaspirated		**dz** [ts]	**dl** [tɬ]	**dj** [tʃ]				
Affricate	aspirated		**ts** [tsʰ]	**tl** [tɬʰ]	**ch** [tʃʰ]				
Affricate	ejective		**ts'** [tsɧ]	**tl'** [tɬ']	**ch'** [tʃ']				
Fricative			**s** [s]	**L** [ɬ]	**sh** [ʃ]	**x** [x]	**xw** [xʷ]	**X** [χ]	**h** [h]
Nasal		(**m** [m])	(**n** [n])			(**ŋ** [ŋ])			
Approximant			**l** [l]		**y** [j]		**w** [w]		

The nasals [n] and [m] occur in loanwords; in native words, Krauss (1965) suggests that they can be interpreted as /l/ and /w/ (respectively) followed by a nasalized vowel. /b/ and /ŋ/ occur only in loanwords. Aspirated stops contrast with unaspirated stops only before vowels.

All consonants may be found stem-initially, except /h/, which is interpreted as zero. /h/ has the allophone [h] only word-initially or directly following a vowel.

Vowels

	Front	Central	Back
Close	**i** [ɪ]		**u** [ʊ]
Mid	**e** [e] / **ɛ** [ɛ]	**A** [ə]	**ɔ** [ɔ]
Open	**æ** [æ]	**a** [a]	

In Krauss's terminology, vowels can be oral or nasal, with further modification by glottalization, aspiration, length, or a combination of glottalization and length. The only unmodified vowels are /i/, /A/ and /u/. Unmodified /A/ varies morphophonemically between [æ] and [e], so /ə/ serves as the basic form of both vowels. When orally modified, the nucleus of /e/ varies between [ɛ] and [æ], the nucleus of /a/ between [a] and [ɔ]. All vowels, regardless of their oral modification, are nasalized following /n/, with the exception of /e/ which is never nasalized.

unmodified	glottal	aspirated	long	glottal long	nasalized glottal	nasalized aspirated	nasalized long	nasalized glottal long
i	i'	ih	i:	i:'	in'	inh	i:n	i:n'
A	e'	eh	e:	e:'				
A	a'	ah	a:	a:'	an'	anh	a:n	a:n'
u	u'	uh	u:	u:'	un'	unh	u:n	u:n'

In written Eyak, length is denoted by double letters and glottalization by ', as in **chi:shg** "sand" or **qi'GA'e'd** "bed".

Prosody

All syllables begin with an onset, so that no two vowels may occur consecutively. Syllables can be counted exactly by number of vowels.

Eyak is not tonal, unlike many of the Athabascan languages to which it is related; nor does it have distinctive pitch. Stems are heavy syllables, whereas affixes tend to be light. Stress usually falls on stems and heavy syllables. In sequences of heavy syllables, the stress falls on the penultimate syllable, as in **q'ahdi'lah** "goodbye".

Morphology

Eyak is an agglutinative, polysynthetic language.

Nouns

With few exceptions, Eyak nouns are morphophonemically invariable. Kinship and anatomical stems are the only noun stems that may take pronominal possessive prefixes, which are as follow:

- First person singular: **si-** (**siya:q'e'**, "my aunt (mother's sister)")
- Second person singular: **'i-** (**'ita:'**, "your (sg.) father")
- Third person singular and plural: **'u-**
- First person plural: **qa:-**
- Second person plural: **lAX-**
- Indefinite: **k'u-**
- Reciprocal: **'Ad-**

Preverbals

Preverbals in Eyak are the category of words made up of preverbals and postpositions. The two are grouped together because one morpheme may often be used as the stem in both categories. Preverbals are individual words that occur in conjunction with the verb. These combinations may almost be said to form lexemes, especially due to the fact that preverbals are rarely if ever used in isolation in natural speech. Preverbals are nearly always unbound and are phonologically separate from the verb, contrasting with the corresponding class in Athabaskan which may be incorporated or not. One preverbal is most common, but combinations of two are equally possible, as in **'uya' 'Adq'Ach' k'udAdAGu'** "hot water bottle" (in it onto self something/someone is kept warm). There are more than 100 Eyak basic preverbal morphemes.

Postpositions relate directly to an object outside of the verb. Current analysis by Krauss has been phonological rather than semantic, but there is at least one semantically grouped category of postpositions to consider, that of comparatives. This grouping includes P-**ga'** "like P", P-**'u'X** "less than P", and P-**lAX** "more than P" where P is any postpositional phrase. Eyak lacks conjunctions and many postpositions assume a similar function, creating subordinate clauses. These postpositions attach to the verb, the most common example being -**da:X** "and" or "if, when".

Verbs

Eyak verb stems take many affixes: there are nine prefix positions before the verb (many of which may be subdivided) and four suffix positions after. All positions may be filled with zero, except the stem, which can be filled by any of several hundred morphemes but not zero.

Affix position

1. Object
A. Direct object: **xu** (1 sg.), **'i** (2 sg.), **ø~A** (3 sg. and pl.), **lAXi:** (2 pl.), **'Ad(A)~'Ad(u)** (reflexive), **'i~'i(dA)** (indeterminate)
B. Indefinite subject or object: **k'u'**
The indeterminate is used where there is no specific object (such as in intransitive verbs), while the indefinite is used where there is a specific but unspecified subject or object.
C. Mark of semitransitive: **'~:**

- 2. Tense/aspect/mood A (inceptive imperfect): **qu'~qa'~qe'~qi'**
- 3. **'i:lih ~ :lih**
  This position is filled only in a few verbs of thought or emotion, such as **ilih**
- 4. Plurality emphasizer: **qA** (subject *and* object)
- 5. Classificatory (nominal) and thematic (verbal) qualifiers: the most variable and characteristically Eyak affix position. **gu, XA, lAXA, dA, yA**, and **lA** may occur singly, the rest occur in combinations of two or three.

  - A. **GA, gu**
  - B. **XA**
  - C. **qi:, lAXA, ti:, ku:n, k'ush, tsin, tsi:**
  - D. **dA, yA**
  - E. **lA~:n**

Only in position C. do the morphemes have specified meaning, and only nominally, for example: **lAXA**, "berry-like, ball-like, eye" or **qi: + dA** "foot". The other morphemes have unlimited, much broader meanings, but tend to concentrate in certain areas. They may be nominal classificatory or verbal thematic.

gu+lA is nominally classificatory and refers to liquid or viscous matter; when **gu** appears by itself it refers nominally to basket-roots, thread, or hair, (but not rope), as well as thematically with -**L-qu**, "chase".

XA+dA may nominally refer to matches or logs (but not sticks) or to clouds, among others. **dA** alone thematically refers to an unusually broad selection including but not limited to hunger, sleds, arrows, noises (only certain types), and non-solid round objects (including eggs, severed heads, and hearts).

This is a very limited sampling of the breadth of the meanings of the possible morphemes in position 5.

- 6. Tense/aspect/mood B1: **GA**, ø ~ **A**, **:** ~ **A**
- 7. Subject: **xw** (1 sg.), ø ~ **y(i)** (2 sg.), **lAX** (2 pl.), ø (all else)
- 8. Tense/aspect/mood B2: *sA* ~ *s* (perfective), **(y)i** ~ ø (inconclusive function)
- 9. Verb voice classifier: ø, **dA~di**, **L**, **LA~Li**
- 10. Verb stem
- 1. Derivational: **g** (habitual action), **X** ~ ø (progressive)
- 2. Aspectival: **L** (perfective); Derivational: **k'** (customary)
- 3. Negative: **G**
- 4. Human subject or object of third person: **inh** (sg.), **inu:** (pl.); non-human object of imperative: **uh**

An artificial but grammatical example presents near-maximum affixal positions filled: **dik' lAXi:qAqi'dAxsLXa'Xch'gLG** "I did not tickle your (plural, emphatically) feet." This gives:

- **dik'**, negative particle
- Prefix position 1: **lAXi:**, direct object, you pl.
- Position 4: **qA**, emphasizing plurality
- Positions 5C & D: **qi' + dA**, pertaining to feet
- Position 6: ø, negative active perfective
- Position 7: **x**, 1st pers. sg. subject
- Position 8: **s**, perfective
- Position 9: **L**
- Stem: **Xa'Xch'**, tickle
- Suffix position 1: **g**, repetitive
- Position 2: **L**, perfective
- Position 3: **G**, negative

Tense, mood, and aspect

There are two moods, optative and imperative, and two aspects, perfective and imperfective. Verbs may be inceptive, 'active,' or 'neuter', such that the possibilities are as follows:

	Inceptive	Active	Neuter
Perfective	is doing, is becoming	did, became	is
Imperfective	will do, will become	is doing	is
Optative	let it do, let it become	let it do	let it become
Imperative	let it do!, let it become!	let it do!	let it be!

Morphemes in prefix position 2 modify the inceptive imperfective; in position 6 the perfective, optative, and imperative in inceptive, active and neuter; in position 8 the inceptive optative, active perfective and optative, and neuter perfective, imperfective, optative, and imperative; in suffix position 2 the inceptive, active, and neuter perfective; and in suffix position 3, negativity.

There are also three derivational modes, a repetitive, a customary, and a progressive. The infinitive takes approximately the same form as the imperative, with some variation.

Syntax

The majority of the Eyak corpus is narrative, with very little spontaneous conversation (and that only when embedded in the narratives). There is a better understanding therefore of the syntax of Eyak narrative style and performance than of natural speech. The basic word order of Eyak is subject-object-verb, or SOV, as in "*Johnny 'uyAqa'ts' sALxut'L*" "Johnny shot his (own) hand." Relatively few sentences, however, follow this exact pattern; it is far more common to find SV or OV. The full word order of a transitive sentence is I S O [[C P] V]:

- I, introductory sector: consists of two parts, a connective (e.g. 'and so,' 'then,' etc.) and one or more adverbs, especially temporal and spatial adverbs.
- S, subject
- O, object
- V, verb sector: includes two subsectors in addition to the verb.

C, complement subsector: in Eyak syntax a complement is a noun or noun phrase (e.g. not a demonstrative pronoun) and does not have the same meaning as the usual use of 'complement' in ordinary syntax. This is due to traditional classifications of Eyak.

P, preverbal subsector: includes preverbals (preverbs and postpositions) and pronouns.

The subject and object categories can consist of a noun, a noun phrase, or a demonstrative phrase. All constituents may be filled by zero, excepting the verb.

There is extreme ambiguity in Eyak syntax, due in large part to homophony (as in the English loss of subjunctive) and lack of distinction (there is the same ambiguity in third-person singular as in English).

References

- - https://www.npr.org/sections/thetwo-way/2014/04/21/305688602/alaska-oks-bill-making-native-languages-official
- - Hammarström, Harald; Forkel, Robert; Haspelmath, Martin, eds. (2017). *"Eyak"*. *Glottolog 3.0*. Jena, Germany: Max Planck Institute for the Science of Human History.
- - Michael E. Krauss 2006. A history of Eyak language documentation and study: Fredericæ de Laguna in Memoriam Archived 2013-08-31 at the Wayback Machine. Arctic Anthropology 43 (2): 172-217
- - ADN.com
- - "Last Alaska language speaker dies". *BBC News. January 24, 2008.*

- • "How Do You Learn a Dead Language?", Christine Cyr, Slate, January 28, 2008
- • John McWhorter,"No Tears For Dead Tongues"[1], Forbes,2/21/2008 @ 6:00PM.
- • "Marie Smith". The Economist. February 7, 2008.
- • Hopkins, Kyle. "Extinct Alaska Native language interests French student". Archived from the original on 10 June 2011. Retrieved 15 July 2011.
- • Gibbins, Jennifer. "Preserving Alaska Native culture". Archived from the original on 27 March 2012. Retrieved 15 July 2011.
- • "Ethnologue".
- • Hintze, Heather (2014-06-25). "Program seeks to revitalize extinct Eyak language". KTVA CBS 11. Archived from the original on 2014-07-05. Retrieved 2014-06-28.

Bibliography

Hund, Andrew. "Eyak". 2004. Encyclopedia of the Arctic. Taylor and Francis Publications. ISBN 1-57958-436-5

Krauss, Michael E. 1965. Eyak: a preliminary report. University of Alaska.

Krauss, Michael E., ed. 1982. *In Honor of Eyak*: The Art of Anna Nelson Harry. Fairbanks: Alaska Native Language Center. ISBN 0-933769-03-2

Krauss, Michael E. 2004. Athabaskan tone. Pp. 51-136 in Sharon Hargus & Keren Rice (eds) *Athabaskan Prosody*. (Current Issues in Linguistic Theory 269). Amsterdam: John Benjamins. ISBN 90-272-4783-8. Based on an unpublished manuscript dated 1979.

Krauss, Michael E., and Jeff Leer. *Athabaskan, Eyak, and Tlingit Sonorants*. Alaska Native Language Center Research Papers No. 5. Alaska Native Language Center, University of Alaska, P.O. Box 757680, Fairbanks, AK 99775-7680, 1981. ISBN 0-933769-35-0

New Yorker, June 6, 2005: "Last Words, A Language Dies" by Elizabeth Kolbert

External links

- dAXunhyuu Eyak Language Project
- Overview of Eyak Language at the Alaska Native Language Archive
- Native Village of Eyak (official homepage of the Tribe)
- An Eyak speaker
- Alaska Native Language Center
- Wrangell's 1839 Comparative Word-List of Alaskan languages (includes Eyak)
- Eyak basic lexicon at the Global Lexicostatistical Database
- BBC News article about death of last native speaker, with her picture.
    - (Article date January 24, 2008).
- Eyak Preservation Council
- From Stewards to Shareholders: Eyaks Face Extinction (interview).
- The Eyak Corporation (ANSCA Corporation)
- Extinct Alaska Native language draws French student's interest
- "In Alaska, a Frenchman Fights to Revive the Eyak's Dead Tongue" Jim Carlton,
    - *The Wall Street Journal*, 10 August 2010

A

Abercrombie, Colonel W.R, 7f, 12, 24f
abortion, 13
Affix, 72, 78, 163f
Ahtna, 4, 17ff, 43f, 49, 55, 71, 88; Atna, 7, 45, 54
Alaganik, 1, 4f, 17, 51, 55, 57, 84, 88, 146, 156
Alaska Native Language Center, 40, 50, 76, 85f, 88, 161
Alutiiq, 27, 36, 40f, 84, 161
Anchorage, 69, 76f, 86f, 157f, 161
Anderson, William, 27*f
Arredondo, Antonio de Tova, 30f
assimilation, 41, 51, 91
Aztec, 46

B

Bagley Icefields, 17, 24
Baranov, Aleksandr, 22, 41*
beaver crest, 15
Bergman, Karl, 78
birchbark canoes, 126
Black, Lydia, 39
Boas, Franz, 4, 25f, 52ff, 60f
Bodega Bay, 40f
Borodkin, Sophie, 68f, 72*, 84f, 91
box, 9, 17f, 57, 97, 102f, 111f
Bristol Bay, 33

C

Calm Weather, 122
Chicago, 64
Chilkats, 15f, 20, 48, 141
Chugach, 4, 15f, 20ff, 32f, 40f, 51f, 61f, 84, 87f, 93, 139, 157
Clam People, 114
clam shell, 8, 123, 131
Cleveland, 90
Colnett, James, 29*
confinements, 11f
Controller Bay, 15f, 20f, 137, 158
Cordova, 3f, 15f, 20f, 32, 38, 41, 48, 50ff, 60ff, 70ff, 84f, 91f, 119, 136f, 142f, 156f, 161f
Cordova Daily Times, 56

D

Dall, William, 25, 48f*
daylight, 63, 102f, 117, 123f, 130ff
devil-club, 11f, 122f; devil's club, 21, 111f
devilfish, 115f, 136*
dolls, 13, 22 (taboo), 71, 132*
dreams, 11, 21, 88, 92, 97, 125, 138
Dry Bay, 15f, 20f, 158
dugout, 2f, 18, 93, 156

E

Eagles, 8, 10, 18, 19*, 20*, 84, 100, 159,
Eyak Corp, 23, 87f, 167
eyeballs, 11, 21, 144

F

Fairbanks, 40, 66f, 73, 76, 87f, 90f, 161
feather, 46, 97f, 107f, 125, 139f, 153
Finno-Ugric-Uralic, 66
first kill, 12, 21
first salmon, 11
first-fish, 21

G

gable, 8, 17
Gallatin, Albert, 34, 43ff, 50
Gibbs, George, 47
glaciers, 17, 90, 93, 119, 129, 152f
graveyard, 8, 18
Grinnell, George Bird, 52
Gvozdev, 26

H

Haas, Mary, 60
hair, 8, 18, 89, 95, 100, 111f, 126f, 131, 142, 148, 151, 165; goat hair, 8
hypothesis, 7, 55f

I

Inupiaq, 32

J

Jackson, Sheldon, 90
Jacobs, Melville, 58
Jacobsen, Johan Adrian, 51*
Jesup Expedition, 52

K

Kari, James, 40
Kayak, 8, 18, 157f
Kayak Island, 7, 15, 22, 27, 33, 44, 137, 140f
Kodiak, 32f, 40f, 50, 83, 88
Kolosh, 25, 38, 46
Kuskov, Ivan Aleksandrovich, 40
Kutchin, 46f, 65

L

Lankard, Dune, 77f, 87, 93
Leduey, Guillaume, 85, 161
Leer, Jeff, 33, 40, 76
Leningrad, 77
levirate, 10, 20
log drum, 12

M

Madras, 28
Madrid, 30f
Malaspina, Alessandro, 15, 24, 30f
Malshaa, 127f
masks, 9, 12, 23
menstruants, 21, 91
Merriam, C. Hart, 53
MIT, 75f
Miwok, 40f
moieties, 8, 10f, 18f, 20*, 84
Monk Gideon, 39
monsters, 13, 22, 119
Mountain Slough, 3f, 156
Muir, John, 52

N

Na-Dene, 4, 7, 59f; Na-Dené, 85, 162
Newman, Stanley, 60
Nuchek, 31, 50, 142f

O

Old Chief Joe, 55, 84, 147
opposite moiety, 10f, 21
Otters > land otters, 9, 74, 117, 134f, 141, 147f, 151; sea otter, 8f, 17f, 32, 137; Land Otter People, 22, 141; sea otter hunters, 158

P

polygyny, 10, 20
porcupine, 135, 147; porky, 109, 135
potlatch customs, 11; death, 21, 78; houses, 8, 11f, 18; name, 11
pottery, 9, 19
puberty, 11f, 21

Q

Qaduwina, 130f

R

rattles, 12, 21
Raven, 95ff, 144
Ravens, 8, 10f, 20*f, 74
Reynolds, Norman, 7, 56f, 84

S

S.O.V., 92
Sakhalin, 66
salmon, 2f, 10f, 20f, 64, 84f, 92f, 100; canneries, 91; eggs, 10; salmonberries, 32; prices, 64
Sapir, Edward, 7, 59ff, 84
Scots, 28
septum, 91
shamans, 8f, 12f, 21f*, 31, 74, 84, 127, 140f; hair, 8, 18
Shumagins, 54
Sicilian ~ Alessandro Malaspina, 29
Sierra Club, 88f
Sitka, 23, 34f, 41f, 52f, 158f
skunk cabbage, 113; skunk-cabbage, 141f
songs, 11f, 21, 53, 104, 118, 126, 146; insulting, 11, 21; leaders 22
sororate, 10, 20
souls, 11, 21, 44, 50
Spaan, Laura Bliss, 77f, 93
Stevens, Scar, 65f, 84f, 129
strawberries, 137, 143, 147*; point, 124
Sun, 11f, 120; theft of, 12, 97*

T

Tanacross, 44f
thumb, 121f, 150
Tikhmenev, Petr Aleksandrovich, 24f, 36, 49*

Tolmie, William Fraser, 48

U

ulu, 9, 19
umiak, 8, 18
unexplained obligation, 71

V

Veniaminov, Ioann Ivan Evseevich Innokentii, 39f, 44f*, 50f, 59
von Humboldt, Alexander, 42f
Yupik, 27f, 31f, 44, 68, 76

W

wakck ~ woman's knife, 126, 129
witches, 9, 11f, 21f, 74, 139

Y

Yakutat, 4, 8, 15f, 20ff, 30ff, 41ff, 50f, 60ff, 70ff, 84f, 88, 124, 135f, 142, 157f, 161
Yale, 60
Yukon, 90, 162

Please help wipe out typo-gnomes!

Report Corrections

Thunderbird Screen, Drum House, Yakutat
drawn by Edward Malin